D0215455

Monsters, Mushroom Clouds, and the Cold War

Monsters, Mushroom Clouds, and the Cold War

American Science Fiction and the Roots of Postmodernism, 1946–1964

M. Keith Booker

Contributions to the Study of Science Fiction and Fantasy, Number 95

Greenwood Press
Westport, Connecticut • London

Library of Congress Cataloging-in-Publication Data

Booker, M. Keith.
    Monsters, mushroom clouds, and the Cold War : American science fiction and the
roots of postmodernism, 1946–1964 / by M. Keith Booker.
    p.   cm.—(Contributions to the study of science fiction and fantasy,
ISSN 0193–6875 ; no. 95)
    Includes bibliographical references (p.) and index.
    ISBN 0–313–31873–5 (alk. paper)
    1. Science fiction, American—History and criticism.   2. American fiction—20th
century—History and criticism.   3. Postmodernism (Literature)—United States.
4. End of the world in literature.   5. Atomic bomb in literature.   6. Cold war
in literature.   7. Monsters in literature.   8. Aliens in literature.   I. Title.   II. Series.
PS374.S35 B66   2001
813′.0876209054—dc21   00–069148

British Library Cataloguing in Publication Data is available.

Library of Congress Catalog Card Number: 00–069148
ISBN: 0–313–31873–5
ISSN: 0193–6875

First published in 2001

Greenwood Press, 88 Post Road West, Westport, CT 06881
An imprint of Greenwood Publishing Group, Inc.
www.greenwood.com

Printed in the United States of America

The paper used in this book complies with the
Permanent Paper Standard issued by the National
Information Standards Organization (Z39.48–1984).

10 9 8 7 6 5 4 3 2 1

For Savannah

for all the right reasons

Contents

Introduction

H. Bruce Franklin begins his 1980 study of the work of Robert A. Heinlein by noting that, during Heinlein's career, "science fiction has moved inexorably toward the center of American culture, shaping our imagination (more than many of us would like to admit)" (3). Of course, Franklin is writing after the *Star Trek* television series (which originally aired on NBC from 1966 until 1969 and which first became a feature film in 1979) had become a major institution of American popular culture. He is also writing after Stanley Kubrick's *2001: A Space Odyssey* (1968) had made science fiction film more respectable as an art form than it had ever been and after George Lucas's *Star Wars* (1977) had made science fiction film bigger box office than ever before. In 1980, the science fiction novel was still regarded as marginal to American literature, but it was considerably more mainstream than it had been in the old days of the 1950s, when it, along with the crazed novels of Mickey Spillane and the offbeat crime fiction of writers such as Jim Thompson, had formed the mainstay of the somewhat disreputable pulp fiction industry.[1] Popular genres such as crime fiction and science fiction were placed in a particularly marginal position within the Cold War climate of the 1950s, when many in the West felt that this war was being waged, not just against the Soviets and communism, but against mass culture as a whole. Indeed, mass culture was widely perceived, even by left-leaning critics such as Dwight Mac-Donald, as a powerful threat to the very survival of the values of the Western high cultural tradition.[2]

There was a mounting horror of popular culture on both the Left and the Right in American intellectual circles of the 1950s, as witnessed by the cultural elitism of groups otherwise as different in their attitudes as the rightest New Critics and the (supposedly) leftist New York Intellec-

tuals. Nevertheless, the growing importance of science fiction, as indicated by Franklin, did begin in the 1950s, which are still often regarded
as the "Golden Age" of the genre. Many of the legendary figures of
American science fiction, including Frederik Pohl, Isaac Asimov, Ray
Bradbury, and Heinlein, did much of their best work in the decade, producing a series of classics that would centrally define the genre for decades to come. Other science fiction writers, such as Alfred Bester and
James Blish, well known among aficionados of the genre, if not so well
known outside the genre, also worked in the 1950s. Still others, who
would become better known for their work in the 1960s, got their starts
in the 1950s, including Kurt Vonnegut, Jr., and Philip K. Dick. Science fiction films from the 1950s are legendary as well, even if some of them (especially those produced late in the decade) are more famous as campy
cult classics than as the thought-provoking cinema science fiction, at its
best, can be. And the 1950s, culturally remarkable as much as anything
for the rise of television, were topped off with the appearance of *The Twilight Zone*, a science fiction series still widely regarded as one of the finest
series ever to appear on television.

Still, as a literary genre, science fiction got little critical respect during
the decade, remaining consigned to the shadows of "popular fiction."
Yet, as popular fiction, science fiction remained strangely unpopular,
producing none of the decade's leading sellers. Similarly, none of the science fiction films of the 1950s are considered among the finest American
films, and none of them were, at the time, among the biggest box office
hits. Yet science fiction captured something very crucial about the first
decade in which it was clear that science had given humanity the power
to destroy itself virtually at the touch of a button. Meanwhile, the decade's obvious anxieties over nuclear holocaust were mixed with a certain
faith in the ability of science to make life better on all levels, from mundane advances in the technology of vacuum cleaners and washing machines, to more seemingly profound improvements in the technology of
communication, transportation, and medicine. On the positive side, the
1950s were the decade in which space flight, long a staple of the science
fiction imagination, finally became a reality; on the negative side, the
same technical advances in rocketry also enabled the development of the
intercontinental ballistic missile (ICBM), thus allowing far more effective
delivery of nuclear weaponry. What was worse, from the American point
of view, the Soviets achieved both space flight and fully operational
ICBMs before the Americans, fueling the fire of American anti-Soviet
hysteria.

The best science fiction of the 1950s, like all of the best science fiction,
was a fiction of ideas, using plot and character to develop these ideas,
but also trying to make a point. Many of these points were political, and,
despite the reputation of science fiction as a politically conservative

genre, some of the best science fiction of the 1950s was produced by left-leaning writers who found Aesopian potential in setting their political commentary in other times or other galaxies, thus allowing them more freedom than they could possibly have to comment on political conditions in contemporary America. This phenomenon helps to explain the marginality of science fiction to 1950s literature, though there were also other factors, including the fact that the genre continued to be viewed by many as being aimed primarily at adolescents.

That reputation has continued to haunt the science fiction of the 1950s, even as a later generation of critics, publishing in scholarly journals such as *Science-Fiction Studies,* has brought a new level of sophisticated critical attention to science fiction as a whole. But the most sophisticated critics of science fiction have tended to focus on more recent works, particularly on the phenomenon of cyberpunk and its relation to the larger context of postmodernism.[3] Even Carl Freedman, whose very useful *Critical Theory and Science Fiction* shows little enthusiasm for cyberpunk, concentrates on science fiction produced after the 1950s. Tellingly, Freedman notes that he first became interested in science fiction through his teenage reading of Asimov. But he also notes that, alas, Asimov no longer figures prominently in his more sophisticated adult vision of science fiction (xi).

Freedman does, however, greatly admire Dick and has some extremely positive things to say, in passing, about 1950s science fiction writers such as Alfred Bester. By and large, there is much to be learned from a more sophisticated — and more political — reading of the science fiction of the 1950s than has generally been attempted. That attempt is the project of this book, which deals with both novels and films from the 1950s. In order fully to capture the phenomena I wish to consider, however, I have taken the liberty of extending my definition of the 1950s to encompass what one might call the "long 1950s," the period from roughly 1946 to 1964. I believe this periodization is far more useful than a slavish adherence to the traditional (but entirely artificial) notion of decades. My definition of the long 1950s allows me to encompass the great period of American Cold War hysteria, beginning soon after World War II and ending sometime around 1964, when nuclear and anti-Soviet paranoia in the United States began noticeably to decline.[4] In the meantime, the long 1950s include the era of Cold War–inspired science fiction films, which essentially came to an end around 1964 after the release of Kubrick's *Dr. Strangelove,* which made it impossible for such films ever again to take themselves entirely seriously. Science fiction writing came to the end of an era at about that time as well with the rise of what has come to be called the "New Wave," spearheaded by British writers such as Brian Aldiss, J. G. Ballard, and Michael Moorcock, but also involving

American writers such as Harlan Ellison, Thomas Disch, and Robert Silverberg.

Though the remarkable outburst of production of science fiction films and novels in the long 1950s is not surprising, given the overall tenor of the decade, it is also not a simple matter to characterize those films and novels as a whole. For one thing, the films were very different from the novels, tending much more toward reinforcement of prevailing ideologies than toward the often critical stance taken by the novels. In the intense political climate of the early 1950s, concerns with themes such as nuclear destruction and alien invasion tended to dominate both novels and films. However, as John Brosnan notes, written science fiction moved on to new themes in the second half of the decade, while "the film genre endlessly repeated itself with cheaper and less impressive variations on the same themes" (73). Still, despite this monotony, both the films and the novels were often filled with ambivalence and contradictions, partly because of the complex nature of the decade itself. In addition, while the science fiction of the long 1950s responds in a particularly direct and obvious way to the threat of nuclear holocaust, it is also the case that this fiction is influenced by a number of other concerns and anxieties that were crucial to the texture of American life in the decade. Indeed, these other concerns and anxieties are ultimately inseparable from the nuclear fears of the decade, the synergies among these various fears accounting for the otherwise seemingly inexplicable level of Cold War hysteria that informed American attitudes during this period — and for the vulnerability of the American populace to manipulation by opportunistic demagogues such as Senator Joseph McCarthy.

In short, the 1950s were far more complex than they have often been pictured to be. Somewhat like the 1790s in France (at least as described by Charles Dickens), the 1950s in America were informed by a radical doubleness. There are special reasons for this doubleness within the context of the 1950s. But doubleness is also a fundamental characteristic of capitalism itself, thus Marx's recognition that only dialectical analysis could comprehend the complexities of the capitalist system. The overt doubleness of American culture in the 1950s can thus be taken as a reflection of the increasing ideological hegemony of capitalism in the decade, as the last remnants of agrarian alternatives to capitalism were swept from the American scene once and for all. This phenomenon, of course, is precisely the one associated by Fredric Jameson with the rise of late capitalism and with its cultural logic, postmodernism. Thus, the consistent doubleness of the science fiction novels and films of the long 1950s can be taken as a sign of the beginnings of late capitalism and of an incipient postmodernism, regardless of the seeming lack of postmodernist formal elements in the works.

Indeed, if doubleness is a consistent characteristic of American life and ideas in the long 1950s, it is also the case that this decade is marked by a monolithic and monotonic growth in the penetration of capitalist, Fordist-Taylorist organization into virtually every aspect of American society. At the same time, the globalization that Jameson associates with late capitalism was also a consistent phenomenon of the decade. Of course, this globalization was partly propelled by the Cold War, which spurred the United States to establish a growing military, political, and economic presence around the globe. Still, as we gain increasing historical distance from (and, presumably, perspective on) the 1950s, it may well become increasingly clear that the fundamental historical phenomenon of the decade was not the Cold War, but the rise of late capitalism, to which the Cold War contributed, but was not an absolute premise.

A troubled decade, the 1950s would come to be regarded, at least after the fact, with great nostalgia as a time of material prosperity and pastoral tranquility. There were more "golden ages" in the 1950s than in any other decade. It was the Golden Age of rock 'n' roll, as new superstars, such as Elvis Presley, combined the established resources of black rhythm-and-blues music and Southern white country-and-western music to produce a new musical form attuned to the tastes and needs of an emergent youth culture. It was also the Golden Age of television, a medium that came into its own during the decade. Indeed, David Halberstam is surely correct when he suggests that the 1950s nostalgia craze of later decades was inspired less by the reality of the 1950s than by the idyllic visions promulgated in the decade's television programming, especially in idealized family sitcoms, such as *Leave It to Beaver* and *The Adventures of Ozzie and Harriet* (*The Fifties* 514).

The 1950s are also widely remembered as the Golden Age of nuclear fear. Indeed, nostalgic visions of the American 1950s as a decade of peace and prosperity notwithstanding, it is clear from the perspective of half a century later that one of the central experiences of the decade was fear, and not just of nuclear war. It is clearly not for nothing that David Caute calls his survey of the decade *The Great Fear*, emphasizing both the decade's fear of communism and the resultant terrorization of the American populace by the witch-hunting forces of anticommunism. And, if the decade's fears surrounding the Cold War confrontation between capitalism and communism went well beyond the central fear of nuclear destruction, it is also the case that the various fears that were so central to the decade went well beyond fear of communists or fear of anticommunist repression. Despite the impressive economic expansion of the decade, many who remembered the Great Depression remained terrified that another economic collapse might be on the horizon. Meanwhile, those who had profited most from the 1950s boom grew increasingly anxious that they might not personally be able to hold onto their gains, even if the overall economy remained sound.[5] White males remained afraid that their jobs might be taken by women and minorities, who, after all, had very successfully helped to fill the labor void during World War II. Women and minorities, on the other hand, were fearful, and rightfully so, that they might lose the gains they had made during the war. Workers in general grew increasingly vulnerable to exploitation as big business took advantage of the anticommunist atmosphere to conduct an all-out war on organized labor, erasing all of the gains that the trade unions had made from the 1930s through the end of the world war.[6]

Despite the reputation of the decade for conservatism and conformity, the unsettling social movements of the 1960s were strongly rooted in the 1950s. June Cleaver, Donna Reed, and Harriet Nelson might have remained the decade's official models for appropriate feminine conduct, but American women were becoming less and less willing blindly to emulate those models. Meanwhile, the rather staid and professorial Alfred Kinsey was laying the groundwork for a vast increase in awareness that the sexual behavior of actual Americans did not match that depicted (or, rather, implied) on television. *Sexual Behavior in the American Male* was published as long ago as 1948; *Sexual Behavior in the American Female* appeared in 1953. The very next year, Hugh Hefner, who saw Kinsey as his great forerunner, followed with the publication of the first *Playboy*, featuring Marilyn Monroe, the decade's central icon of female sexual allure. Meanwhile, Margaret Sanger struggled throughout the decade, with financial support from Katharine McCormick and help from scientists such as Goody Pincus and John Rock, to develop a viable oral contraceptive for women, resulting in FDA approval of "the Pill" in May 1960. In addition, the experiences of young women such as Betty Friedan in the 1950s were preparing them to lead the women's movement of the 1960s. Thus, a book such as *The Feminine Mystique*, published in 1963, is strongly rooted in the previous decade and began as an article for *McCall's* magazine in 1957.

If attitudes toward gender and sexuality were getting all shook up in the 1950s, traditional attitudes toward race, especially in the South, were becoming even less viable. It was, for example, in May of 1954 that Chief Justice Earl Warren announced the decision of the U.S. Supreme Court in the *Brown v. Board of Education* case, making illegal the widespread practice of segregated education in the United States. This decision was, Halberstam claims, "perhaps the single most important moment in the decade" (*The Fifties* 423). In December of 1955, Rosa Parks declined to move to the back of a Birmingham bus, launching the Birmingham Bus Strike and the career of Dr. Martin Luther King as a civil rights leader. By the fall of 1957, *Brown v. Board of Education* had led directly to the enforced integration of Little Rock Central High School in a televised confrontation between the 101st Airborne Division of the United States Army, called out by a reluctant Eisenhower, and the Arkansas National Guard, called out by Governor Orval Faubus. Thus, both the civil rights movement and television news simultaneously came of age in the national consciousness.

Americans, in the 1950s, were only just learning to think globally, but it is clear, in retrospect, that African Americans of the decade drew at least some inspiration from anticolonial movements in Africa and elsewhere. The influence of Mahatma Gandhi's techniques of nonviolent anticolonial resistance on civil rights leaders such as Dr. King is well known.[7] It is also clear that white Americans, who felt threatened by the inchoate civil rights movement, felt even more threatened when they saw nonwhite peoples demanding their rights around the world. The 1950s began with the near-disastrous American adventure in Korea, a conflict that many Americans saw as a battle against, not just communism, but also barbarian hordes of yellow Asians, whose steadfastness in battle was interpreted as a sign, not of courage and determination, but of typical Oriental fanaticism. The decade ended with a revolution in Cuba that led to the expulsion of American businesses (many of them controlled by organized crime) and eventually to the 1962 missile crisis, for most observers the closest the world would come to nuclear war. In between was a decade of anticolonial activism around the world, much of which was also anti-American, given the strong support of the Americans for their colonialist allies in Britain and France. Much of the anticolonial struggle, especially the Mau Mau rebellion in Kenya, was seen in the U.S. as a demonstration of primitive savagery in the non-Western world, though it was also (and often without good reason) associated, in the American mind, with the threat of communism.

Robert Coover captures many of these anxieties extremely well in *The Public Burning*, a 1977 novel about the trial and execution of the Rosenbergs, featuring Richard Nixon as the protagonist and capturing well a 1950s America gone mad with Cold War anxiety. Thus, Coover, in one telling passage, describes the "children of Uncle Sam" slipping into uneasy sleep and experiencing nightmares of all of the horrors facing American capitalism in a hostile world. These nightmares draw much of their imagery from 1950s science fiction films and feature

Soviet tanks in Berlin, dead brothers lying scattered across the cold wastes of Korea, spreading pornography and creeping socialism. Phantomized black and yellow people rising up in Africa and Asia ... the Rosenbergs, grown monstrous ... breaking out of their cells, smashing down the walls of Sing Sing with their tentacles, and descending on the city like the Beast from 20,000 Fathoms. ... They are joined by ... John Reginald Halliday Christie, his huge organ bloody and gangrenous; a big black white-eyed giant with SUPER MAU MAU emblazoned on his savage breast; thousands upon thousands of groaning victims, blinded, their flesh eaten away, from Hiroshima and Nagasaki; and Chairman Mao, swirled about by fumes from the dens of vice, like a bloated gold-toothed Fu Manchu. (107)

Such horrors could not be avoided as the United States increasingly assumed the global role formerly played by the British Empire, and "American" corporations became increasingly transnational as capitalism shifted into its global postwar phase. Indeed, though the American public was not aware of the full extent of such activities, many of which were covert, the United States repeatedly intervened in Third World politics during the 1950s. Of course, the American government justified its efforts around the world as an attempt to contain the spread of communism. However, the American claim to be intervening on behalf of democracy and human rights did not square well with the engineering of coups against elected governments in Iran and Guatemala in order to protect the interests, not of freedom, but of British Petroleum and the United Fruit Company.

Ultimately, the most important of these interventions was the staunch American support for the French forces in colonial Indochina. Not only did the American government spend more than $3 billion financing the French effort to maintain their colonial rule, but the Americans eventually stepped in altogether for the exhausted French in a sort of colonialist tag-team effort that nearly tore apart American society in the 1960s. Meanwhile, in the 1950s, the siege of the French garrison at Dien Bien Phu, so seemingly reminiscent of Indian attacks on frontier forts in American Westerns, served in the American mind as a powerful image of civilized white settlers under attack by savage natives.[8] Indeed, one could see the French outpost at Dien Bien Phu almost as an allegory for Cold War America itself, surrounded by a hostile world full of crazed enemies who simply refused to fight by Western rules.[9]

Cold War fears of Soviet expansionism were directly related to the legacy of colonialism. Indeed, as I have discussed in more detail elsewhere, the Americans, stepping into the shoes of the British as the major Western global power, also often followed in the footsteps of the British in the rhetoric with which they justified this global power (*Colonial Power* 174–83). William Pietz thus describes the rhetoric of the Cold War as a sort of "substitute for the language of colonialism" and notes in particular how many Western stereotypes of the Soviets seem to have been almost direct reinscriptions of the attitudes toward the East that Said describes in *Orientalism* (55). For Pietz, the mapping of certain traditional Orientalist stereotypes onto the Russians not only helped to "justify the practical policy of containment, but it contributed to a new theory of the neurotic psychological basis of all 'ideology,' that is, of all left political argument." Further, such stereotyping was offered as an explanation for the "component of state-backed social terror so prominent in twentieth-century European history" (69).

In the classic Orientalist gesture, negative characteristics from which the West sought to dissociate itself were projected onto the Soviets, who were then depicted as radically different from Westerners. Much early American Cold War propaganda was specifically designed to make Russia seem as foreign as possible, thus distancing Americans from the negative characteristics associated with Russians while making the Soviet menace seem more terrifying as a threat to the American way of life. Science fiction films of the 1950s famously participated in this phenomenon, with the aliens in films such as *Invasion of the Body Snatchers* (1956) often bearing suspicious resemblances to Cold War depictions of communists. But this strategy went well beyond popular culture. J. Edgar Hoover's remarkable *Masters of Deceit* (1958), for example, reads almost like a scenario for films such as *Invasion of the Body Snatchers* or for novels such as Heinlein's *The Puppet Masters* (1951).

Aliens in the science fiction of the 1950s often resembled Others from the Third World as well. Of course, Thomas Disch is correct when he points out that there is a long tradition of equating aliens with "bad guys from the Third World" in American science fiction, a tendency Disch attributes at least partly to a national bad consciousness over the genocidal destruction of Native Americans by white settlers in the United States (185–207). At the same time, this motif has a special urgency in the 1950s, when American paranoia about all kinds of aliens reached an unprecedented peak.

Meanwhile, the fears and anxieties of the 1950s resembled those that were earlier associated with colonialism in ways that went beyond an association of Soviets or communists with the colonial Other. For example, one of the most important anxieties suffered by Westerners at the end of the nineteenth century concerned the possibility of "degeneration," or backward evolution. Perhaps the central expression of this anxiety was Max Nordau's 1895 book *Degeneration*, an enormously popular work that helped to fuel the widespread fascination with the concept of degeneration. Indeed, as Kershner notes, the concept of degeneration captured the popular imagination of the time perhaps more than any other. Nordau was a student of Cesare Lombroso, the physician and criminalist who had developed the concept of inborn criminal traits, which he believed could be detected through phrenological and other physical examinations of would-be criminals. Nordau's book bears a clear relationship to Lombroso's work, and the degeneration craze as a whole draws upon both the pseudoscience of Lombroso and the genuine science of Charles Darwin.

Thus, the turn-of-the-century concern with degeneration was, like the various fears and anxieties of the 1950s, largely fueled by scientific research and discovery. It thus may not be surprising that fears of degeneration underwent a remarkable resurgence in the 1950s. Vaguely aware that evolution was driven by mutation and that mutation could be caused by radiation, Americans in the 1950s put two and two together and concluded that radiation could cause evolution, or (more probably, given the negative resonances of radiation in the decade) degeneration. Late Victorian literature is filled with images of degeneration, of which Robert Louis Stevenson's *Dr. Jekyll and Mr. Hyde* (1886) is perhaps the classic example; the science fiction of the 1950s, especially in film, quite often displays a concern with degeneration as well.

As the dark side of the Victorian fascination with evolution and progress, the fascination with degeneration represents a classic case of the doubleness of the Victorian era. The same can be said of the 1950s, when the fear of radiation and nuclear destruction represented the dark side of what in many ways was a growing faith in the ability of science to provide the knowledge required to produce better living. Even the various golden ages of the decade had dark sides that were often drenched in fear. Golden Age science fiction often turns the optimistic utopian dreams of the Gernsbackian 1930s into visions of coming dystopian nightmares. Elvis and the Golden Age rock culture he represented were terrifying to many adults, who not only perceived the emergent rock culture as an emblem of a total breakdown in American morality, but also often saw it as a sort of cultural miscegenation that could be taken as a symptom of the negrification of American culture, itself part of the general collapse of simple polar oppositions during the decade. Similarly, the idealized television programming of the 1950s was designed largely as an attempt to assuage the various fears of the decade. The Nelsons, the Cleavers, and all those other perfect television families lived in entirely white middle-class worlds, where issues of race and class simply did not exist. There simply were no African Americans in the worlds of these shows, nor were their poor workers or labor unions. Nor was gender an issue. There were women, because they were required to complete the family structure, but these women were perfectly happy to live in entirely patriarchal worlds, where men were men, and women knew their place.[10] There were no economic tensions or worries about nuclear war.

The almost complete repression of social problems in the television programming of the 1950s has often been interpreted as merely another symptom of the blind complacency and mindless conformism with which the decade has been so widely charged. After all, the 1950s were also the Golden Age of American standardization and homogenization, as Fordist-Taylorist mass production techniques reached new heights of sophistication and new levels of penetration into every aspect of American life. While television helped to homogenize the thoughts and dreams of the rapidly expanding American population, General Motors, the great industrial juggernaut of the decade, achieved unprecedented success in the business in which Ford's techniques had originally been developed. At the same time, Bill Levitt's Levittown brought mass production to the housing industry, ushering in the great age of suburbanization, perhaps the single most important step in the commodification of the American dream.[11] The 1950s were also the Golden Age of branding and franchising, as standard brands, aided by television advertising, installed themselves in the collective American consciousness, while chain franchises spread across the nation, informed by the central driving idea of homogeneity—selling identical products in identical ways at thousands of identical franchises across the country. Thus, if Levitt's vision helped to homogenize the American home, Kemmons Wilson's Holiday Inn chain made identical lodgings available to Americans wherever they drove on the nation's rapidly expanding (and more and more homogeneous) highway system in their increasingly powerful, standardized automobiles. Similarly, Ray Kroc made homogeneous food available on the road when he took the fast-food production techniques pioneered by the McDonald brothers and made standardized hamburgers an indispensable part of everyday cuisine in America.

And so on. It is thus not for nothing that the 1950s developed such a reputation for homogenization, not only of material life, but of thought itself. Thus, when Herbert Marcuse topped off the long 1950s with the publication, in 1964, of *One-Dimensional Man*, a study of the impoverishment of human experience within the growing conformism of "advanced industrial society," it is not surprising that he began his book with an introduction entitled "The Paralysis of Criticism: Society without Opposition." It was not, however, the case that the 1950s were a time in which American society had no critics. In fact, the decade was one of intense self-examination and critique, so much so that it might even be considered a Golden Age of American social criticism, or at least of engagement of American intellectuals with public issues. In the decade, one analyst after another excoriated American society for, not only its complacency and conformism, but also its shallow materialism. And these critics gained considerable public attention. As Richard Pells notes, intellectuals in the decade were often hampered by the conservative climate in which they worked, but nevertheless they fulfilled "the central function of the intellectual in a modern society" by translating their scholarly work in various disciplines "into a form of general communication" (vii–viii). Pells then goes on to argue that the works of figures such as Hannah Arendt, David Riesman, William Whyte, John Kenneth Galbraith, Paul Goodman, Daniel Bell, Dwight MacDonald, Louis Hartz, Daniel Boorstin, and C. Wright Mills are "superior in quality to any comparable collection of works produced in America during other periods of the twentieth century" (x).

Vance Packard, though not among the intellectuals Pells means here, even converted social criticism into a new genre of bestseller.[12] Clearly, the problem was not a lack of critique or even a lack of attention to this critique, but a lack of ultimate effectiveness, in which these critiques were unable to stem the tide of the phenomena they were criticizing. Of course, the inefficacy of many of these critiques can be attributed largely to the fact that, within the context of the 1950s, any truly damning critique of capitalism immediately made its author suspect as a potential communist. Thus, perhaps the most important critic of 1950s capitalism was C. Wright Mills, who managed, in works such as *White Collar* (1951) and *The Power Elite* (1956), to provide an important oppositional voice, but had to perform a delicate balancing act by appearing anti-Marxist as well. Still, Mills went further than most cultural critics in the 1950s in attributing the ills of the decade to fundamental structural flaws in the American system. Especially in *The Power Elite*, he even comes close to suggesting that class inequality is the most important social problem in America, though he assures his readers at several points that his concept of a powerful elite, constantly pulling the strings of ordinary Americans, differs in crucial ways from the Marxist notion of a ruling class. Indeed, Mills's critique is ultimately typical of 1950s cultural criticism in its focus on specific institutions rather than class or the basic economic system. For Mills, there is a powerful elite of individuals in corporations, government, and the military, who determine the basic course taken by American society, while the vast majority of Americans are immersed in a "mass society" that leaves them in a state of passivity and ignorance relative to the real forces that drive the world around them.

Ultimately, Mills's critique is not all that different from Eisenhower's famous later warnings about the growing power of the American "military-industrial complex." And it arises from a firmly American perspective, its most serious concerns being based on a loss of individualism in the face of the increasing power of institutions and the elite who run them. At times, in fact, Mills even seems to anticipate Michel Foucault's later, more poststructuralist (and postmodernist) description of the modern carceral, or disciplinary society, in which individual life is penetrated and controlled by large impersonal forces to an unprecedented extent. Mills, for example, notes that Americans pride themselves on their unmatched individualism, but that "among them the impersonal corporation has proceeded the farthest and now reaches every area and detail of daily life" (*The Power Elite* 120).[13]

Other critics focused on more specific phenomena, while still refusing to attribute any of the ills associated with those phenomena to fundamental flaws in capitalism as a system. In particular, as Jackson Lears notes, the social scientists of the 1950s tended to perform elaborate feats of reification, in which they attributed a variety of material consequences to the agency of abstract concepts (42–43). Thus, for David Riesman, in *The Lonely Crowd* (1950), personality types cause individuals to act in certain ways and contribute to the inability of individual Americans to develop any genuine sense of personal identity. He sees America, at the beginning of the 1950s, as being in the process of a fundamental shift from the dominance of "inner-directed" personality types (who act out of a sense that what they are doing is right) to the dominance of "other-directed" personality types (who act primarily out of the hope that others will approve their action), especially among the affluent middle classes. *The Lonely Crowd* thus becomes an extended warning against creeping conformism, a warning that, in the course of the coming decade, would be echoed again and again by social scientists. At the same time, as his title indicates, Riesman warns that this shift to an emphasis on approval by the Other is fraught with a number of inherent difficulties, including a tendency for individuals to feel unauthentic and inadequate in their quest for approval.

Riesman draws upon a number of disciplines, "juggling" them, as Pells puts it, "with spectacular dexterity" (238). But Riesman is typical of the 1950s in this regard, and particularly in his reliance on psychology and psychoanalysis for the examination of what are essentially social and historical phenomena. Similarly, David Potter, in *People of Plenty* (1954), goes out of his way to relate his historical thesis to fields such as psychology. For Potter, however, American abundance in the 1950s does not represent a new historical phase, but is merely an extension of the culture of abundance that he sees as central to American life from the very beginning. For Potter, abundance may have its down side, but any problems associated with the American emphasis on wealth are caused, not by capitalism, but by a personified notion of abundance itself. Meanwhile, Potter's concern with the role of abundance in the formation of the "American character" focuses on an object of fascination for the cultural critics of the 1950s, who made this topic a key locus for a demonstration of American exceptionalism. In any case, the problems caused by America's culture of abundance (such as the creation of high expectations that are bound to lead to disappointment for some citizens) are, for Potter, relatively minor and secondary. Indeed, Potter's book is essentially a paean to Americanism, repeatedly declaring that America's unprecedented abundance arises as much from the hard work and ingenuity of the American people as from ample natural resources. On the other hand, Americans work hard because they learn, growing up in a culture of abundance, to be productive and competitive from the very beginning. Potter does offer some warnings about the potentially sinister power of the advertising industry in the abundant 1950s, but, by and large, the American character he associates with abundance is a positive character indeed, unrivaled in its productive capacity.

Not surprisingly, given the paranoid climate of the 1950s, critics of American society in the 1950s were fairly consistent in maintaining a strongly pro-American stance, arguing that the ills they described were deviations from genuine Americanism. Even Lewis Mumford, one of the most strident cultural critics of the 1950s, characterized the negative consequences of an almost hysterical emphasis on "national security" amid the anticommunist hysteria of the early 1950s as a loss of traditional American values (and civil liberties). As the title of his main work in this vein, *In the Name of Sanity* (1954), clearly indicates, Mumford saw this hysteria as a sort of mass, officially encouraged, psychosis. But Mumford carefully couches his seemingly bitter criticisms of American society in terms that avoid any indication of a preference for the Soviet alternative. Indeed, one of Mumford's central tropes in *In the Name of Sanity* is an expression of fear that the United States might become as bad as the Soviet Union. Meanwhile, in his other works, Mumford also became a leading critic of the homogenization and standardization of American life, carrying on a particularly violent battle with Bill Levitt, whose Levittown was for Mumford the very embodiment of enforced mind-numbing conformity.[14]

Such conformity was also supposedly a key consequence of the massification of culture in the decade, as addressed by critics such as Dwight MacDonald. Indeed, one of the remarkable phenomena of the 1950s is the consistency with which American cultural critics who were supposedly on the Left expressed a horror of mass culture, as opposed to a great admiration for high culture, now epitomized by modernism. Of course, this suspicion of mass culture has a legitimate leftist pedigree in the work of Frankfurt School critics such as Max Horkheimer and Theodor Adorno, whose essay, "The Culture Industry," is the seminal text in this field. But Horkheimer and Adorno focused their critique on the corporate powers that controlled mass culture, using it to further their own ends. American critics of the 1950s, particularly the New York Intellectuals and other critics associated with the journal *Partisan Review*, seemed horrified by the very idea of mass culture — or even of the masses themselves.

Meanwhile, the Frankfurt School tradition was carried on directly in the long 1950s by Marcuse, who became an important figure with the publication of *One-Dimensional Man*, which looked back on the 1950s, but ultimately helped to make its author, who seemed to recommend nonstandard sexual conduct as a potential form of subversion, a key figure in the 1960s. Marcuse's study draws heavily upon Marx, but is Freudian enough to avoid seeming all that Marxist, instead merely appearing European. On the other hand, Marcuse's critique also recalls concerns of the American cultural critics of the 1950s, especially William Whyte, whose book, *The Organization Man* (1956), is described by Lears as the "locus classicus of the 1950s critique of conformity" (44). Whyte argues that the growing regimentation of corporate culture in the 1950s is producing a population of corporate clones, virtually bereft of any genuine individual identity. However, far from attributing this phenomenon to capitalism, Whyte essentially suggests that the enforced conformism of the 1950s represents a betrayal of the true individualistic values of capitalism in favor of an emphasis on the group.

The Organization Man was widely read in the 1950s, though the concerns it expresses were more firmly associated in the popular imagination with a novel, Sloan Wilson's *The Man in the Gray Flannel Suit*, one of the top bestsellers of 1955. Wilson's book comes as close as anything we have to being the decade's signature novel, despite having received relatively little critical attention and even less critical respect as a work of literature. Wilson's title image, for example, became an emblem of the decade's drive for conformism, a drive that threatened individual identity but that also offered a certain comfort level for those (mostly male WASPs) who were able to fit in. Indeed, *The Man in the Gray Flannel Suit*, despite some criticism of the era's corporate culture, with its emphasis on the drive for success at the expense of all else, is ultimately an affirmative work that assures Americans that they can succeed and still be themselves.

Less affirmative was Erving Goffman's *Asylums* (1961), perhaps the decade's most chilling account of the suppression of individuality by impersonal institutions. Goffman focuses not on corporations, but on "total institutions," such as mental hospitals and prisons, the inmates of which are completely in the control of institutional authority. Again anticipating the work of Foucault, Goffman's characterization of total institutions is consistently accompanied by subtle suggestions that these institutions are not extreme cases, but are in fact representative of life in the highly regimented corporate culture of modern America. Moreover, Goffman's suggestion that conditions in total institutions lead to the fragmentation of the psyches of their subjects tends to anticipate postmodern descriptions of subjectivity as a whole, though postmodern accounts of this phenomenon often gave it a positive spin, as in the celebration of psychic fragmentation in the work of Gilles Deleuze and Félix Guattari.

Among other things, Goffman's focus on mental hospitals is indicative of the growing preoccupation, in the America of the 1950s, with mental illness and with psychoanalysis as a technique for separating "normal," mentally healthy (and thus reliable) citizens from those who were mentally ill, and thus were abnormal and unreliable. Freud became a virtual icon of American popular culture in the 1950s, and the language and images of psychoanalysis became very much a part of the popular jargon and imagination. Meanwhile, mental illness became a major public health issue as never before — witness the campaign to promote awareness of mental health that lies at the center of the depiction of the advertising industry in *The Man in the Gray Flannel Suit*. And, not surprisingly, the rhetoric of psychoanalysis strongly informed the social criticism of the period, particularly in the work of European imports such as Marcuse, Erik Erikson, Bruno Bettelheim, Karen Horney, and Erich Fromm, who also drew upon vaguely Marxian resources in his declaration that American society itself, by placing more value on material wealth than on people and their emotional well-being, was in danger of insanity. No matter, however: the good news, according to Fromm, was that it was, in fact, possible to have both individual happiness and material abundance.

Though the points of view of individual critics can vary dramatically, virtually all of the social and cultural criticism of the long 1950s had to do in one way or another with the very American notion of suppression of individualism. At the same time, no matter how non-Marxist this criticism strove to be, most of it can be subsumed under the various basic Marxist categories described by Jameson as "mediatory codes," including Max Weber's notion of "rationalization," as well as "social class, mode of production, the alienation of labor, commodification, the various ideologies of Otherness (sex or race), and political domination" (*Political Unconscious* 226). Herein surely lies at least part of the explanation for the inefficacy of social critique in the 1950s: not only were the Marxist terms of this critique displaced into an alien, non-Marxist context, but they lacked the crucial element that lends Marxist critique its unique strength—the ability to envision a specific, well-articulated utopian alternative (namely, socialism) to the capitalist system.

This lack is part of a general weakness in utopian thought in the 1950s. It is, in many ways, a version of Daniel Bell's well known diagnosis of the "exhaustion of political ideas" in the 1950s, an exhaustion that for Bell centrally involves "the exhaustion of utopia," a topic that for him means the exhaustion of *socialist* utopias and that occupies approximately one-third of his seminal volume, *The End of Ideology* (1960). It is my thesis in this volume that the science fiction of the long 1950s, in both novel and film, closely parallels the social criticism of the decade in the terms of its critique of American society—and in the ultimate limitations of this critique. This phenomenon can be traced via any of the mediatory codes listed above, but I focus primarily on two of them: alienation and rationalization, though I prefer the term "routinization" to indicate the latter.

If the long 1950s are the decade in which late capitalism begins not only to assert its global hegemony, but also to complete its dominance in the "advanced" countries" of the West, then it should also be the decade when the consequences of capitalism, such as alienation and routinization, reach full fruition. Alienation, of course, was self-consciously a central issue of the 1950s, beginning with the focus on that motif in Riesman's *The Lonely Crowd*. It was a great theme of the Beats and of the decade's literature as a whole: Ellison's Invisible Man and Salinger's Holden Caulfield are nothing if not alienated. Meanwhile, central cultural icons of the decade, such as Marlon Brando and James Dean, owed much of their popularity to their ability to radiate alienation on the screen. In his biography of Brando, Richard Schickel notes the self-conscious preoccupation with alienation in the 1950s, relating it to the cultural criticism of such figures as Riesman, Mills, and Whyte, while at the same time suggesting the impotence of this criticism, no matter how widely disseminated:

The Lonely Crowd was anatomized in 1950, and the fear of drifting into its clutches was lively in us. *White Collar* was on our brick and board bookshelves, and we saw how the eponymous object seemed to be choking the life out of earlier generations. *The Man in the Gray Flannel Suit* stalked our nightmares and soon enough *The Organization Man* would join him there, though, of course, even as we read about these cautionary figures, many of us were talking to corporate recruiters about entry-level emulation of them. (6)

Given the pervasive concern with alienation in the culture of the 1950s, it should come as no surprise that the science fiction of the decade was often concerned with this issue. For example, Mark Jancovich notes that the fiction of writers such as Ray Bradbury and Richard Matheson and the films of Jack Arnold are centrally concerned with the phenomenon of alienation (3). Similarly, Marc Scott Zicree, introducing his *Twilight Zone Companion*, argues that the popularity of the show was largely due to its strong focus on the theme of alienation, which he describes as "the great dilemma of our age" (n.p.). Actually, the phenomenon described by Schickel as "alienation" is at least partly a matter of routinization, and the two phenomena are in fact extremely difficult to separate in the long 1950s.

Routinization is closely related to the decade's concern with conformism, where by routinization I refer to Weber's indication, in *The Protestant Ethic and the Spirit of Capitalism* (1904–1905), of the way in which, under modern capitalist society, every aspect of life becomes regimented, scheduled, and controlled for maximum economic efficiency, leaving little room for elements of life that might lie outside the realm of the economic. Sensing this phenomenon, the very economic successes of the 1950s were felt as a threat by many, as middle-class families ran up more and more debt and got more and more firmly locked into the capitalist system. For many, greater material wealth only meant that they had more to lose within the unstable fabric of a rapidly moving and changing American society. Indeed, many American sociologists in the long 1950s recognized the relevance of Weber's work to their own context. Riesman refers to Weber repeatedly and admiringly. Whyte declares that the phenomena he associates with the rise of the "organization man" in 1950s

America "stem from a bureaucratization of society" that was described in the work of Weber (4). And Daniel Bell, looking back from the perspective of the mid-1970s, declares *The Protestant Ethic and the Spirit of Capitalism* to be "probably the most important sociological work of the twentieth century" (*Cultural Contradictions* 287).

As Jameson points out in his discussion of mediatory codes, Weber's notion of rationalization is very much the same phenomenon described by Georg Lukács, especially in *History and Class Consciousness*, as reification (226). The phenomenon indicated by Weber is also very much a part of what Michel Foucault has more recently described as "carceral" or "disciplinary" society. I prefer the term routinization because it well captures the sense of stultifying pressure to conform that was central to this experience in America in the long 1950s. Meanwhile, Weber's discussion of this phenomenon places a special emphasis on the way in which the modern capitalist world has become bereft of magic and of any sense that the marvelous can occur. The diminished utopian imagination of the 1950s can thus be seen as a consequence of routinization, while the growing popularity of science fiction in the 1950s can be related, at least in part, to a desire to recover some sense of the marvelous, to gain some reassurance that the very technologization that was helping to make life routine might also help to make it magical once again. Jancovich has very clearly made this point in relation to the "horror" films of the 1950s, a category that, for him, includes many of the best known science fiction films of the decade. Noting the growing sense of Americans that their lives were in the grip of large, impersonal forces, Jancovich argues that the principal threat out of which the horror films of the decade grew is "the process of rationalization," by which he means "the process through which scientific-technical rationality is applied to the management of social, economic and cultural life, a process in which rational procedures are used to examine and reorganize social, economic, and cultural practices in an attempt to produce order and efficiency" (2–3).

Jancovich places special emphasis on the growing power of science and of the penetration of Fordism and Taylorism into all aspects of American life in the 1950s, but his notion of rationalization is essentially the same phenomenon that I am calling routinization. Indeed, though Jancovich does not mention Weber in his discussion, he uses Weber's terminology, which had, in fact, earlier been used by Marx and even Hegel to describe much the same phenomenon. Meanwhile, critics such as Jameson have long argued that science fiction and other forms of nonrealist literature derive much of their energy from a desire to escape routinization and to restore some of the romance and magic that this capitalist phenomenon has removed from everyday life. Science fiction certainly participates in this project, even as it is also part of the popular culture that many have seen as a symptom of routinization. As Bell points out, the various critiques of mass society and mass culture that were so prominent in the social criticism of the 1950s were often really focused on "the mass as bureaucratized society," which is simply another name for the phenomenon of rationalization or routinization (*End* 24).

The following chapters explore the science fiction novels and films of the 1950s, focusing on the engagement of those works with their social and cultural contexts. This engagement naturally includes a concern with the scientific developments of the decade and with the possibility of nuclear war. However, it also includes a central concern with other issues, including the issues of alienation and routinization, both of which are also crucially involved in the decade's complex attitude toward the Other. The particular form of alienation that was so prevalent in America in the long 1950s can be described as a fear of exclusion, as a fear of not fitting in. Surrounded by a pressure to conform, individuals feared their own inability to do so; they feared being identified as different, as being, in fact, the Other. Conversely, routinization in the long 1950s involves a sense of being forced into conformity, at a loss of individual identity. In short, Americans in the long 1950s suffered from two principal fears: the fear of being different from everyone else and the fear of being the same as everyone else.

Given the complex imbrication of these two seemingly opposed fears, it is not surprising that the decade's attitude toward the Other is complex and ambivalent. Indeed, one can see the intensity of the "Us versus Them" logic that was so central to the Cold War as an attempt to recover the firm sense of separation between self and Other that was otherwise becoming so unstable in the 1950s. Indeed, even within the context of Cold War Manicheanism, it became extremely difficult to determine with any certainty just who was Us and who was Them, a problem that is most clearly expressed in all those science fiction films, such as *Invaders from Mars* (1953) and *Invasion of the Body Snatchers* (1956), in which alien invaders could make themselves or their agents indistinguishable from "normal" Americans.

Among other things, the erosion of stable polar oppositions in the 1950s can be taken as a sign of incipient postmodernism. Indeed, numerous aspects of the 1950s anticipate the postmodern condition in ways that have yet to be fully appreciated by critics of the phenomenon of postmodernism. David Harvey, for example, views the 1950s as the heyday of "Fordist modernism," and sees the political unrest of 1968 as a "harbinger" of the coming of postmodernity, which he sees as emerging into full view by around 1972 (38). More specifically, Harvey argues that postmodernism involves "the cultural evolution which has taken place since the early 1960s, and which asserted itself as hegemonic in the early 1970s" (63). On the other hand, Harvey does not fundamentally disagree with Jameson's important thesis that postmodernism is the "cultural logic" of late capitalism, where late capitalism is the latest, global phase of capitalist development as described by Ernest Mandel.

For Jameson, late capitalism is capitalism in its phase of global dominance, when modernization has swept over the globe, and transnational corporations have become the world's most powerful and important entities, accompanied by a number of other phenomena, including

the new international division of labor, a vertiginous new dynamic in international banking and the stock exchanges (including the enormous Second and Third World debt), new forms of media interrelationship (very much including transportation systems such as containerization), computers and automation, the flight of production to advanced Third World areas, along with all the more familiar social consequences, including the crisis of traditional labor, the emergence of yuppies, and gentrification on a now-global scale. (*Postmodernism* xix)

Jameson argues that the global hegemony of capitalism leads to the global homogeny of culture, with postmodernism as the dominant mode worldwide. This does not, of course, mean that no other cultural forms survive in the postmodern age, only that the postmodern forms are the dominant ones. Thus, for Jameson "the only authentic cultural production today has seemed to be that which can draw on the collective experience of marginal pockets of the social life in the world system," a category that for him includes such heterogeneous entities as Third World literature, African-American literature, British working-class rock, women's literature, gay literature, and the *roman québecois* (*Signatures* 23). In this sense, by the way, Jameson oddly echoes the neoconservative arguments of Bell that, with ideology exhausted in the West, the best hope for new sources of utopian ideas lies in the Third World (*End* 403).

Nevertheless, Jameson's model clearly implies a continually diminishing distance between the cultures of the First and Third worlds in the era of late capitalism. Meanwhile, the globalization of capitalism means that America and the Third World are now part of one large economic system, thus obscuring the sense that Americans are somehow unique and apart from the rest of the world, especially the "backward" areas of the Third World. In addition, the global hegemony of modern capitalism, by wiping out all vestiges of older social systems and modes of productions, contributes to an overall loss in the ability of postmodern subjects to imagine alternatives to the current system, and thus the diminution of utopian thinking after World War II. And, if it is impossible to imagine alternatives to the present, then it is impossible to think historically, to imagine that, with time, things might become fundamentally different. The historical imagination is further crippled by the confusion and bewilderment of the individual subject as he or she attempts to map his or her place in the huge system of global capitalism. Indeed, this difficulty in cognitive mapping is central to a virtual dissolution of the stable subject altogether. Thus, for Jameson, in a move that recalls the work of Goffman from the 1950s, the postmodern era is characterized, among other things, by a continual increase in the level of alienation of individual subjects under capitalism, to the point that alienation is no longer the word for it: by the time of full-blown postmodernism, the individual subject experiences a "psychic fragmentation" so radical that individuals no longer have a stable enough psyche to undergo the fundamentally modernist experience of alienation (*Postmodernism* 90).

This loss of historical sense and the fragmentation of subjectivity contribute to the production of postmodernist "schizo-texts," which are themselves highly fragmentary and which tend to be spatial in form, with postmodernist authors no longer being able to construct coherent narratives that can provide a stable temporal structure for their works. These phenomena also contribute to a destruction of individual style. For Jameson, postmodernist authors no longer have stable and distinctive identities, so it only makes sense that, surrounded by a world of simulacra and ever-flowing, interchangeable media images, all they can produce are pastiches of a variety of pre-existing styles, tending to switch rapidly from one style to another, or even one genre to another, within a single work.

All of these consequences emerge in their full form only in the postmodernist culture of the 1970s and beyond, a culture in which science fiction films and novels have played a central role. Importantly, however, Mandel locates the beginnings of late capitalism in the 1940s and 1950s, essentially in the new world capitalist order that arose after World War II. Following Jameson's thesis, then, it makes sense that one should be able to locate at the least some of the roots of postmodernist culture in the long 1950s. And, of course, such roots can be found. William S. Burroughs's *Naked Lunch* (published in Paris in 1959, though not appearing in the U.S. until 1966) grew out of the Beat movement and was thus very much a representative work of the 1950s. It is also widely regarded as postmodernist. And, if Burroughs's book reaches back from the Beats to the avant garde and forward from the Beats to postmodernism, it is also the case that postmodernist icons such as William Gaddis, with *The Recognitions* (1955), John Barth, with early works culminating in *The Sot-Weed Factor* (1960), and John Hawkes, with a series of novels that include *The Beetle Leg* (1951) and *The Lime Twig* (1961), also got their starts in the 1950s, even before postmodernism was recognized as a phenomenon — which partly explains why these novelists were not widely recognized as important figures at the time.

However, if Jameson's view of the organic relationship between postmodernism and late capitalism is correct, one should see even more widespread signs of the birth of postmodernism in the culture of the long

1950s. I believe those signs can be found in a number of places, including film noir and the crime fiction of Jim Thompson. They can also be found in the science fiction of the decade, even in the seemingly formulaic efforts of science fiction film. Vivian Sobchack, essentially adopting Jameson's vision of postmodernism, argues that science fiction film in the 1980s, including such seminal works as Ridley Scott's *Blade Runner* (1982) and James Cameron's *The Terminator* (1984), can be taken as one of the central instances of the postmodernist culture that Jameson describes. But Sobchack also argues that certain beginnings of postmodernism appear in the science fiction films of the 1950s, which can be seen as an attempt at "mapping" the new world of late capitalism and as "the first socially symbolic cinematic representation of late American capitalism's new expansion toward its 'purest' state" (252).

In a similar way, if cyberpunk is a central instance of postmodernist fiction, then it is also the case that the science fiction novels of the long 1950s often show signs of incipient postmodernism. The following chapters, while exploring the political engagement of the science fiction films and novels of the 1950s, also pay attention to the way in which these films and novels announce the beginnings of postmodernism. Of course, postmodernism is notoriously difficult to define or characterize in simple terms — which is why its very name suggests that it is simply something rather vague and undefined that comes after modernism. However, it is probably useful, in order to facilitate my exploration of the beginnings of postmodernism in the science fiction of the 1950s, to at least suggest some of the general phenomena that I mean to encompass when I use the word "postmodernism."

I should say, first of all, that I believe Jameson's characterization of postmodernism as the cultural logic of late capitalism is basically sound and that his work is the principal influence on my own view of what constitutes postmodernism. I would, however, go a bit further than Jameson in his description of postmodernism as what happens culturally when capitalist modernity has triumphed entirely. For one thing, I would put more emphasis than Jameson does on the canonization of modernism in the long 1950s as evidence of this triumph of modernity, despite the antagonism often shown toward capitalism by modernist art. I would suggest that this canonization was largely a matter of appropriation and that it occurred partly because the modernist art of the first half of the twentieth century continued, in its treatment of themes such as alienation and routinization, to respond very well to the concerns of the first two decades after World War II. But I would also suggest that the canonization-appropriation of modernism in the long 1950s was largely a phenomenon of Cold War propaganda, in which modernism was conscripted as the High Art of the West so that it could be favorably opposed to the presumably less impressive and sophisticated socialist real-

ist art of the Soviet Union. There was, of course, a great irony in this con-
scription, given that modernism had largely defined itself in opposition
to the bourgeois culture of capitalism (and given that the modernists had,
as a result, been held largely in disrepute by the capitalist powers that
were). Modernism having thereby been stripped of its critical function in
relation to capitalism, postmodernism then arose as an attempt to recover this critical position, but as a largely ineffectual attempt, because
the postmodernists had no new aesthetic resources at their disposal other
than the modernist techniques that had already been conscripted by capitalism as a tool of Cold War propaganda (not to mention advertising and
popular culture). After all, the late consumer capitalism of America in the
1950s was not a new historical phenomenon, but merely the completion
of the rise of consumer capitalism in the first two decades of this century,
a rise that had helped to inspire modernism.

This particular historical conjuncture, in which postmodernist art
seeks to find an identity for itself in opposition to a modernism it is
doomed aesthetically to echo, leads to a number of particular characteristics that are crucial to my understanding of postmodernism. First, I
would argue that postmodernism itself is difficult to define now, partly
because it has always been difficult to define. The movement itself has
been in the midst of an identity crisis from the very beginning, and
postmodernist artists, except perhaps for the special case of postmodernist architects, have never had a very clear idea of what it was they were
trying to achieve. And this confusion is central to what I see as a number
of other basic characteristics of postmodernist literature and film, listed
below.

1. Postmodernism participates in a general crisis in belief of the kind indicated in
   their different ways by Jean-François Lyotard's influential suggestion that
   postmodernism is informed by a radical suspicion toward "totalizing
   metanarratives" and by Daniel Bell's argument that the period following
   World War II was informed by a general loss of belief in specific, well-defined
   "ideologies." Of course, this crisis, in the versions of both Lyotard and Bell,
   grows out of a number of historical events, including the traumas of World
   War II; the final realization of the West soon after the war that colonialism had
   been immoral, brutal, and unethical all along; and the rapid growth of technology during and after the war. This growth included, not only the development of nuclear weapons, which, for many, made human life so tenuous as to
   appear pointless, but also major innovations in communications, transportation, and automation. Importantly, many of these innovations served to enable
   and trigger still more rapid innovations, in a dizzying spiral of accelerating
   change that seemed to bear out once and for all the warning of Marx and
   Engels that, under the pressure of capitalist innovation, nothing lasts long
   enough to acquire any real meaning, and "everything solid melts into air"
   (Marx and Engels 476). It should also be stated, however, that this collapse of
   belief in totalizing ideological systems was greatly enhanced by Cold War as-

saults on Marxism, the leading example of such a system. Once again, then, postmodernism proves to be far more a product of the Cold War than has typically been acknowledged by critics and theorists.

2. The vertiginous pace of change in the long 1950s also contributed to the era's increasing sense of the instability of personal identity, which accompanied the growing sense of alienation experienced by individuals during the decade. After all, individual identity attains its stability through a perception of continuity of selfhood over time. This perception was increasingly difficult to maintain in a decade in which so many things changed so radically over such short periods of time.

3. This schizophrenic sense of a loss of individual temporal continuity also contributed to a larger loss of any sense of historical continuity. Individuals in the 1950s increasingly felt that they were living in unprecedented situations to which the experience of the past was irrelevant. For example, how could anything that had happened before the bomb really apply to a world in which the bomb made sudden global annihilation a constant threat? Moreover, the pace of change was so rapid that the present also became disconnected from the future, which became more and more unpredictable. Thus, the totalizing systems that were called into question during the long 1950s included any and all scientific and theoretical models of history.

4. The loss of faith in historical metanarratives was accompanied by a weakening of the utopian imagination, and in particular by a loss of faith in the possibility that utopian dreams might actually be realized. If history did not make sense, how could it be expected to lead to an ideal conclusion? Thus, the era's sense of rapid, and even terrifying change was accompanied by an equally horrifying sense that, within the routinized context of late capitalism, nothing ever really changes after all. Again, routinization combined with alienation. That these two fears seem opposed and contradictory is itself an indication of the ambivalence of the decade and of postmodernist thought as a whole.

5. Also closely related to the collapse of belief in totalizing systems was a collapse of the tradition of Aristotelian logic, through which Western society had long defined itself via a series of polar oppositions, the central of which were Good versus Evil and Us versus Them—both of which ultimately amount, in the Western tradition, to pretty much the same thing. Without such clear distinctions to rely on, postmodernist thought tends toward a radical relativism, in which no point of view can be maintained as absolutely superior to any other point of view. This collapse, of course, has been more strongly associated with poststructuralism than with postmodernism, and is crucial to poststructuralist phenomena such as Derridean deconstruction. Meanwhile, the critique of the social implications of polar thought is crucial to the works of Foucault, a central thinker of both poststructuralism and postmodernism, which are, in this sense at least, very much congruent phenomena, even if it is an exaggeration to say that they are the same thing.

6. This collapse of belief in polar oppositions has a number of aesthetic consequences, including a growing sense of doubt about the distinction between art and reality. Of course, this particular crisis was furthered by the increasing aestheticization of life in the 1950s, as new communications and media technologies made it possible for culture to penetrate everyday life in an unprece-

dented way. The unstable boundary between fiction and reality is a key element of what Brian McHale has described, in his *Postmodernist Fiction* (1987), as a general postmodernist confusion of ontological levels and boundaries. But a blurring of this boundary is also, in many ways, a key element of science fiction as a genre.

7. Related to this confusion of levels is a questioning of the traditional distinction between high and low culture. Many critics, such as Andreas Huyssen, have seen this aspect of postmodernism as a sign that it is more democratic than an elitist modernism. On the other hand, it is also the case that the institutionalization of modernism in the 1950s was furthered by a sense for a need to establish new standards of high art amid the general collapse of aesthetic values that many saw as a consequence of the massification of American society during the period. If nothing else, this deconstruction of the boundary between high and low art opened opportunities for popular genres, such as science fiction, to assume a new importance in American culture.

8. The postmodernist questioning of traditional standards of aesthetic judgment leads to a general mode of playfulness and parody in which postmodernist art, often resorting to the campy self-parody, seems to have difficulty taking itself seriously. Moreover, in the absence of reliable standards of aesthetic value, works of postmodernist art tend to be informed by a multiplicity of styles and genres. Again, one can see this multiplicity as democratic and as an attempt to generate a Bakhtinian dialogism among the different styles and genres. But one can also see it as a sign of a lack of faith in the appropriateness or effectiveness of any one style or genre.

All of these characteristics, especially as they are rooted in the cultural and historical context of the long 1950s, inform my readings of science fiction in the coming chapters. The first chapter surveys the politics of a range of novels by major science fiction writers such as Asimov, Pohl, and Heinlein. It also looks at the work of writers such as Bester, Vonnegut, and Dick, who are also politically engaged, but who serve more clearly as harbingers of postmodernism. Chapter 2 looks at the post-holocaust theme in both novels and films of the long 1950s, demonstrating the ways in which these works engage issues such as alienation and routinization, in addition to the obvious theme of the threat of nuclear destruction.

Chapter 3 surveys science fiction films that concentrate on the theme of alien invasion, while chapter 4 looks at monster movies. In both cases, the films engage a number of issues that are representative of American culture in the long 1950s, going well beyond their obvious Cold War resonances to explore themes related to race, gender, and the increasing involvement of the United States in the Third World. Partly because of their limited budgets, these films do not tend toward postmodernism in style to the same extent as do many of the science fiction novels of the period. Nevertheless, these films show a strong awareness of, and thematic engagement with, phenomena, such as the globalization of capital, that are crucial to the development of postmodernism. From this point of view, these films are not the naïve and dated productions they are often seen to be: they are the direct predecessors of sophisticated postmodernist productions such as *Blade Runner* and *The Terminator*. Meanwhile, this continuity sheds new light on the nature of postmodernism itself, which appears to be rooted far more in the political climate of the long 1950s than it has typically been seen to be.

1

Politics in the American Science Fiction Novel, 1946–1964: Science Fiction as Social Criticism

Darko Suvin's suggestion that the central strategy of science fiction is "cognitive estrangement" has been one of the most influential formulations in the history of science fiction criticism (*Metamorphoses* 3–15). Essentially an extension of the Russian formalist concept of defamiliarization, this notion suggests that science fiction is not primarily concerned with distant times or distant galaxies, but instead uses these unusual settings to provide fresh perspectives from which to view the author's (or reader's) own time and place. Drawing upon Suvin, I myself have argued that this defamiliarizing technique is particularly effective as a method of political commentary in dystopian fiction and other overtly political science fiction (*Dystopian Impulse* 19). More recently, Carl Freedman has extended Suvin's formulation to argue that the dominance of cognitive estrangement in science fiction as a genre makes that genre a particularly potent form of political commentary, one that has much in common with critical theory. In particular, Freedman argues that "critical theory itself, especially in its most central, Marxian version, does implicitly privilege a certain genre; and the genre is science fiction" (30). Further, he concludes that "science fiction enjoys a unique affinity with Marxism as well as with other varieties of critical theory" (86).[1]

Freedman, who sees the work of Philip K. Dick as the leading example of the critical potential of science fiction, provides a convenient framework within which to begin to explore the political engagement of the science fiction of the long 1950s. Meanwhile, the emphasis on cognitive estrangement in science fiction as a whole suggests a potential affinity between the genre and postmodernism. I am thinking here of Fredric Jameson's well known suggestion that one of the principal experiences of postmodernity is a difficulty with "cognitive mapping," in which individual subjects find it more and more difficult to establish a stable sense of their own place amid the growing complexity of the postmodern world. For Jameson, then, any genuinely political form of postmodernist culture must attempt to surmount this difficulty and will thus "have as its vocation the invention and projection of a global cognitive mapping, on a social as well as a spatial scale" (*Postmodernism* 54).[2]

If postmodernist fiction needs to explore new modes of cognitive mapping, and if cognitive estrangement is the principal strategy of science fiction, then it only makes sense that science fiction should be a paradigmatic mode of postmodernism. This connection may help to explain why Jameson himself is among those who have seen cyberpunk science fiction as a quintessential form of postmodernist culture, as when he declares cyberpunk "the supreme *literary* expression if not of postmodernism, then of late capitalism itself" (*Postmodernism* 419). Jameson also sees a potentially powerful political role for science fiction, declaring science fiction "a historically new and original form which offers analogies with the emergence of the historical novel in the early nineteenth century" (*Postmodernism* 283). Freedman does not share Jameson's belief in the importance of cyberpunk, but he does extend the analogy between science fiction and the historical novel as he argues the political relevance of science fiction as a whole. Moreover, he agrees that cyberpunk is essentially a postmodern phenomenon, proposing, in fact, a Lukácsian-Jamesonian model of the literary history of science fiction in which "the 'Golden Age' work typified by Heinlein and Asimov amounts to the science fictional equivalent of realism, with modernism represented by such authors as Le Guin and Delany of the *Dangerous Visions* era, and postmodernism represented by that more recent science fictional tendency known as cyberpunk" (195).

This model has its merits, though it seems to suggest that the historical evolution of science fiction is somewhat out of phase with the larger culture, recapitulating in three decades or so a literary history that spanned two centuries in the mainstream fiction of the West. In short, Freedman's model places science fiction at the height of its realist phase just as modernism is being enshrined as the official high culture of the West and just as modernism itself is already being supplanted by the early works of such postmodernism as William Gaddis's, *The Recognitions* (1955) and John Barth's *The Sot-Weed Factor* (1960). Indeed, even such "later" postmodernists as Thomas Pynchon and E. L. Doctorow were already publishing in the long 1950s. This situation does not necessary obviate Freedman's model, but it does suggest that the seeds of later modernist and postmodernist developments were already present in the Golden Age science fiction of the long 1950s, thus spurring the particularly rapid movement of the genre from one phase to another.

Dick is a particularly important figure here. Often seen as a crucial forerunner of cyberpunk, Dick is certainly the science fiction writer, prior to William Gibson, who has been most widely associated with the phenomenon of postmodernism.[3] Dick's fiction, with its consistent confusion of ontological levels, overtly thematizes many of the central concerns and characteristics of postmodernism. For example, in *The World Jones Made* (1956), Dick projects a post–nuclear holocaust world, in which attempts to avert the kind of fanaticism that can lead to nuclear war have resulted in an officially mandated relativism, which makes it literally illegal to proclaim the absolute truth of one's own position relative to the untruth of other competing positions. This situation, however, creates a population so hungry to believe in something without question that it becomes susceptible to the machinations of the future-reading demagogue Jones. The implications of this defamiliarizing scenario as a diagnosis of the American political scene in the 1950s are entirely clear. Among other things, it suggests that the seemingly excessive fervor of American anti-communism may have grown partly from a deeply felt need, amid the relativism of values in modern consumer society, to believe in something, even if in a negative way. Meanwhile, Dick himself shows his own post-modernist stripes by out-relativizing his own relativists, refusing to present relativism as clearly superior to belief, or vice versa.

Dick also thematizes the growing 1950s confusion between reality and simulation in *Time Out of Joint* (1959), a book to which Jameson devotes an entire chapter of *Postmodernism*. Ostensibly set in the late 1950s, Dick's novel presents a vivid picture of life in small-town America during the Eisenhower years. However, there is something not quite right about this setting, as the protagonist, Ragel Gumm, begins to realize after he finds some faded magazines in an abandoned ruin. Despite appearing quite old, these magazines have what seem to be contemporary dates. More-over, they contain certain information that seems inconsistent with Gumm's experience of reality. Gradually, contradictions begin to arise between Dick's fictional 1950s and our existing historical record of that period: Tucker cars are a commercial reality; Marilyn Monroe is com-pletely unknown; Jack Daniel whiskey does not exist. Meanwhile, Gumm himself begins to experience a personal crisis that leaves him doubting the reality of any of the things he sees around him.

The confusion between reality and illusion in *Time Out of Joint* exem-plifies the uncertain boundary between supposedly different levels of re-ality that McHale, in *Postmodernist Fiction*, sees as typical of a postmod-ernist sensibility.[4] It also resonates with the prominent thesis of Jean Baudrillard that the postmodernist world is one in which the conven-tional distinction between authentic reality and simulation has lost all meaning, because of the proliferation of "simulacra" — essentially, copies of which there are no originals. Baudrillard's notion of simulacra is largely a theory of signs, a vision of a world in which signifiers no longer correspond to signifieds. In Dick's case, much of the ontological confu-sion similarly involves a destabilization of language and of the relationship between signs and their referents, signifiers and the signified. In-deed, Gumm's investigation into the true nature of his surroundings is triggered by a growing uneasy awareness that words do not necessarily match the reality they supposedly represent. In one key scene Gumm sees a soft-drink stand vanish before his eyes, leaving in its place a slip of paper on which is printed the designation "SOFT-DRINK STAND" (54-55). And Gumm has similar experiences with a variety of other objects as well, leading him to wonder whether there is a reality apart from our representations of it: "Relation of word to object ... what is a word? Arbi-trary sign. But we live in words. Our reality, among words not things" (60).

It turns out that Gumm, like so many characters in Dick's novels, has a history of mental illness, which might explain his strange experiences with disappearing objects. But the line between sanity and insanity in Dick's work is also unstable. Gumm's sense of unreality turns out to have an identifiable cause: the 1950s town in which most of the book's action takes place is actually a simulation constructed by the government of earth in the late 1990s to allow Gumm to live in the environment of his childhood. This soothing atmosphere keeps the unstable Gumm in a mental state that allows him (unknowingly) to exercise his uncanny abil-ity to predict the locations of upcoming rocket strikes from a moon col-ony that is at war with earth. The unstable relation between reality and illusion that informs most of the book thus turns out to have a perfectly logical explanation, but there is nevertheless a clear implication that all "reality" is to a certain extent a fiction promulgated by the powers that be and that Gumm's situation is merely an exaggerated version of what we all experience every day. One lingering implication of the book is the possibility of infinitely nested realities: if the 1959 town is a simulation created by the 1998 external world, then that world itself might be a simulation created by still another world, and so on.

The world depicted by *Time Out of Joint* is dystopian in a number of ways. For one thing, when Gumm finally manages to escape the artificial 1950s town and to reach the "real" world, he discovers there a nightmar-ish police state that is haunted not only by high-tech warfare, but also by a variety of social problems such as roaming gangs of delinquents like those who were so feared in the "real" 1950s. At first glance, the reality of this dystopian world seems especially harsh when contrasted with the seemingly utopian artificial world in which Gumm has been living. But this artificial world also has a dystopian aspect: its utopian surface cloaks the dark reality of its simulated origin, clearly suggesting that Dick's own 1950s America was itself not all it appeared to be.

As Jameson points out, the relation between the artificial 1950s town and the external 1990s world of *Time Out of Joint* can be read as an alle-gorical duplication of the relation between America (as placid utopia) and the external world (as dangerous dystopia) that prevailed in the American imagination in the 1950s (*Postmodernism* 281). In that sense, Dick clearly intends to suggest that this popular Manichean vision was false. Meanwhile, Dick's inquiry into the nature of reality in 1950s America strikingly anticipates the wave of nostalgia for the 1950s that would follow in subsequent decades. As Jameson points out, Dick's depiction of a simulated 1950s not only foreshadows the way concepts of "the fifties" would come to be packaged in the popular imagination, but also indicates the conventionality of all period concepts. From our future perspective, the artificiality of Gumm's "1950s" environment suggests that the nostalgic reminiscences of the fifties that would become popular in subsequent decades might be similarly false. It also implies that all utopian figurations of ideal past periods may be distortions of reality. Moreover, Dick's clear sense of a lurking menace beneath the surface of his own ostensibly peaceful and prosperous 1950s America serves as a clear warning that a seemingly utopian present can hide a dystopian core as well.

Most of Dick's novels from the long 1950s are, in fact, dystopian in nature. The majority contain strong postmodernist elements as well, particularly in the way they challenge the polar opposition between fiction and reality. This challenge often takes the form of an exploration of the points of view of schizophrenics, which provides a special form of cognitive estrangement. This is particularly the case in a work such as *Martian Time-Slip* (1964), which builds upon the notion that schizophrenics experience time in totally different ways than "normal" people, a motif that anticipates Jameson's later suggestion, especially in the essay "Postmodernism and Consumer Society," that schizophrenia provides an apt metaphor for the postmodernist disengagement from historical time. This focus on schizophrenia also demonstrates the way in which Dick's deconstruction of polar dualities during this period tends to focus specifically on the opposition between the normal and the abnormal, a concern that makes his work very typical of the long 1950s.

For example, Dick begins *The World Jones Made* (1956) with the portrayal of a group of experimental mutants, engineered to live on Venus, but forced, while on earth, to live in a special, environmentally controlled "Refuge." But he ends the book on Venus, where the mutants live in harmony with nature, while a family of "normal" humans now lives in a new Refuge that duplicates the environment on earth. The opposition between Us and Them has been precisely reversed, a motif that is also crucial to Dick's great alternative-history dystopia, *The Man in the High Castle* (1962), which presents a post–World War II United States occupied by the victorious Germans and Japanese. This reversal provides great opportunities for politically charged cognitive estrangement, as Freedman emphasizes in his extensive discussion of the book, leading to the conclusion that the book is "one of the crowning masterpieces by the most end-lessly fascinating master of the genre" (180).

As this high praise indicates, Dick is a special case. But it is also true that the more "mainstream" Golden Age science fiction writers of the long 1950s were often quite political—and often in ways that foreshad-owed the development of postmodernism. Of course, these "main-stream" science fiction writers were still quite marginal within the larger literary culture, as the case of Asimov, long at the center of the science fiction canon, amply illustrates. A notoriously bad stylist, Asimov has been especially popular among adolescents, thus seeming to verify both the notion that science fiction is subliterary and the idea that it is kid stuff. For example, Asimov's legendary *Foundation Trilogy* appears, at first glance, to be little more than a particularly grand example of the space opera subgenre, depending for its effect on plot twists and the creation of suspense, showing obvious signs of its genesis in fanzine cul-ture. But the trilogy addresses a number of important issues of relevance to the 1950s.

The tales that make up the trilogy were originally published in serial form over the period 1942 to 1950, though they can still be regarded as phenomena of 1950s science fiction, having been polished up and pub-lished as the integral volumes *Foundation, Foundation and Empire,* and *Sec-ond Foundation* in 1951, 1952, and 1953, respectively.[5] A sort of science fic-tion reinscription of Gibbon's *Decline and Fall of the Roman Empire* (set in the distant future), the *Foundation* novels are in a sense post-holocaust works, in that they detail a time after the collapse of the mighty Galactic Empire plunges the galaxy into a new Middle Ages. But the novels were typical of much of the science fiction of the 1950s in their assurances of the ultimate beneficial effects of science and technology in expanding the possibilities of humankind (and making these new Middle Ages as brief, and as bright, as possible). A similar pro-technology theme was central to Asimov's robot fiction, including such novels as *The Caves of Steel* (1954) and *The Naked Sun* (1957), which combine science fiction with detective fiction. In such works, Asimov addressed a number of issues related to artificial intelligence long before it became a real technological possibil-ity, again ultimately endorsing robots as aids to humanity.

Asimov's famed Laws of Robotics presumably ensured the benevo-lent nature of his robots, though even he occasionally depicted renegade robots, as in *The Caves of Steel.* Thus, his robots represented particularly comforting visions of Otherness: easily distinguished from human be-ings, but entirely pro-human in their behavior. Such useful, but lovable, machines would eventually culminate in the charmingly chubby robot of the *Lost in Space* television series of the mid-1960s. Other science fiction robots were not necessarily so benevolent, however, and writers like Dick, in works such as *Dr. Futurity* (1960), *Do Androids Dream of Electric*

Sheep? (1968), and *We Can Build You* (published in 1972, but written in 1962), would eventually extend the robot theme in the postmodernist direction of android simulacra, indistinguishable from humans by all but specially trained experts. Such creatures, of course, precisely reversed Asimov's assurances, blurring the boundary between the animate and the inanimate and introducing the frightening (especially in the 1950s) possibility that technology might advance to the point where we cannot tell ourselves from our own machines.

Asimov's robot stories were tremendously influential, but it is probably in the *Foundation* trilogy that Asimov made his most important contributions to the development of science fiction as a genre. The trilogy is really more a sequence of loosely connected sketches than a series of novels. It is set several thousand years in the future, after humans, emanating from earth, have established a vast galactic empire, only to have that empire crumble into competing local fiefdoms. However, despite this decline-and-fall scenario, the trilogy is basically optimistic in its suggestion that human beings have the ability to conquer the stars through judicious use of technology. The fall of the empire, meanwhile, is brought about essentially by a growing conformism and routinization, thus linking Asimov's vision to the persistent concerns of the 1950s. As Hari Seldon, founder of the science of psychohistory and thus the greatest scientist figure in the entire trilogy, explains in the first volume, the fall of the empire is "dictated by a rising bureaucracy, a receding initiative, a freezing of caste, a damning of curiosity" (27).

Unlike most science fiction of the 1950s, however, the *Foundation* trilogy is relatively unconcerned with the question of Otherness. There are, in fact, no nonhuman aliens in Asimov's galaxy whatsoever, while the humans of the trilogy seem no different from humans of the mid-twentieth century.[6] The closest Asimov comes to depicting an alien Other in the trilogy is in the figure of the Mule, a human mutant whose psychic powers give him such control over the emotions of others that he is able, in the middle volume of the trilogy, to establish a growing empire of his own. The Mule, a physically inferior freak whose charismatic power makes him able to disrupt the flow of history, might almost be a character from the pages of Dick. As such, one is tempted to read him as a figure of Adolf Hitler, especially given that the original tales were begun during World War II. On the other hand, the Mule sometimes becomes a vaguely sympathetic figure. In particular, he represents the trilogy's most vivid picture of the alienated individual, especially given that most of the other characters have no psychic depth whatsoever. A one-of-a-kind mutant, he is entirely alone in the universe—he is even sterile (thus the name) and therefore unable to pass on his mutation. Further, he is specifically identified as psychologically abnormal even beyond his mutation: we are told that the combination of his psychic and physical abnormalities have left him with "an intensely psychopathic paranoia" (*Second Foundation* 70). His empire building is motivated, in fact, primarily by a desire to wreak revenge "on a Galaxy in which he didn't fit" (*Second Foundation* 8).

Psychic powers or no, the Mule is easily defeated early in the third volume by the forces of the Second Foundation, which have considerable psychic resources of their own. This defeat may again link the Mule with Hitler, Asimov himself having stated that he began composing the stories that make up the trilogy largely as a way of projecting the inevitable victory of the anti-Nazi forces in World War II (Gunn 260). Thus, the two foundations of the trilogy (the forces that protect the galaxy from a descent into barbarism) might be equated with the anti-Nazi forces of World War II. One is even tempted to wonder whether the First and Second foundations can be related to the United States and the Soviet Union (the first with superior technical and material resources, the second with a firmer theoretical understanding of history). There is little in the trilogy to support such a thesis directly, though it would not have been so farfetched when the trilogy was begun, in the midst of the American-Soviet alliance against fascism.[7] In any case, the vaguely anti-Nazi tone of the trilogy does carry echoes of Asimov's background in Popular Front politics, and the association of the two foundations with the Americans and the Soviets, respectively, would have all sorts of ramifications. For example, throughout the trilogy, these two foundations are described as residing at opposite ends of the galaxy. In the end, however, they turn out to be in the same place, the galaxy being a circle—just as the Americans and Soviets, once thought to be diametrically opposed, wound up on the same side in World War II. Meanwhile, from the point of view of the 1950s, this motif could be taken as a plea for détente and as a suggestion that the differences between the Americans and the Soviets, both big believers in the modernizing power of science and technology, are not so dramatic after all.

Despite its fragmentary structure, the trilogy shows a tremendous faith in precisely the kinds of grand historical metanarratives suspicion of which has been identified by observers such as Jean-François Lyotard as a central characteristic of postmodernism. Americans were certainly beginning to question such metanarratives in the 1950s. Such metanarratives were, after all, inescapably reminiscent of the work of Karl Marx, and it is almost impossible not to see echoes of Marx in Asimov's Seldon, the genius whose psychohistory is a new form of scientific historiography that allows him, not only to understand the past, but even to predict the broad outlines of the future as a sequence of well-defined stages of historical development. In this ultimate pro-intellectual and pro-scientific statement, it is Seldon's plan that ameliorates the historical impact of the decline and fall of the Galactic Empire. And it is the work of the scientists at the foundations set up by Seldon that enables the plan to stay on course, despite everything. In other words, the plan is not automatic, though it does suggest certain broad parameters in which the drama of history is played out. Here, as in Marx's *Eighteenth Brumaire*, "men make their own history, but they do not make it just as they please; they do not make it under circumstances chosen by themselves" (Marx and Engels 595).

Numerous critics have noticed the parallels between Marx's and Seldon's visions of history. James Gunn, coming to praise Asimov, not to analyze him, thus feels, in his 1996 book on Asimov, the need to defend Asimov from suspicions of Marxist influence. Starting from the premise that Marxism is bad and Asimov is good, Gunn then proceeds to use these basic assumptions to argue their differences. As late as 1979, Asimov was thus able to convince the gullible Gunn in an interview that, even then, he had "never read anything" about Marxism (255). Gunn, in fact, presents this statement as evidence that Asimov's conception of psychohistory could not possibly have been influenced by Marxism in any way, ignoring all those years (including the years when the tales on which the trilogy would eventually be based were being composed) in which Asimov participated in the Futurians, a Marxist-oriented group of science fiction writers and enthusiasts.[8] Gunn even goes so far as to try to explain Asimov's depiction of humans thousands of years in the future as identical to humans of the twentieth century as an intentional refutation of the Marxist notion that human beings change with their social and historical context, meanwhile producing the weird argument that Asimov's seemingly simplistic vision is "defensible" precisely because it is opposed to Marxism (37).

On the other hand, Donald Wollheim, one of Asimov's fellow Futurians (and thus perhaps in a position to know), sees a clear influence of Marxism on Asimov's construction of psychohistory. Wollheim, however, argues that psychohistory is intended as an advance beyond Marxism. In fact, he argues that the psychohistory developed by Asimov's Seldon is "the science that Marxism never became" (40). Wollheim, exorcising his own youthful attraction to Marx, then descends into a typical Cold War diatribe against Marxism, which he sees as a pseudoscience that "never successfully predicted anything" (40). Charles Elkins, noting Wollheim's unsophisticated caricature of Marxism, nevertheless agrees that Marxism is often deployed as a sort of pseudoscience by those who fail to understand its complexities. And this, he believes, is just what Asimov does in the trilogy. Elkins thus argues that Seldon's new science is not what Marxism wanted to be, but what Marxism used to be, describing it as a reinscription of "the vulgar, mechanical, debased version of Marxism promulgated in the Thirties" (104). Elkins, of course, is merely repeating the description of 1930s Marxism that became current

in the 1950s, when left liberal groups such as the New York Intellectuals
(and others associated with the journal *Partisan Review*) sought to distance themselves from their own Marxist past by depicting themselves as
having moved beyond the "bad" Marxism of the earlier decade.

Recent work by scholars such as Barbara Foley, Cary Nelson, James
Murphy, and James Bloom has demonstrated that this *Partisan Review*
model of Marxist history is seriously flawed, if not downright falsified.
But Elkins is right that the historical model put forth by Asimov as psychohistory is rather simplistic, even if Marxism never was. In fact, Asimov's model of history differs from Marxist historiography primarily in
being substantially less complex and sophisticated. Most notably, despite
the prefix "psycho," the model of history attributed by Asimov to Hari
Seldon shows little comprehension of the fundamental Marxist insight
that the basic characteristics of human beings, especially the psychological characteristics, are largely the products of historical circumstances
and thus change over time. As Marx puts it in *The German Ideology*, "The
nature of individuals thus depends on the material conditions determining their production" (Marx and Engels 150). Further, Marx argues that
"men, developing their material production and their material intercourse, alter, along with this their real existence, their thinking, and the
products of their thinking. Life is not determined by consciousness, but
consciousness by life" (155).

The ability to understand that fundamental characteristics of human
beings change over time is surely central to the ability to think historically. Conversely, as Georg Lukács points out in *The Historical Novel* (the
work that strongly informs both Jameson's and Freedman's understanding of the historical novel as a genre), the failure to recognize that humans change over time is one of the first signs of a loss of historical sense
or of any sense of a "living connection between the past and the present"
(Lukács 62). Thus, for Lukács, one of the central signs of failure in a historical novel is the phenomenon he refers to as "modernization," in
which characters from the past are given entirely modern psychologies,
while the past is depicted as disconnected from the present, as an exotic
and foreign realm into which readers (and writers) can "escape from the
triviality of modern bourgeois life" (192). In the *Foundation* trilogy, there
is certainly a longing to escape from the trivialities of the routinized present through a fantasy of escape into another time. Moreover, there is no
suggestion of real historical change from one time to another. Characters
from thousands of years in the future have absolutely the same psychological makeup as individuals from the mid-twentieth century, even
though they live in a world so distant from ours in time that they cannot
even remember humankind's origins on earth except through vague leg-
ends.

In short, Asimov, via Seldon, seems unable to envision any real historical change: one reason why Seldon can presumably predict the future is that people in the future are no different from people in the present. Indeed, the one time Seldon's predictions fail is when the Mule, whose mind does work differently, comes along. Ultimately, then, Asimov's psychohistory is neither an extension of Marxism to greater scientific validity, per Wollheim, nor a reversion to the vulgar Marxism of the 1930s, per Elkins. It is, instead, a simplistic, essentially ahistorical model that has nevertheless clearly been influenced by grand historical metanarratives of the sort proposed by Marx. Some of this ahistorical simplicity might be attributed to Asimov's own lack of sophistication. After all, he began writing the tales of the trilogy in his early twenties. By the time the volumes of the trilogy were published in book form, he had a doctorate in chemistry, but that is hardly the kind of education designed to give him a sophisticated understanding of the historical process.

Not that science fiction (or any fiction) writers tend to have such an understanding in general, but Asimov, through the very premise of the trilogy, asked to be taken seriously as a historical thinker.[9] Moreover, freed from the bounds of verisimilitude in the usual sense, even science fiction works with less ambitious premises have a genuine opportunity to project potential future solutions to current problems, to suggest utopian alternatives to the troubled present. As Freedman puts it, science fiction by its very nature "insists upon historical mutability, material reducibility, and utopian possibility" (xvi). Thus, Marxist critics have often seen a special promise in science fiction as a genre. Jameson, for example, has lamented the loss of utopian vision in recent decades, relating that loss to a general decline in the historical imagination during the postmodern era. But Jameson also argues that science fiction may retain a vital utopian imagination, even if it is only through a demonstration of our waning ability to imagine a genuine utopian alternative in the postmodern era ("Progress or Utopia" 153).

Of course, by Jameson's reckoning, the more postmodernist a work of science fiction is, the less likely it is to maintain this utopian imagination. One might thus note here Andrew Ross's complaint of the inability of William Gibson to imagine a future that differs in any significant socially progressive way from the present (145-56). Of course, Gibson's fictions are set in the near future, so Asimov's failure to imagine much difference after thousands of years is even more problematic. In Asimov's case, it is particularly problematic that, even in such a pro-technology work as the trilogy, there is little hint of technology advanced much beyond that of the 1950s—except for the obligatory hyperspace drive, which is necessary to make the scenario of the trilogy feasible at all. On the other hand, the failure of utopian vision in Asimov is fairly typical of the 1950s, when all sorts of writers, not just science fiction writers, had problems believing things were ever going to get substantially better. In short, the failure of Asimov's historical imagination is part of a larger phenomenon, and one which clearly participates in the beginnings of a postmodern loss of historical sensibility in the science fiction of the 1950s.

The remoteness of psychohistory from genuine Marxist historiography was one of the reasons why Asimov's work could thrive in the repressive climate of the 1950s. Most readers would see little in the way of political statement, Marxist or anti-Marxist, in the *Foundation* trilogy other than an antipathy toward religion as a form of superstition and an endorsement of science (including atomic science) as the rational solution to human problems. Asimov even goes so far as to suggest that rule by a scientific elite, who would exercise reason (rather than emotion or prejudice) in making their decisions, might be the best form of human government. Indeed, it is in this pro-technology stance, not in any appeal to vulgar Marxism, that Asimov's trilogy recalls the 1930s, when science fiction as a phenomenon, led by the guiding hand of Hugo Gernsback, tended to believe that science and technology held the keys to the solution of the dismal difficulties of the Depression decade.[10] Interestingly, the two foundations of the trilogy not only represent a scientific-technological elite, but also precisely the technologies about which Americans in the 1950s were most anxious: atomic power and mind control. The primary tool of the First Foundation is atomic power, presented in the trilogy as entirely benevolent, a sort of *sine qua non* of advanced civilization. The primary tool of the Second Foundation, presented by Asimov as even more powerful (and ultimately more beneficial) than atomic power, is scientific mind control, a technique they use not for totalitarian domination, but for gentle nudges that help to keep human history on its proper course.

Asimov thus assures us that we have nothing to fear from science: we get into trouble only when we descend into religion or otherwise ignore the guidance provided by science. Frederik Pohl is not so sure about the promise of technology, though it is also the case that Pohl, especially in the 1950s, tended to write in a satirical mode that was very different from the straightforward science fiction of Asimov.[11] Pohl's science fiction, while often set in the future, was very clearly not about the possibilities of the future, but about the foibles of the present. Thus, the lack of a strong utopian dimension in his work is not surprising. Meanwhile, Pohl was substantially more daring and less reassuring in his science fiction political statements than was Asimov. One of the movers and shakers of 1950s science fiction, Pohl had been active as an editor, agent, and writer since his teenage years in the 1930s. From 1938 to 1945, he was a leading member of the leftist Futurians. Even after the breakup of that group as a formal entity, Pohl wrote much of his work in collaboration with others, including a series of anticapitalist satires in the 1950s. For example, in

1955, Pohl and Lester Del Rey (writing together under the pseudonym Edson McCann) published a searing satire of the insurance industry in *Preferred Risk*. That same year, Pohl and former Futurian C. M. Kornbluth published *Gladiator-at-Law*, a send-up of organized sport that serves as a commentary on the competition-based ethos of American society as a whole. But Pohl's most important satire from the 1950s, written with Kornbluth, is undoubtedly *The Space Merchants* (1952), which is widely recognized as one of the all-time classics of the science fiction genre.

The Space Merchants presents a vivid picture of a future world dominated by huge multinational corporations, the most powerful and influential of which are media and advertising firms. In this sense, the book strikingly anticipates the direction of the next fifty years of world history, presenting a future world system much along the lines of that analyzed by Jameson and other contemporary Marxist theorists as "late capitalism." Ad executive Mitch Courtenay, who works for the huge Fowler Schocken advertising conglomerate, receives a major (and sudden) boost to his career when he is unexpectedly put in charge of the company's project to colonize Venus, a planet to which the firm has been granted exclusive access through bribery and other political manipulations. Courtenay's job is not only to oversee the development of the technologies that will make this colonization possible, but also to develop an advertising campaign that will make colonists want to go to Venus, where the whole planet can then be turned into a new source of profit for Fowler Schocken. Courtenay's job is complicated, however, by his difficult personal life (his temporary wife, Dr. Kathy Nevin, wants to break off their trial marriage) and by the fact that rival Fowler Schocken executive Matt Runstead seems to be sabotaging all of his efforts.

Courtenay goes to Antarctica to confront Runstead with his treachery but is knocked unconscious and awakes on a transport that is taking him as a contract laborer to a huge high-rise protein plantation in Costa Rica. There, the formerly wealthy and powerful Courtenay gets a taste of how the working class (largely relegated to the Third World, but collectively referred to in this consumer capitalist society as "consumers") lives. He is also contacted by a secret organization of "Conservationists," or "Consies," who are working worldwide to try to prevent environmental destruction of the planet by industrial capitalism. From this point, the plot's various twists and turns become too numerous to be worth summarizing, but Courtenay eventually returns to New York, learns that both Kathy and Runstead are Consie agents, and discovers that they have shanghaied him to Costa Rica both to try to teach him something about working-class experience and to prevent him from being killed by a rival advertising agency that hopes to wrest the Venus contract away from Fowler Schocken. In the end, the Consies manage to load the only Venus rocket with their people and to blast off with the hope of building on Venus a new world free of the greed and corruption that capitalism has spread across the earth.[12]

All in all, the plot of the book is rather contrived, but also beside the point, as is often the case with satire. What is important is the book's satirical thrust, which quite effectively comments both on the overall direction of consumer capitalism as a system and on the specific political climate of the United States in the early 1950s. The Consies (although somewhat reminiscent of the modern Greenpeace organization) are rather transparent stand-ins for communists, and their role in the book serves as part of an effective satire of the anticommunist oppression of the McCarthy era in which the book was written. Even more striking, however, are the depictions of the negative consequences of the growing power of consumer capitalism and the increasing dominance of media and advertising in enforcing uniformity in the thoughts and desires of people around the world. These depictions are effective in the best tradition of literary satire—seemingly exaggerated in sometimes comical ways, they turn out on reflection to be much closer to reality than one might first have imagined. Thus, Fowler Schocken's marketing tactics seem extreme until one compares them with tactics already in use in the 1950s. One of their favorite techniques is to employ subtle forms of subliminal suggestion so that consumers will associate their products with sexual attractiveness and success and the products of their rivals with sexual frustration or deviance. Meanwhile, one of their most lucrative accounts involves the marketing of a drink called "Coffiest," which is laced with an addictive chemical to ensure that consumers will be hooked for life—which seems extreme only until one considers recent revelations of the addictive effects of the caffeine in ordinary coffee or the nicotine in cigarettes.

John Pierce's description of the book as an effective combination of "satirical exaggeration and logical extrapolation" is thus entirely appropriate (192). *The Space Merchants* shows a profound understanding of the direction in which consumer capitalism was already headed in 1952 and suggests interesting forms of complicity between the corporate manipulation of consumers for profit and the official promotion of anticommunist hysteria in the Cold War. Through the Consies, the book also suggests a potential utopian alternative to industrial capitalism, though the program of the Consies does not always accord well with the ideology of communism or socialism. The book maintains an essentially comic tone throughout, but it also includes some horrifying scenes to suggest the underlying seriousness of its message. At times the humor may become so glib that this seriousness is obscured, but as a whole the book is an effective satire that serves as an important counter to all those science fiction allegorizations of the communist menace for which the 1950s are notorious.

Another particularly effective science fiction satire of the 1950s was *Player Piano* (1952), an early work of Kurt Vonnegut, Jr. *Player Piano* responds to a number of anxieties in American life in the early 1950s with its depiction of an administered society in which human labor has been made superfluous by advanced technology, resulting in a populace that itself feels superfluous and without purpose. But Vonnegut's projections of the future are more social than technological—the technology depicted in his book is in fact not particularly advanced. Still, *Player Piano* addresses a growing fear of American workers that they are in danger of being replaced by automation, while it also provides a counter to Marxist arguments about the value of freeing humans from physical labor.[13]

To an extent, Vonnegut begins by dismissing many of the anxieties of the 1950s by constructing a future world in which America stands unchallenged as the world's leading superpower, having triumphed through superior technology and organization in a third world war. With the Soviets and other foreign enemies removed from the equation, America is able to turn its energies inward—with less than utopian results. Machines have replaced almost all human workers, except a small elite of engineer-managers who are still required to make the system operate smoothly. But the real political power of Vonnegut's engineer-managers is rather limited. Ultimate planning decisions in this machinelike society are made by a giant computer, EPICAC XIV, making *Player Piano* one of the surprisingly few 1950s science fiction novels to deal in a central way with advances in computer technology. Indeed, there are signs in the novel that growing computerization will eventually replace even the top engineers and managers, resulting in a society ruled entirely by machines and a populace left entirely without purpose.

Meanwhile, computers like EPICAC already play an ominous role in this society. In the America of *Player Piano* citizens are carefully screened, tested, and categorized during their schooldays so that they can be slotted for their proper place in society. And computerized systems keep up with these test results to ensure that their recommendations are followed. Meanwhile, even the most minor deviations from accepted normal behavioral patterns are recorded and stored in a massive police information system, so that potential "saboteurs" (which basically means anyone outside the rigidly defined norm) can be closely watched. Vonnegut's book thus anticipates the power inherent in modern computer information systems as tools of enforced routinization, though even EPICAC is not all that advanced by the standards of half a century later. Computerized data processing in *Player Piano* still relies on punched cards and paper tape, and the computers of the book are still based on vacuum tube technology—EPICAC is thus so large that it must be housed in Carlsbad Caverns. The relatively banal technological developments depicted in *Player Piano* might be attributed to a failure of Vonnegut's imagination, but perhaps they are more properly related to a failure of imagination of the machinelike future America described in the book. Moreover, the very similarity of the dystopian society of the book to the society of Vonnegut's contemporary America increases the power of Vonnegut's satire by making his warnings all the more urgent and believable.

Player Piano focuses on the travails of Paul Proteus, a high-level engineer-manager in Ilium, New York (Vonnegut's reinscription of the real town of Troy, New York), who becomes disillusioned with his own life and with a system that renders the lives of most citizens pointless. The loneliness, emptiness, and alienation felt by Proteus and the other characters in *Player Piano* would have already seemed all too familiar to his contemporary audience. Such symptoms are, in fact, results of the Industrial Revolution that had already been diagnosed nearly a century earlier by Marx and Engels. But the Marx-Engels critique of industrialization is primarily focused on production and on the dehumanizing conditions to which workers were exposed in the attempts of nineteenth-century factories to turn out larger and larger quantities of goods. Vonnegut moves this critique into the realm of consumer capitalism, recognizing that modern technology has made production so efficient that humans are becoming more and more necessary not as workers who produce goods, but merely as consumers who buy them. Moreover, Vonnegut extends the Marxist analysis of the Industrial Revolution, suggesting that the technological developments depicted in *Player Piano* are part of a Second Industrial Revolution: whereas in the original Industrial Revolution human muscle was replaced by machines, in this new Industrial Revolution routine human thought is replaced by machines. In addition, the book suggests that a Third Industrial Revolution, in which even the most sophisticated intellectual work would be done by machines, making human beings obsolete altogether, may be just around the corner.

If *Player Piano* thus recalls a number of sophisticated analyses of modern culture and society, it includes less sophisticated elements as well. In particular, the book seems to romanticize labor, depicting even work on a factory assembly line as spiritually fulfilling without paying attention to the fact that much of such work is degrading, mind numbing, and alienating in its own right. Rather than contrast his technological dystopia with some romantic primitivist vision of nature, Vonnegut presents as an alternative, not a time without machines, but one when machines still required human operators to do their work. A principal image of the replacement of human workers by machines involves the story of Rudy Hertz, a gifted lathe operator whose movements are recorded on tape so that the machines can be programmed to function as if under his control but without his presence, resulting in a dehumanization that Vonnegut evokes with a string of sentimental clichés: "The tape was the essence distilled from the small, polite man with the big hands and black fingernails; from the man who thought the world could be saved if everyone read a verse from the Bible every night; from the man who adored a collie for want of children" (9-10).

Hertz is depicted more as an artist than as a factory worker, consistent with the central player piano metaphor—after all, player pianos represent a replacement of human artistic performance by mechanization, and a player piano is not far from the musicometers and versificators of Zamyatin's *We* and Orwell's *Nineteen Eighty-four*. And the emphasis on industrial efficiency and mass production in Vonnegut's dystopian America leads to the overt mechanization of culture that is reminiscent of the visions of Zamyatin and Orwell. Vonnegut's America is Benjamin's age of mechanical reproduction with a vengeance: efficient manufacturing techniques causes books to be extremely inexpensive, and mass production similarly makes reproductions of the paintings of the Great Masters accessible to all. "It's the Golden Age of Art," proclaims government bureaucrat Ewing J. Halyard, "with millions of dollars a year poured into reproductions of Rembrandts, Whistlers, Goyas, Renoirs, El Grecos, Dégas, da Vincis, Michelangelos" (210). This mechanical reproduction of art contributes to the shattering of the aura lauded by Benjamin. However, the loss of this aura is simply another aspect of the removal of all magic from this thoroughly routinized world. In this text, at least, auraless art leads not, as Benjamin hoped, to a critical-minded populace, but merely to mindless conformity.

Echoing the warnings of Horkheimer and Adorno about the workings of the modern Culture Industry, culture in Vonnegut's dystopian America is completely banal, consisting mainly of insipid soap operas and works of official propaganda. Moreover, like everything else in this society, culture is thoroughly managed for industrial efficiency. But this efficiency requires strict censorship, and one episode in the book involves a loyal wife who has been forced to turn to prostitution to try to support herself and her novelist-husband, whose career has been ruined by his unfortunate encounters with official censorship. In particular, his writing has been rejected by the National Council of Arts and Letters because it is too well written for the literacy level of the average reader, because it has an antimachine theme, and because it is twenty-seven pages longer than the maximum length decreed by the council for optimum economic efficiency (211). Like Adorno, Vonnegut seems to see in art (and particularly in the craftsmanship of skilled workers like Rudy Hertz) a potential resistance to the tyranny of technology. However, by depicting Hertz more in the mold of a medieval artisan than of a modern factory worker, Vonnegut ignores the fact that modern factory work is in general not nearly the creative activity that the book associates with Hertz's deft artistlike operation of his lathe.

Vonnegut's use of Hertz as a romantic foil to the excessively tech-
nologized dystopia of the book suggests that (like most of the science fiction of the 1950s) *Player Piano* does not denounce science and technology
themselves as unequivocal evils; the dehumanizing effects described in
the book occur only because technological development and the con-
comitant bureaucratic management have simply gotten out of control. In
particular, Vonnegut depicts a society in which industry and technology
have themselves become a sort of substitute religion; the citizens of his
projected dystopia worship above all else industrial efficiency and pro-
ductivity. Thus Kroner, a top industrial manager, is described as a rather
incompetent engineer who serves primarily as a sort of spiritual leader,
as an "evangelist" who "personified the faith, the near-holiness, the spirit
of the complicated venture" of industrial capitalism (38). On the other
hand, one of the principal leaders of the "Ghost Shirt Society" (a group
that rebels against Vonnegut's technocratic dystopia) is Reverend James
J. Lasher, a Protestant minister who espouses traditional human values
against the dehumanization of an increasingly automated society that is
threatening to render humans obsolete. However, Lasher himself winds
up as a symbol of the disengagement of religion from the individual lives
of real people. The revolution fails miserably, with dire consequences for
many of its participants, but Lasher himself is "contented." In the traditional spirit of Christian sacrifice (a spirit the sadomasochistic nature of
which is encompassed in his name), Lasher had known all along that the
revolution could not succeed, but merely wished to use it to make a point
and to gain an opportunity for martyrdom: "A lifelong trafficker in symbols, he had created the revolution as a symbol, and was now welcoming
the opportunity to die as one" (295). Vonnegut makes it rather clear,
however, that the martyrdom of Lasher and his followers will produce
nothing but their own suffering.

Proteus represents a more moderate reaction to the dystopian present
of the book. His nostalgic visions of the past are focused not on agrarian
fantasies but on a shop in "Building 58," a building left over from the
early days of the plant that Proteus now manages. This shop was once
used by Thomas Edison, who functions for Proteus not as a villain whose
work contributed to the routinized technologization of American society,
but as a heroic image of human capability and ingenuity. Proteus has restored the shop as a sort of museum, where he can occasionally go to
view its clumsy and antiquated machines and thus to recharge his spirits,
to remind himself that the present has progressed far beyond the past
days of Edison: "It was a vote of confidence from the past, he thought—
where the past admitted how humble and shoddy it had been, where one
could look from the old to the new and see that mankind really had come
a long way" (6). But this progress is purely technological, and when Proteus views a photograph of the shop's workers from the days of Edison,

he is reminded of the relative spiritual impoverishment of the present; he sees in their faces a strength, a determination, and a spirit that he himself has lost (7).

The book's title image reinforces this same sort of nostalgia for a simpler past that was still somewhat mechanized. A player piano is precisely a machine designed to perform work that would normally be performed by a human, and its perforated rolls are analogous to the punched tapes that program the lathe once operated by Rudy Hertz. Yet player pianos are typically regarded in the popular consciousness not as warnings of the growing danger that mechanization will render humans obsolete but as quaint reminders of a simpler past. Hertz himself seems fascinated by the player piano in the bar that he frequents, though his description of the machine to Proteus carries ominous undertones: "Makes you feel kind of creepy, don't it, Doctor, watching them keys go up and down? You can almost see a ghost sitting there playing his heart out" (28).

Vonnegut's appeal to a time of more limited technology as an alternative to his dystopia is probably more realistic than would be a similar appeal to raw nature. On the other hand, *Player Piano* ultimately suggests that the development of technology may in fact be inherent in human nature. Late in the book a group of Luddite-like subversives (who recruit Proteus as their titular leader) violently revolt against the system; though the revolt fails in most of the country, the revolutionaries do manage to take control of Ilium, where they begin to smash every machine in sight. Yet, by the book's end, these same subversives are already beginning to repair the machines, simply to give themselves something interesting to do. This ending indicates that, even had the revolution succeeded, the progressive industrialization that brought it about would simply have been repeated. And the book as a whole suggests that the oppressed citizenry of America brought about their own predicament. As Wymer puts it, "Vonnegut goes beyond a simple attack on technology by suggesting that the real tragedy is that man has defined himself in a way that makes him replaceable by machines, that man has defined his own value as he defines the value of an object" (44).

The computerized surveillance of individual behavior depicted in *Player Piano* is clearly reminiscent of contemporary concerns over the impact of the McCarthyite inquisitions on the lives of individual citizens. McCarthyism is taken on even more directly in James Blish's *They Shall Have Stars* (1956, republished in 1970 as the first volume in the *Cities in Flight* tetralogy). Blish's book begins in 2013, but it depicts an America in the throes of a repressive political climate that is clearly derived from the early 1950s. Indeed, Blish himself has suggested that "about a third" of the novel is devoted to "a personal attack on Sen. McCarthy" (*More Issues* 34). Thus, a central figure in the book is Francis Xavier MacHinery, who, as the "hereditary head of the FBI," is a sort of composite of Senator Joseph McCarthy and FBI chief J. Edgar Hoover. In Blish's book, the Cold War is still raging, and the Soviets seem to have the upper hand. One reason they do is that America has been essentially paralyzed by Mac-Hinery's inquisitions and the resultant freeze on the free flow of information. Scientific advancement has particularly stagnated, unable to flourish in such a repressive climate. For one thing, scientists are unable to share their findings with others, and are thus unable to take advantage of the traditional collaborative spirit of scientific research. For another, many talented individuals are discouraged from even going into science, not wanting to work in a sensitive area that might draw MacHinery's attention. Thus, top scientist Giuseppe Corsi (clearly a stand-in for J. Robert Oppenheimer)[14] is branded an "unreliable" after "the repeated clearance hearings, the oceans of dubious testimony and gossip from witnesses with no faces or names" to which he is subjected in senate hearings orchestrated by MacHinery (8).

Nevertheless, scientists in *They Shall Have Stars* are on the brink of two major breakthroughs, and much of the plot of the book involves attempts, spearheaded by Senator Bliss Wagoner, to bring these breakthroughs to fruition by evading MacHinery and his security apparatus long enough to get the necessary research completed. These attempts turn out to be successful, resulting in the development of two seemingly unrelated technologies: a practical method for the negation of gravity and a drug to prevent aging. These technologies are, however, more closely interrelated than they first appear: the first enables antigravity drives that can carry spacecraft on interstellar journeys, while the second extends human life essentially without limit, meaning that crews will be able to survive the incredibly long duration of interstellar flights.

In the meantime, these breakthroughs, especially the immortality drug, are so revolutionary that Wagoner and his followers expect them to result in the complete collapse of the capitalist world, which is all the more reason the work must be hidden from MacHinery. For Wagoner, however, the research is so significant for the future of humanity that its immediate negative impact on one particular political and economic system is beside the point. Echoing the look beyond earth in *The Space Merchants* and *The World Jones Made*, he is willing to cede earth to the Soviets, both because humanity's real future is in the stars and because the West has become so repressive in its opposition to communism that it is no longer preferable to communism, anyway. In the end, the research is successfully completed, and Wagoner is, as expected, called to task for it. He is, in fact, executed, not only for his support of the research, but also for making the results of the research known to Corsi so that they can be made public and not suppressed by MacHinery.

Religion is one potentially charged issue that hovers in the margins of *They Shall Have Stars*. Throughout the book, many of the central characters are forced to work their way through civil disruptions caused by the activities of the Believers, a fanatical religious cult with millions of followers. The members of this radically evangelical cult are charged with spreading the good word by any means necessary, a task they take very seriously, blocking traffic, interfering with the normal flow of commerce, and obnoxiously forcing themselves on anyone who comes near them. And these aggressive tactics have paid large dividends: by the time of the book's action, one in ten people in the United States is a Believer. The Believers are essentially conservative Christians; they espouse absolute faith in the truth of literal interpretations of the Bible, and they expect the Second Coming of Christ to occur at any moment. Events in the book, however, identify them as deluded and misguided and as symptoms of the decadence of American capitalism. Meanwhile, Blish's major characters tend to regard the Believers merely as nuisances. As one of them, spaceman Paige Russell, points out, "I think when the experts talk about 'faith' they mean something different than the shouting kind, the kind the Believers have. Shouting religions always strike me as essentially like pep-meetings among salesmen; their ceremonies and their manners are so aggressive because they don't really believe the code themselves" (30).[15]

The subsequent volumes of *Cities in Flight* follow the results of this research, which enables entire cities to fly through the galaxy in search of work, in a motif that is directly compared to the migrant Okies of the 1930s. In this sense, Blish's sequence cannot fail to recall John Steinbeck's *The Grapes of Wrath* (1939), one of the great classics of American leftist literature. But Blish's own political stance, however opposed it may be to McCarthyism, is not so clearly leftist. Indeed, Blish, despite his extensive association with the leftist Futurians, sometimes identified himself as a supporter of the theory, though not the practice, of fascism (Knight 155).

One of the most overtly leftist of the "American" science fiction novels of the 1950s was Ben Barzman's *Twinkle, Twinkle Little Star* (1960), also published in the United Kingdom in 1960 as *Out of This World* and reissued in the United States in 1962 as *Echo X*. The Canadian-born Barzman became a successful screenwriter in the United States in the 1940s. He was then identified by informers as a communist and subsequently blacklisted, receiving no further screen credits in the United States between 1952 and 1963. In 1949, he and his wife went into exile, living at various times in France, Britain, and Spain until they returned to the United States in 1976. Barzman scripted several French and British films during the period of the blacklist, working frequently with director Joseph Losey. He also helped write the screenplay for the award-winning 1961 film, *El Cid*, but was not credited due to the blacklist.

Described by Alan Wald as a "Marxist science fiction classic" (72), *Twinkle, Twinkle Little Star* is a whimsical and entertaining piece (somewhat reminiscent of the earlier novels of Vonnegut) that nevertheless addresses some important political issues. In particular, the book is a critique of both the economic inequality of Western capitalist societies and the paranoid and belligerent mentality that prevailed in those societies during the Cold War. The story is narrated by a nameless narrator, who begins by describing much of his own Canadian background, then proceeds to the main plot, which revolves around a scientific research project that results in the establishment of a transport beam between earth and another planet that is its double. These two earths are physically identical, though certain historical developments have led to social differences. In particular, the second earth was able to avert the rise of fascism and therefore did not experience World War II. As a result, this world has developed a far more advanced civilization than our own, free of economic injustice and of the competition and social hostilities to which that inequality inevitably leads. The other earth sends a delegation to ours, the members of which are doubles of their counterparts on our earth, although some of these counterparts are no longer alive, having been killed in World War II. The delegation examines our planet to determine whether it is safe to remain in contact with us and to share with us their more advanced technology. Unfortunately, however, they conclude that our planet is too primitive and warlike to use that technology properly. The delegation then returns to the other earth and breaks off the beam, though they promise to keep an eye on future developments here, awaiting the day when future contact will be appropriate.

Though this conclusion may be somewhat predictable, recalling such classic 1950s science fiction films as *The Day the Earth Stood Still* (1951) and *It Came from Outer Space* (1953), the narrative is in general an engaging one that keeps the reader's interest while making a number of subtle political points about racism, economic injustice, McCarthyism, and the Cold War. The book is thus a good example of the attempt of many leftist writers in the post–World War II period to reach a larger audience by writing in popular genres. It also demonstrates the way in which such writers sought to convey their political messages with a light touch, given the climate of anticommunist hysteria in which they were forced to work. It thus confirms Wald's argument that postwar radical writers tended to shift to such popular genres as science fiction and detective fiction, continuing to convey leftist political messages in the oppressive political climate of that era, but in a more oblique fashion than that which characterized the proletarian fiction of the 1930s.[16]

If Asimov, Pohl, Vonnegut, and (especially) Barzman leaned heavily to the Left, it is also the case that major figures such as Ray Bradbury and, especially, Heinlein leaned to the Right. Heinlein, who seems often to have been motivated by a desire to produce anticommunist propaganda, is in that sense a particularly representative figure of the 1950s, even though he would achieve his maximum popularity in the 1960s, when his Hugo Award-winning *Stranger in a Strange Land* (1961), still politically right-wing, but seemingly pro drugs and sex, was adopted as a sort of fictional manifesto of the presumably leftist 1960 counterculture.[17] This phenomenon, to an extent, demonstrated the counterculture's lack of political sophistication and coherence, but it also derived from the fact that Heinlein's extreme right-wing attitudes were more libertarian than fascist, a fact that can perhaps be seen most clearly in his 1966 novel of libertarian revolution, *The Moon Is a Harsh Mistress*, which won Heinlein's fourth and final Hugo Award.[18] But, before these important works of the 1960s, Heinlein had already established a major reputation in the science fiction world with extremely representative 1950s novels such as *The Puppet Masters* (1951) and *Starship Troopers* (1959).

Though ostensibly set in 2007 (after a third world war has failed to settle the differences between the United States and the Soviet Union), *The Puppet Masters* is one of the quintessential alien-invaders-as-allegory-for-communism texts of the 1950s.[19] Here, parasitical alien slugs (from Titan, a moon of Saturn) land in Iowa and begin attaching themselves to the backs of human hosts, whose minds they then control. Using these human puppets to do their bidding, the alien masters quickly move forward on a program of global conquest. Most of the plot of the book involves the efforts of narrator-protagonist Sam Cavanaugh (a.k.a. Elihu Nivens) and other members of a top secret U.S. intelligence force to thwart the alien conquest. Meanwhile, plot complications are provided by a romantic involvement between Sam and his fellow agent, the beautiful Mary, and by the somewhat Oedipal relationship between Sam and the "Old Man," head of the intelligence force and also, as it turns out, Sam's father. Extra interest is also added by a number of scenes of sophomoric ogling as various individuals, especially women, are forced to strip to prove that they are not carrying a parasite. Sex and violence are, in fact, often equated in the text, as when Sam, having been freed of his parasite, feels "warm and relaxed, as if I had just killed a man or had a woman" (91).

Given that the alien invaders take over and control the minds of innocent humans, who then become deadly foreign agents, despite looking just like everyone else, there is an obvious parallel between the parasite "masters" and the standard American 1950s view of communists, whom J. Edgar Hoover would famously characterize as "masters of deception."[20] Indeed, much of the book reads like pure McCarthyite fantasy, especially when the slugs work to infiltrate the highest levels of the U.S. government and military as part of their takeover plan. But propaganda only works if its recipients get the message, so Heinlein is careful to ensure that this connection will indeed be made, even by the most literal-minded of readers. Not only does Heinlein label the area controlled by the parasites as "Zone Red," but the slogan of the slugs is "we are the people," and Heinlein repeatedly emphasizes the collective nature of the slug society, which has no concept of individual identity, and in which "each slug is really every other slug" (239).

Even more directly, Sam, as Heinlein's narrator, notes that "the parasites might feel right at home behind the Curtain" (148). Further, he reports that the "Cominform propaganda system" immediately goes into action when the American media start to report on the invasion, characterizing the reports as "'American Imperialist fantasy' intended to 'enslave the workers.'" Then, Sam wonders why the parasites did not attack the Soviets first, given that "Stalinism seemed tailormade for them. On second thought, I wondered if they had. On third thought I wondered what difference it would make; the people behind the Curtain had had their minds enslaved and parasites riding them for three generations. There might not be two kopeks difference between a commissar with a slug and a commissar without a slug" (205). Heinlein also gets in a few shots at fellow travelers, noting that the only thing more disgusting than a human mind in the grip of the slugs are the few humans who work in complicity with the slugs, even without having a parasite directly attached (251).

As it turns out, the slugs did, in fact, invade Russia and China first, taking over quickly, precisely because no one noticed the difference. And Heinlein is able to exercise a bit of anticommunist fantasy when he reports that the slugs, not understanding human sanitation, suspended all sanitation procedures behind the Iron Curtain, leading to an epidemic of the black plague that wipes out the entire population of Asia and Russia. And good riddance, too, especially since the deaths finish off, not only hundreds of millions of commies (and lots of slanty-eyed foreigners), but also the parasites who were riding them. Meanwhile, the valiant (and resourceful) Americans manage to defeat the slugs through the use of germ warfare, a controversial weapon in the 1950s, and one the use of which Heinlein here wholeheartedly endorses.

In this sense, *The Puppet Masters* calls attention to the topic of biological warfare, which was probably second only to nuclear warfare among the Cold War fears of the 1950s. In the U.S., such fears involved the assumption that the Soviets would stop at nothing, including the use of germ warfare, in their all-out effort to destroy American capitalism. Of course, just as the United States was the only nation ever actually to use nuclear weapons in combat, there is also ample evidence that the U.S. was the only nation actually to use germ warfare in the 1950s, as an experimental weapon during the Korean conflict.[21] Heinlein would have presumably had no objection to this use, on the basis of *The Puppet Masters*. Indeed, one of the central messages of the book is that we need, not only to remain eternally vigilant, but also to be willing to use any resources at our disposal to defeat our enemies.

Sam, who has at one point been taken over by one of the slugs, bears them a particular animosity, and his "kill-all-slugs" expressions of racial hatred can be taken as a pretty clear expression of Heinlein's attitude toward America's communist enemies. It is thus with particular satisfaction that Heinlein (through Sam) reports the apparently complete destruction of all slugs on earth, even though he warns that we still need to be alert, lest there be others lurking in some obscure Third World hideout, like the Amazon (321). Meanwhile, the Americans prepare to launch an all-out genocidal assault on Titan itself so they can wipe out the slugs once and for all. Sam and Mary go along on the mission, Sam gleefully ending his narrative with the announcement, "Puppet masters — the free men are coming to kill you! *Death and Destruction!*" (340, Heinlein's italics).

For Sam, as for Heinlein, the only good alien is a dead alien, but this hatred of the alien Other is intensified by the particularly horrifying nature of these Others, whose strategies make it impossible to tell Us from Them — one of the ultimate nightmares of the 1950s. Of course, Heinlein's happily bloodthirsty vision of racial extermination might threaten to backfire in a propagandistic sense, making one wonder if we have correctly identified the good guys and the bad guys in this text.[22] It is, however, a telling statement on the texture of life in the early 1950s that no such difficulty seems to have occurred to Heinlein, who could be pretty confident that his readers would endorse these harsh measures against such an unremittingly alien enemy. Heinlein's enthusiasm for the death and destruction of all enemies of the American way comes through even more clearly in the Hugo Award-winning *Starship Troopers*, widely regarded as the text that did the most to feed the suspicions of some that Heinlein was a warmongering fascist.[23]

Described by Franklin as "a bugle-blowing, drum-beating glorification of the hero's life in military service," *Starship Troopers* includes a number of battle scenes, but it actually has very little in the way of plot, being primarily a celebration of militarism and a concerted attempt to indoctrinate readers into accepting this celebration (111). Clearly a response to Heinlein's belief that the U.S. was going soft in the late 1950s, *Starship Troopers* is essentially a call to arms, a reminder that some enemies can be defeated only by force. Indeed, the book presents a pseudo-Darwinian vision of life as a struggle for survival of the strongest, thereby urging Americans to seek greater military strength so that they can survive. The book presents a future world in which a period of high crime (especially among juvenile delinquents) has preceded a final near-apocalyptic confrontation among different world powers, leading to a collapse of existing social systems, but also to the establishment of the

Federation, a new world government ruled by a military elite.[24] Indeed, under this new system, only veterans of the military enjoy full citizenship, including the right to vote. Yet, horrifying as this system might sound, Heinlein presents it as a utopia. The military rulers of this global system are described as the best and wisest rulers in human history, leading to unprecedented freedom and prosperity for all, including the vast majority, who have never served in the military.

Structured as a bildungsroman, *Starship Troopers* is didactic in the most literal sense. Most of the text simply describes the military education of the narrator and protagonist, Juan Rico, as he goes through boot camp and then officer candidate school (OCS). In the process, Rico learns the nature and value of militarism, presumably teaching readers the same lesson as well. Indeed, Rico's education in militarism begins even in high school, where his history teacher, Mr. Dubois, a former military officer, inundates him with right-wing expositions on various issues that show the book's origins in the 1950s, despite the fact that the book is ostensibly set in the distant future. For example, Dubois's expositions on the centrality of violence to the course of human history serve as a critique of those who would call for co-existence with the Soviets. He proclaims to his students that "violence, naked force, has settled more issues in history than has any other factor, and the contrary opinion is wishful thinking at its worst. Breeds that forget this basic truth have always paid for it with their lives and freedoms" (26).

Dubois's teachings also include a response to the 1950s fear of juvenile delinquency. At one point, he extols the virtues of flogging and other forms of corporal punishment as a means of straightening out wayward juveniles, a method he compares to spanking puppies to try to housebreak them (114–20). Meanwhile, during this same speech, Dubois dismisses the notion of inalienable rights, explaining that juvenile delinquency occurs because society is too soft on young people, encouraging them to demand their rights, when in fact they should be urged to learn to do their duty, duty being the basis of all morality. Dubois, in fact, dismisses the whole notion of inalienable rights as nonsense: for him, people have only the rights they are willing to fight and die for (119).

Dubois's lectures also include the obligatory Cold War critique of Marxism, which he supposedly demolishes with a ludicrous argument that is not only silly, but hopelessly naïve and ignorant in its presentation of Marx's theories. Heinlein apparently understood Marx even less than he did Darwin. He has Dubois claim, for example, that Marx's labor theory of value implies that human labor can transform anything into anything else, like some sort of alchemy. He further interprets Marx as believing that any human action always increases the value of whatever is being acted upon. Given this kind of radical misinterpretation, perhaps it is little wonder that Dubois describes Marx as a "disheveled old mystic ... neurotic, unscientific, illogical, this pompous fraud" (92).

Rico's military training is physically rigorous and demanding. Those who fail are apt to suffer severe punishment, including floggings in front of the other troops. In fact, several trainees are killed in the course of their training. On the other hand, soldiers can leave the service at any time, and Heinlein continually extols the virtues of an all-volunteer army, whose members serve freely and thus learn the twin values of duty and responsibility far better than could a force of conscripts. Rico's education also includes considerable indoctrination, culminating in the declaration by Major Reid, one of his instructors in OCS, that rule by veterans of the military is the ideal political system because these veterans have learned, via their voluntary military service, to place "the welfare of the group ahead of personal advantage" (182). But, having learned this valuable lesson, the new ruling class also performs far better than any ruling class in history, because they understand full well that the very nature of human beings is to struggle for power through the use of force. Force, then, lies at the heat of all politics: "To vote is to wield authority; it is the supreme authority from which all other authority derives. ... *Force*, if you will! — the franchise is force, naked and raw, the Power of the Rods and the Ax. Whether it is exerted by ten men or ten billion, political authority is *force*" (183, Heinlein's emphasis).

Rico learns this lesson well, ultimately accepting its sinister message without question — after all, the instructors at OCS are described by Heinlein as being able to demonstrate the correctness of their point of view through mathematical proofs and symbolic logic. Rico thus emerges from his education as a trained killing machine, ready to go forth to defend his planet as a member of the Mobile Infantry (M.I.), described by Franklin as a sort of "interstellar Green Berets" (116). And defend the planet Rico must, for, as ideal as the system there might be, eternal vigilance is still required. In a rather transparent allegorization of the position of the United States in the world system of the 1950s, the prosperous earth is surrounded by sinister enemies, who threaten to take away its wealth and freedom. Central among these are the "Bugs," whose insect-like nature makes them the ideal Other, because they are so obviously inhuman. The Bugs are also imperialistic, hoping to add the earth to their empire, thus forcing the earthlings to fight to defend their way of life.

In fact, the Bugs and their ideology are virtually identical to Western Cold War visions of communism and the Soviet Union, though their alienness considerably simplifies the Us vs. Them terms of the Cold War. Noting this use of the Bugs as stand-ins for communists, David Seed suggests that "political difference is thereby naturalized into the threatening alien" (37). Theirs is a communal society of unfeeling creatures who forgo all individualism in favor of the collective good. Indeed, they are formidable precisely because they work so smoothly as a collective unit, with no consideration for individual needs and concerns. Heinlein, through Rico, makes the connection to communism explicit: "Every time we killed a thousand Bugs at the cost of one M.I. it was a net victory for the Bugs. We were learning, expensively, just how efficient a total communism can be when used by a people adapted to it by evolution; the Bug commissars didn't care any more about expending soldiers than we care about expending ammo" (152–53).

Of course, Heinlein is careful to qualify his seeming admiration for Bug communism by explaining that the Bugs are adapted to it by evolution, implying that, on the other hand, communism is unnatural for human beings, who are by nature driven by blind self-interest. For Heinlein, only military discipline can harness this natural survivalist tendency in human beings and put it to good use, though Heinlein here gets entangled in the contradictions of his own arguments. On the one hand, he presents military discipline as involving first and foremost a willingness to sacrifice the individual in the interest of the group—which makes the human military seem rather similar to the Bug communists. On the other hand, he makes a sharp distinction between the liberality with which the Bugs sacrifice individual soldiers and the willingness of the human military to sustain huge losses to rescue even one of their number who happens to be in trouble. In fact, he suggests that the ultimate strength of humanity derives from "a racial conviction that when one human needs rescue, others should not count the price" (223). Yet Heinlein fails to explain how this "racial conviction" arose in a race he characterizes as naturally driven only by self-interest; nor does he explain how the military morality of favoring the group over the individual fits in with the willingness to sacrifice entire platoons to try to rescue a single human soldier.

Of course, Heinlein was never a very clear thinker—just clearly promilitary and anticommunist. But the contradictions in his thought are not merely problems with his personal logic. They are, in fact, highly representative of popular American thought in the 1950s, which consistently found itself entangled in such contradictions. Thus, communists could be both naïve bumpkins and coldly scientific eggheads. Meanwhile, Americans could celebrate both individual liberty and personal sacrifice, culminating, in the 1950s, in a distinctive simultaneous fear of being like everyone else and of not being like everyone else. In any case, if the contradictions in Heinlein's arguments threatened to explode his position, his fans on the anticommunist right failed to notice. Nevertheless, the extremity of Heinlein's vision in *Starship Troopers* was such that two popular science fiction novels, Harry Harrison's *Bill, the Galactic Hero* (1965) and Joe Haldeman's *The Forever War* (1974, winner of the Hugo and Nebula Awards), were written at least partly as parodies of Heinlein's book.

Even Paul Verhoeven's 1997 film adaptation of Heinlein's novel is done as big-budget camp, with tongue in cheek. The film thus largely lampoons Heinlein's militaristic vision and glorification of violence, though it sometimes seems to get caught up in its own spectacular special effects, becoming a spectacle of violence in its own right. Verhoeven drops the anticommunist rhetoric, but his extremely realistic Bugs are so menacingly alien that there is little chance of audiences truly sympathizing with them, even though the murderous humans have vastly superior weapons and the film hints that it may have been the humans who provoked the war. Meanwhile, it is a measure of the extremity of Heinlein's ideology that Verhoeven, in his dystopian depiction of the militaristic Federation, does not exaggerate Heinlein's vision, but in fact mediates it. Women, for example, seem to enjoy full equality in Verhoeven's Federation, whereas they serve primarily as sexual objects in Heinlein's. Thus, in the film, women serve in the M.I. alongside men. In Heinlein, women do not go into combat, but serve only aboard the navy's starships, where they can hold some important jobs (such as pilots), but where they are mostly glorified camp followers, to keep up the men's morale and give them a "living, breathing reality" to fight for (204).

If the exact nature of Heinlein's rightism is sometimes hard to pin down, the political visions of other writers in the decade were vague enough that it is difficult to determine whether they are right-wing or left-wing. Clifford D. Simak is a representative figure here; his work provides critiques of capitalism that sometimes sound almost Marxist, but also are some of the clearest science fiction explorations of a nostalgic longing for the pre-capitalist past that informed much conservative thought in the decade, including that of the New Critics. The key text here is *Ring around the Sun* (1953), a quintessential early–Cold War novel. Here, Simak not only neatly summarizes the nostalgia of the period, but does so within a constellation of images that focus on alienation, routinization, and attitudes toward the Other.

The protagonist and narrator of *Ring around the Sun* is Jay Vickers, a writer whose feelings of loneliness and isolation make him a very representative figure of the alienated intellectual. Vickers has somehow always felt apart from other people. He is convinced, for example, that his fellow passengers always seem intentionally to avoid sitting next to him on the bus; earlier when he had worked in an office, he concluded that the other workers avoided talking to him, excluding him from both their office conversations and their social activities outside of work. Thus, he became a writer, allowing him to work at home alone. But, not surprisingly, this retreat from humanity only reinforces his feeling of not fitting in. He wonders if he is somehow different from other people. In fact, he

notes that he has essentially built his entire life out of "the feeling of loneliness which he had always had—not the occasional twinges that everyone must feel, but a continual sense of 'differentness' that had forced him
to stand apart from his fellow humans, and they from him" (58).

Thus, as so often happened in the 1950s, Vickers's sense of alienation
takes the particular form of suspecting that he himself is the Other of
which the normal people of the decade are so afraid. He cannot fit into
their routine, so he establishes a separate routine of his own, protecting
himself from his own seeming paranoia by settling into "a rut of his own
devising, a polished and well-loved rut" (58). But this is a science fiction
novel, so in this case his paranoia is justified, and his routine will soon be
interrupted. Actually, there have already been times in his life when he
has escaped the humdrum everyday. He has at least two vague memories of having, in his childhood and adolescence, momentarily escaped
into "enchanted" realms rich in the magic that his real world so sadly
lacks. As the book begins (in 1987), Vickers has concluded that these
memories simply derive from his immaturity at the time the events occurred, as nothing similar has happened in his adult life. However, odd
things have begun to happen in the world at large. In particular, some
mysterious firm has begun producing commodities, such as razor blades,
cigarette lighters, and light bulbs, that apparently last forever. Further-
more, these items are sold at ridiculously low prices, precipitating the
collapse of the industries that originally manufactured these items.

When these "forever" goods are soon expanded to include cars, housing, and clothing, it becomes obvious that someone is attempting to un-
dermine those industries as well, threatening to lead to a global economic
collapse. On the other hand, someone has also begun producing syn-
thetic carbohydrates, which are distributed free of charge, thus amelio-
rating the crisis by at least ensuring that everyone has food. The forces of
capitalism, led by the corpulent Mr. Crawford, head of North American
Research Corporation, respond by organizing to oppose the spread of
these new goods. Vickers then enters the scene when he is asked by
Crawford to write a propagandistic book urging the public to shun the
new goods. He refuses, however, preferring to concentrate on his own
independent writing, apparently fiction.

But Vickers cannot settle back into his old routine so easily. Odd
things begin to happen, and Vickers is soon forced to flee his suburban
home to escape a lynch mob that has somehow become convinced that he
murdered an old man, Horton Flanders, who recently disappeared from
the neighborhood. This event triggers a series of adventures that leads
Vickers to discover that the new goods are being manufactured by a race
of mutants, using robot labor in factories located on a parallel earth. The
mutants have a variety of special mental skills, including the ability to
pick up transmissions from advanced civilizations in other solar systems,

thus their access to superior technology. The mutants have also been using their mental abilities subtly to intervene in the course of human history throughout modern times. Among other things, the intervention of
these mutants is responsible for the fact that the Cold War never became
hot. Nevertheless, the mutants have been unable to prevent modern society from decaying to the point that correction of its course seems hope-
less. In still another science fiction vision of abandoning the original earth
in order to seek a fresh start, the mutants are carrying out a plan gradually to transfer the population of the original earth to their parallel earth
(or to one of a whole series of other parallel earths, all uninhabited, to
which they have learned to travel), there to replay the course of modernity, presumably with better results. The original earth would eventually
be depopulated altogether, "its hide cleansed of the ravening tribe which
had eaten at it and gutted it and mangled it and ravished it" (130).

However, Simak makes it clear that the source of this destruction is
not humanity or human nature per se, but rather the particular course
taken by human history from the Renaissance forward. Thus, on their alternative earths, the mutants plan to restart human history in feudal
times, moving forward from there, but this time with better planning and
direction. In other words, they conclude that civilization can be saved
only by starting over in a time before the advent of capitalist modernity,
which is thereby identified in the text as the culprit that has led to the
current sad state of affairs on the original earth. Indeed, the text is
strongly and explicitly dystopian in its characterization of modern capitalist culture on the original earth, with its ethic of competition and cor-
responding animosity toward the Other. This culture is described in the
text as "founded on hatred and a terrible pride and a suspicion of everyone who did not talk the same language or eat the same food or dress the
same way as you did. It was a lop-sided mechanical culture of clanking
machines, a technological world that could provide creature comfort, but
not human justice nor security" (167).

Not surprisingly, given this xenophobic culture, the humans on the
original earth react violently when they learn of the existence of the mutants, leading to widespread outbreaks of mob violence. After all, the
mutants are not just different (and threateningly superior), but they are
also difficult to distinguish from normal humans, making them one of
the ultimate nightmares of the 1950s. Simak is careful to suggest that his
target is not just capitalism, but modernity as a whole, which encom-
passes communism as well as capitalism. It is interesting, however, that
this mob violence includes suspicions that the mutants might somehow
be part of a communist plot, while others dream of using the mutants to
"blow these Commies plumb to hell" (166). Thus, Simak, while clearly
including communism in his critique of modern "mechanical" society,
comments on the McCarthyite anticommunist hysteria of the early–Cold

War years, implicating it as a symptom of the dehumanizing hatred of the Other that he sees as central to the ideology of the modern world.

It is also interesting that many of Simak's critiques of modern society so closely resemble various Marxist critiques of capitalism. For example, much of his indictment of the modern world is extremely reminiscent of the famous critique leveled against the instrumental reason of the Enlightenment by Max Horkheimer and Theodor Adorno of the Frankfurt School. One could, in fact describe Simak's principal target as the Enlightenment and its legacy of rationality and technological domination of nature. Thus, Vickers is told that one of the secrets of the mental superiority of the mutants is their willingness to play hunches and their refusal to be bound by "the old machine-like reasoning that the human race has relied on since it left the caves" (138). Here, however, Simak runs into a bit of a contradiction: if this legacy of reason goes back to caveman days, then presumably the mutants would have to go back that far in their attempt to start over. Of course, one could argue that such contradictions are perfectly consistent with Simak's apparent rejection of logic. However, he is not always able to abandon logic so easily. At times, he equates reason and rationality with civilization itself, failing to recognize precisely the historical model on which the mutants have based their plans. But such an equation is itself a characteristic of Enlightenment thought, with its tendency toward universalization and naturalization of its own historicized attitudes. Indeed, Simak sometimes goes so far as to picture this reliance on reason as a universal human attribute, as "the old awkward normal human way," surmountable by the mutants only because they have moved to a new level in their biological evolution, thus changing their nature.

Simak's utopian vision of an idealized life on the alternative earth is a bit confused as well. He describes the system there as "paternal feudalism," and indeed the mutants rule the alternative earth like benevolent aristocrats, supplying whatever their subjects need while also gently educating the subjects to accept and participate in the plan that the mutants have laid out for them (128). On the other hand, Simak also describes this world as being like the "old American frontier," its inhabitants resembling the early American pioneers. Yet the subjugation of the American frontier was a principal example of precisely the ideology the mutants are supposedly seeking to destroy. Further, the potentially sinister aspects of the historical engineering being carried out by the mutants is quite clear, though presumably they are so superior to humans that they will not abuse their power. Yet the text also indicates that they may plan to carry out experiments in which they try out different historical plans on various alternative earths, attempting to discover which version works best. They thus seem to accept the scientific problem-solving strategies of the very Enlightenment they are seeking to circumvent, while the very notion that there are problems to solve suggests that the mutants do not know what course they should take. They are, then, playing dice with the world and with the fates of the entire population of the earth.

Such contradictions are exacerbated by the fact that the "scientific" premise of the book is difficult to believe and that the plot becomes increasingly bizarre as the book goes along. It is no surprise when we discover that Vickers himself is unknowingly a mutant, which explains his lifelong sense of differentness. But it gets a bit more weird when we learn that he is not exactly a mutant, but rather an android containing one-third of the life force of an original source mutant, the other two-thirds having gone into Flanders and Crawford. Here, the contradictions in Simak's vision become particularly problematic. Not only is Crawford, the leader of the antimutant forces of capitalism, himself a mutant, but it turns out that most of the members of his board of directors (and most of the world's business and government leaders) are mutants as well, though they do not know it. In other words, the earth has been guided into its present dire condition under the leadership of mutants, which tends to call into question the ability of the mutants to re-engineer history so that things work out better the second time around.

But Simak does not need to be bothered with such problems. *Ring around the Sun* is in no way a realistic work. It is not really even science fiction, but a parable about the dangers of modernity and a fantasy of escape from the problems of the modern world. In the final analysis, the most striking and important aspects of the book are the passion with which it rejects the values of modern America and the intensity of its longing for an escape into a pastoral alternative. In this sense, *Ring around the Sun* resembles Ray Bradbury's *Fahrenheit 451* (discussed in the next chapter), even though it is more humane in imagining a carefully engineered cleansing of the earth, as opposed to Bradbury's cleansing nuclear holocaust. Simak's book, like Bradbury's, is thus closely related to the post-holocaust fictions that, for obvious reasons, were so prominent in the decade, though Simak's holocaust is particularly clean.

Simak's vision of a re-engineering of history by an enlightened elite is really a fantasy of escape from history altogether. Indeed, the book comes close to denying that history even exists. For one thing, Simak, like Asimov, has trouble imagining that normal historical processes can bring about fundamental changes in human beings or human behavior. Therefore, he must posit a mutation in order to provide the change that kicks his plot into gear. Further, Vickers discovers in the course of the book that time does not really pass. Instead, each alternative world exists in a given instant for all eternity. Thus, the only kind of time travel is travel from one world to another (145). This vision of an eternal present has sometimes been associated with modernism, as when Jürgen Habermas, attributing the attitude originally to Nietzsche. argues that an "exaltation of the present" is a central element of aesthetic modernity (5). Jameson, however, has seen this loss of a sense of temporal progression as a central aspect of postmodernism. In this light, one might identify the timelessness of Gibson's cyberspace, in which individuals can move through virtual distances instantaneously, as a clear expression of a postmodernist sensibility. It is also, in the early twenty-first century, a postmodernist experience shared by millions of Internet users every day.

One of the writers of 1950s science fiction who is most often seen as a crucial predecessor of Gibson and other writers of cyberpunk science fiction is Alfred Bester, notable, among other things, as the winner of the first Hugo Award for his 1953 novel, *The Demolished Man*. Here, Bester envisions a future society in which people with telepathic ability, called Espers (also known as "peepers"), perform crucial roles. They are, for example, ideal psychiatrists. They are also good policemen, so much so that there has not been a murder for more than seventy years, because policemen would be able to detect murderous intentions in advance, or, in the worst case, at least be able to identify the killer. Yet *The Demolished Man* is essentially a murder mystery, taking its plot structure (and much of its tone) from hard-boiled detective fiction, just as Gibson's *Neuromancer* would later do.

Like much hard-boiled fiction, *The Demolished Man* is rather cynical about capitalism. Its murderer is, in fact, America's leading capitalist, Ben Reich, who concocts an elaborate plot to kill D'Courtney, his principal business rival. Police prefect Lincoln Powell, a First-Class Esper, is able to use his abilities to convince himself that Reich is the killer. Unfortunately, he is unable to make a case that will stand up in court because Reich seems to have no motive: D'Courtney, shortly before his killing, had apparently agreed to a merger that would have ended his business rivalry with Reich. Ultimately, however, Powell, aided by a concerted effort of others in the Esper Guild, is able to re-engineer Reich's perception of reality to the point that he breaks down and reveals the truth, which had been hidden even from Reich himself and thus not discernible through conventional telepathic techniques.

Reich is convicted of murder and sentenced to be "demolished," which, in this society, means not physical execution but psychological reconstruction, which will remove his murderous impulses but preserve his considerable talents, making him a productive member of society. Indeed, in a slap, not only at capital punishment, but also at 1950s conformism, Bester is careful to point out that the reconditioning will not wipe out the characteristics that have made Reich a unique individual. Dr. Jeems, spearheading the treatment, explains that it would be crazy to execute a man like Reich, as they might have done in the past. After all, Reich's very ability to go against the rules of society suggests a rare and valuable gift that should not be repressed. "Do that enough," Jeems says, speaking of such repression, "and all you've got are the sheep." "Maybe in those days they wanted sheep," replies Powell, and readers are clearly meant to interpret "those days" as indicating their own context in the 1950s.

If this final statement in favor of individualism sounds like rather conventional 1950s liberalism, there is surely something problematic in the way Reich's unique natural abilities are to be identified and preserved through the imposition of an unnatural and involuntary psychological manipulation. Indeed, both the re-engineering of Reich's reality and the subsequent rebuilding of his mind anticipate the (postmodern) cyberpunk notion of individual identity (and reality itself) as tenuous, contingent, and provisional. Bester's other novel of the 1950s, *The Stars My Destination* (1957, originally published in Britain in 1956 as *Tiger! Tiger!*), anticipates cyberpunk even more directly. Here, Bester again shows his characteristic concern with telepathic powers, building the novel around the ability of individuals in his vision of the twenty-fifth century to teleport themselves for distances of up to a thousand miles merely by mental visualization, or "jaunting," so called after a scientist named Jaunte, who initially discovered the technique. Jaunting, of course, is a direct anticipation of cyberspace, the only difference being that individuals travel about physically as well as mentally.

In addition to its obvious advantages, jaunting, Bester notes, has led to numerous social and ideological upheavals, including a resurgence of Victorian repression of female sexuality, as the new mobility makes it all too easy for randy males to get access to likely females, and vice versa. The newfound mobility provided by jaunting also contributes to the spread of disease, economic crises, and crime waves. In addition, it has led to economic imbalances that have caused an all-out war between the Inner Planets (Venus, earth, and Mars) and the Outer Satellites (seven inhabited moons of Jupiter, Saturn, and Neptune). Yet Bester notes, in good dialectic fashion, that the clashes between extremes brought about by the age have a great potential for leading eventually to "a human explosion that would transform man and make him the master of the universe" (14).

Having suggested these high stakes in a prologue, Bester then turns to the story of the lowly Gulliver Foyle, a mechanic's mate 3rd class in the space service and the unlikely hero of the novel. As the book opens, Foyle has been stranded in space for 170 days, trapped aboard the wreckage of his ship, the *SS Nomad*, owned by the giant Presteign conglomerate. Then, to his great relief, he discovers that another Presteign ship, the *Vorga*, is approaching the wreckage. He signals the *Vorga*, and they clearly realize that he is on board the *Nomad*. Yet they veer off into space rather than attempting rescue. Foyle dedicates himself to revenge against the *Vorga*, a project that drives the remainder of the plot as Foyle, driven by rage, goes to superhuman extremes to try to track down the responsible party and exact his revenge.

In the process, he encounters a number of colorful adventures and misadventures, though Foyle's quest for revenge (clearly based on the similar quest of Edmund Dantes in Alexandre Dumas's *The Count of Monte Cristo*) turns out to be somewhat beside the point, merely providing a framework within which Bester can present his vision of twenty-fifth-century society. For one thing, Foyle's efforts bring him into contact with individuals from a wide range of social situations, including the rich and powerful, such as Presteign himself. Much of the focus is on Presteign and his ruthless management of his clannish conglomerate (his slogan is "blood and money"), both recalling the depiction of Ben Reich in *The Demolished Man* and anticipating the giant *zaibatsus* of Gibson. Much of the satirical treatment of Presteign resonates strongly within a 1950s context. For example, the firm demands absolute loyalty and conformity among its employees. Thus, in a commentary on both the gray-flanneled mentality of 1950s corporate America and the rise of chains of identical retail outlets throughout the country, each of Presteign's 497 retail outlets is managed by one of 497 Mr. Prestos, each made physically and mentally identical to all the others by "six months of surgery and psycho-conditioning." Moreover, we are told, other firms use similar procedures. Presteign's Mr. Presto is paralleled by "the Kodak clan's Mr. Kwik and Montgomery Ward's Uncle Monty" (47).

These commentaries on the workings of capitalism again anticipate many of the motifs of cyberpunk science fiction. One thinks, for example, of Neal Stephenson's *Snow Crash* (1992), in which every aspect of life is administered by various corporate franchises, including the Mafia-run CosaNostra Pizza, Inc., the Central Intelligence Corporation, Meta Cops, Inc., and Hoosegow, Inc., an operator of franchise jails. *The Stars My Destination* anticipates cyberpunk in other ways as well, as when Foyle, in the course of the book, has much of his body replaced by mechanical and electronic parts, making him a formidable fighting machine: "Every nerve plexus had been rewired, microscopic transistors and transformers had been buried in muscle and bone, a minute platinum outlet showed at the base of his spine. ... 'More machine than man,' he thought" (128). This motif clearly addresses the 1950s fears that the increasing technologization and routinization of everyday life were turning people into machines, a fear that had only grown stronger (and more literal) by the 1980s, when Gibson began to produce characters augmented by an array of high-tech implants.

Bester's focus on the economic dimension extends to his commentary on the war between the Inner Planets and the Outer Satellites when he notes that "this war (like all wars) was the shooting phase of a commercial struggle" (124). Further, Presteign is depicted as a profiteer who will gain significantly from the war, no matter which side wins, because "rich men like Presteign never lose" in wars (58). The atmosphere that informs this war is also paralleled directly to the Cold War paranoia of the 1950s. During the war, individuals use the jaunting technique to avoid being drafted either into the military or into work in war industries. Meanwhile, "spy scares and invasion scares spread. The hysterical became informants and lynchers. An ominous foreboding paralyzed every home from Baffin Island to the Falklands" (124).

Ultimately, however, the most striking political statement made in *The Stars My Destination* occurs when Foyle, having obtained the world's only supply of PyrE, a deadly thermonuclear weapon, refuses to turn the material over to the powers that be for use in the their war against the Outer Satellites, but instead distributes it among the common people around the world. This choice may lead to all-out nuclear destruction, Foyle realizes, but for once it will be up to the people to make that decision for themselves, rather than being at the mercy of a power elite. Among other things, this motif provides a telling commentary on the American political system, which makes so much of democracy, but which isolates the general population from life-and-death decisions through an elaborate security apparatus that gives ordinary individuals essentially no role in the decision-making process.

However impractical Foyle's solution of distributing nuclear weapons to the masses might appear, it nevertheless makes a strong symbolic point. Meanwhile, this motif, along with the numerous apocalyptic images that provide much of the texture of *The Stars My Destination*, again links this novel to the genre of the post-holocaust narrative. Such narratives, within the context of the 1950s, were one of the central means through which science fiction writers engaged in dialogues with their political context, as will be explained in the following chapter.

2

The Beginning or the End?:
Post-Holocaust Novels and Films,
1946–1964

Given the Cold War political climate of the long 1950s, it is not surprising that many of the most important science fiction works of the decade dealt with the possibility of nuclear holocaust and its aftermath. Such works took a variety of forms in both novel and film, and as a group these works constitute a large and diverse assemblage. Some works can be taken as cautionary tales and seem genuinely designed as attempted interventions in contemporary debates concerning the Cold War arms race. Others function in a largely satirical vein, using their depictions of post-holocaust worlds as devices of cognitive estrangement that add critical force to the author's commentary on the ills of his or her own contemporary society. These ills, as with other science fiction works of the decade, can quite often be encompassed within the twin topics of routinization and alienation. Indeed, a number of post-holocaust works succumb to the temptation to see nuclear war as an almost positive event that interrupts the growth of alienation and routinization in American society. In addition, as Joyce Evans notes, post-holocaust works of the 1950s, especially films, tended to draw upon the kind of survivalist narratives that were widely promulgated in the media at the time, narratives that actually tended to act as "an extension of the American belief in its own invulnerable omnipotence" (136). The post-holocaust world in such works often becomes a new version of Frederick Jackson Turner's American frontier that offers renewed possibilities for adventure that are no longer available in the routinized world of contemporary America.

In some ways, the predecessor of all of the post-holocaust works of the long 1950s was not a fictional work at all, but John Hersey's *Hiroshima* (1946), a graphic nonfiction account of the effects of the American atomic bombing of the Japanese city of the title. Hersey's book, described by the science fiction novelist and critic Thomas Disch as "the single most influential document of the atomic age," brought home the horrors of nuclear war to an American populace that had hitherto had very little knowledge of those horrors (80). In fact, as Disch further notes, Americans in general remained largely ignorant of the details of nuclear war throughout the decade, as the American government maintained an extremely restrictive, even repressive control of the dissemination of such information. Granted, as detailed in the 1982 film *The Atomic Café*, images related to nuclear destruction were widely disseminated in the decade, but the images tended to be greatly sanitized, assuring Americans that everything will be fine if they will only resist the seductions of communist propaganda and remember to duck and cover in the event of an attack by the nefarious Russians.

The Atomic Café also does a good job of capturing the hysterical anticommunism of the Cold War years, presenting documentary footage ranging from widespread demands that nuclear weapons be deployed in Korea, to the McCarthyite purges of suspected communists in virtually all sectors of American life, to the questionable conviction and execution of the Rosenbergs. The film also includes propaganda footage of American affluence and of American homes being blown apart by Soviet bombs, making the point that our wonderful life is seriously threatened by our evil (and envious) Russian enemies.

Given the careful control of nuclear-related images by the American government, it is not surprising that much of what Americans learned about the impact of nuclear war during the long 1950s had to come from science fiction. One of the most respected post-holocaust novels of this period, George R. Stewart's *Earth Abides* (1949), appeared very early in the long decade and dealt, not with the impact of nuclear war, but with a mysterious plague (perhaps caused by a mutant virus), that sweeps across America (and, presumably, the world) killing virtually everyone within a matter of days. Thus, Stewart's work is a representative work of the early–Cold War years in its concern about the possibility of a widespread holocaust that would wipe out most of the human race. It is not, however, typical of the period in that it does not attribute this holocaust to political rivalries between the Americans and the Soviets. In fact, Stewart's vision is entirely centered on North America, and there is no mention of the rest of the world at all other than vague hints that the plague has probably struck there as well. In this sense, Stewart's work is atypical of Cold War fiction, which, to an extent unprecedented in American literature, tends to deal in central ways (and for obvious reasons) with relationships between the United States and the rest of the world.

In Stewart's plague-decimated United States, there are scattered survivors, who for some reason are immune to the plague. One of these is Isherwood Williams, a graduate student in ecological science and the protagonist of the novel. Ish, in the woods doing research when the plague hits, is bitten by a rattlesnake. He falls ill and nearly dies, but soon begins to recover. He makes his way back to civilization, only to discover that virtually everyone in the San Francisco Bay area (he lives in Berkeley, where he goes to school) seems to have vanished. At this point, the first section of Ish's adventures begins , as he travels across America seeking other survivors. He finds only a few, and none with whom he feels that he wants to make common cause, though he does adopt a beagle. Always a solitary type, Ish is well suited for this new life. As the first section continues, he returns to Berkeley and begins to build a new life for himself, somewhat along the lines of Defoe's Robinson Crusoe. Indeed, this first section of the novel alludes to *Robinson Crusoe* several times, making the connection explicit. At one point, Ish even takes a copy of Defoe's novel from the public library and begins to read it, though he finds its preoccupation with religion "boring and rather silly" (82).

Despite this rejection of Crusoe's Protestantism, *Earth Abides* clearly participates in the science fiction subgenre of the "Robinsonade," perhaps the most explicit example of which would be Byron Haskin's much-admired 1964 film, *Robinson Crusoe on Mars*, which directly transplants Defoe's novel onto the red planet. Most post-holocaust novels participate in this genre in one way or another, and *Earth Abides* well illustrates the problematics of this participation. Ish's efforts, like those of the survivors in many works of post-holocaust fiction, are seen as a testament to human ingenuity, giving the book an upbeat tone that makes the holocaust itself sometimes seem almost like a positive, quasi-Darwinian development, wiping out the weak so that the strong (like Ish) can better survive. Such positive notes are typical of the Robinsonade, though there is a clear irony in this use of Defoe's protagonist as a role model for individuals in the post-capitalist world. After all, Defoe's novel is a sign of the rise of capitalism, not its demise, and Crusoe has been described by critics from Marx onward as a typical example of the capitalist individual.[1]

Such ironies are especially strong in the case of *Earth Abides*, which is informed by a radical rejection of capitalism — which may be why Stewart depicts Ish as rejecting Crusoe as a role model. In any case, for Stewart, the fall of capitalism is not caused by external enemies (such as the Soviets) or by the internal contradictions in capitalism itself (as Marx predicted). Instead, Stewart, in explaining the plague, again returns to Darwin, meditating, not on the origin, but on the demise of species. He gives no explanation for the plague other than natural cycles that, according to the italicized segments that are inserted as commentaries at points throughout the narrative, tend periodically to wipe out any species that is too successful and thus increases its numbers beyond a level that is naturally sustainable. According to these segments, the decimation of humanity is long overdue: *"During ten thousand years his numbers have been on the upgrade in spite of wars, pestilences, and famines. This increase in population has become more and more rapid. Biologically, man has for too long a time been rolling an uninterrupted run of sevens"* (8).

Eventually, Ish moves beyond the lone survivor phase and meets a woman, Em, with whom he feels he can build a life. Indeed, he feels a connection with Em that he has never felt with anyone before: "In the old world it might well never have happened. Out of destruction had come, for him, love" (104). With the capitalist order destroyed, the crippling psychic effects of capitalism are destroyed as well, making it possible even for the previously alienated Ish to feel a genuine sense of connection with others. And this connection goes beyond his sexual bond with Em. The two are gradually joined by others, soon building a thriving community, which they refer to as the Tribe. This community is highly egalitarian, though all of the members of the community tend to look to Ish, as the only intellectual among them, for a certain amount of leadership. Indeed, Ish seems to be the only member of the group who really thinks about the future, trying to plot a course that will help them to restore civilization as soon as possible. Ultimately, however, this plan fails, though in a way that presents this failure as a sort of success. Indeed, all movements toward a restoration of the former structures of civilization are presented as falls from the edenic condition of the post-holocaust community. Thus, when a dangerous, disease-ridden outsider comes among them, the members of the Tribe conclude that their only recourse is to put the man to death, lest he threaten the survival of the entire group. The man is quickly executed, but Ish recognizes that the Tribe has thereby lost a certain innocence and made a potentially crippling move back toward the establishment of laws and their enforcement, toward the regimentation and routinization from which the holocaust has freed them (257–58).

One of the reasons that the life of the Tribe seems so edenic is that the individuals who make up the group are freed of the restrictions and categorizations that had made up life in the former world. In their new life, there is no distinction between work and play, no class inequality, no rules that force individuals to conform to preexisting schedules, dividing their lives into sharply differentiated segments based on rigid timetables. As one of the italicized segments notes, this lack of routine greatly enriches their lives in comparison to their former lives under American capitalism: *"The turning out of the light and the ringing of the alarm-clock were not so much the symbols of man's dual life as were the punching of the time clock and the blowing of the whistle. Men marched on picket-lines and threw bricks and exploded dynamite to shift an hour from one classification to the other, and other men fought equally hard to prevent them. And always work became more laborious and odious, and play grew more artificial and febrile"* (189).

In short, Stewart's analysis of American capitalism is essentially neo-Marxist, building upon Marx's discussion of the centrality of the division of labor in creating alienation, class difference, and exploitation of labor. It also resembles Georg Lukács's concern over the spiritually impoverishing effects of the fragmentation of experience brought about by the reification and categorization of all human activities under capitalism. Indeed, for Lukács, this fragmentation of experience is one of the principal negative psychic consequences of capitalism, surmountable only by a totalizing mode of analysis that treats all aspects of life as parts of an interrelated totality. Thus, in *History and Class Consciousness*, he argues that "the capitalist separation of the producer from the total process of production, the division of the process of labour into parts as the cost of the individual humanity of the worker, the atomization of society into individuals who simply go on producing without rhyme or reason, must all have a profound influence on the thought, the science and the philosophy of capitalism" (27).

In a similar, but non-Marxist, way, Stewart envisions the life of the tribe as a unified whole, freed of the categorical separations that had been forced by modern capitalism. This post-holocaust society thus has a strong utopian dimension, and, as such, it may not be surprising that, in the end, Ish abandons his attempt to rebuild American society, instead encouraging the Tribe to move in the other direction, to return to a simpler life as hunter-gatherers. They begin to reject the remnants of American technological culture, relying instead on their own homemade implements. They grow their own food, using ancient methods of agriculture; they also hunt, but with bows and arrows, rather than leftover rifles. Moreover, in a highly symbolic move that directly allegorizes the rejection of American capitalism, they make their arrowheads by beating old coins, a convenient source of malleable metal, into the proper shape (311). Money has now lost its magical power as the measure of exchange value, but the metal in the coins still has use value once it has been properly processed.

By the end of the text, Ish is the last remaining "American," that is, the last survivor of the pre-holocaust world. And, as he fades toward death, he realizes that the Tribe is now moving down a path that does not seem likely to bring them back to the America he had known. For example, the young men of the Tribe have absolutely no understanding of the former function of the coins that they are beating into arrowheads. Ish concludes, however, that it is all for the best. In his last moments, "he was almost certain that he did not even desire that the cycle should be repeated. He suddenly thought of all that had gone to build civilization—of slavery and conquest and war and oppression" (336).

This reference gains power from the fact that the Tribe is in so many ways clearly returning to the lifestyle of the Native Americans whose culture was virtually destroyed by the advance of modern American civilization. Indeed, Ish's own name is a reference to Ishi, a Native American known in California history for being, in the early years of the twentieth century, the last living member of a tribe destroyed by the modernization of the state. Of course, Stewart was able to get away with such a radical rejection of modern American capitalism, even in the early Cold War years, partly because his solution of a return to the primitive past is not a real alternative and thus poses no particular threat to the existing system.[2] Stewart's solution, which rejects, not only capitalism, but modernity altogether, is also ultimately opposed to Marxism, which is just as thoroughly tied to modernity as is capitalism. Nevertheless, it is also probably the case that Stewart could get by with such radical social critique because he was writing in a marginal genre that tended not to be taken seriously.

Judith Merril's *Shadow on the Hearth* (1950) serves as a useful corrective to the heroic vision of post-apocalypse life presented by Stewart. Merril's book builds directly upon the tensions of the Cold War, presenting an apocalypse that arises precisely from a surprise nuclear attack on the United States, though it does not specifically identify the attackers as Soviets. But Merril's book is highly unusual among post-apocalypse works of the 1950s in its focus on a female protagonist, housewife Gladys Mitchell. The book also concentrates almost entirely on Gladys's domestic sphere, focusing on her attempts to cope with the aftermath of the nuclear assault, not by exploring the surrounding area or attempting to rebuild society, but simply by keeping her household running and taking care of her two daughters, Barbara and Ginny.[3]

This focus is made possible by the fact that the destruction depicted in this book is not nearly so complete as that depicted in many other postholocaust works. Gladys's suburban neighborhood seems relatively untouched by the disaster, even though nearby New York City was one of the central targets. Indeed, she is alone at home with the kids throughout the book because her husband, Jon, was in the city on business at the time of the attack. Jon finally returns home at the end of the book, relatively unscathed, though he has been shot and wounded by security forces, which have run amok in a reign of terror in the neighborhood. In the meantime Gladys has successfully dealt with a string of crises, including fears that both daughters have contracted serious radiation sickness. It appears, however, that the girls will be fine, as will Jon. The family is thus restored. Meanwhile, the enemy has been defeated, and life seems headed back almost toward normalcy.

But *Shadow on the Hearth* is a relatively daring novel despite this recuperative ending. In its presentation of Gladys's struggles, *Shadow on the Hearth* shows nuclear holocaust as anything but a heroic adventure; however, Gladys is presented as a strong individual, able to cope well in the absence of her husband. Indeed, as Berger points out, a central aspect of the narrative is Gladys's growing ability to act as an independent agent, outside the realm of her husband's influence (292). In the meantime, she encounters no evil foreign invaders; her only human tormentors are a few burglars and (primarily) the American security forces, who take charge in the wake of the attack, allowing them to act out their right-wing male fantasies of domination and control. Her main antagonist, in fact, is neighbor Jim Turner, who, it turns out, has been secretly training with the civil defense forces for some time. When the long-anticipated attack finally occurs, Turner takes control of the neighborhood almost as his private domain, and it is quite clear in the text that he is enjoying the experience immensely. Meanwhile, he begins to make not-so-subtle sexual overtures to the attractive Gladys, while conveniently shipping his own wife off to a hospital for radiation victims.

This presentation of Turner identifies *Shadow on the Earth* as an essentially left-wing work, even though it does seem to verify right-wing fears of an unprovoked Soviet nuclear attack, especially coming, as it does, one year after the explosion of the first Soviet atomic bomb in 1949. However, Merril implies that this attack may not be unprovoked at all, but may have come as the inevitable result of rising tensions in which Americans were equally culpable. Far from heroizing the flag-waving patriots who defend us from that attack, it suggests that there are opportunists among us who are anxious to use such an attack (or, by extension, even the threat of such an attack) as an excuse for establishing their own repressive measures. This stance, on the part of Merril, is not surprising, given her own association with the left-wing Futurians. She was, in fact, married to Frederik Pohl at the time she wrote and published this novel, her first, and she later collaborated with Futurian C. M. Kornbluth on two additional science fiction novels, *Outpost Mars* (1952) and *Gunner Cade* (1952).

Shadow on the Hearth is often fairly subtle in its indication of its political position, even though Merril stated in a later interview that she intended the work as anti-arms-race "propaganda" (cited in Seed 57). For example, when Gladys first hears radio reports of the nuclear attack and realizes that Jon is in Manhattan, a central target, she remembers "a description, read and shuddered over" of the imagined impact of a nuclear blast in such a city, "the buildings that had not gone up in thin air at the instant of the explosion, reduced by inconceivable heat to a glassy expanse of poisoned wasteland" (17). Merril does not identify the source of this description, but, as David Seed points out, it appears to have been inspired by a passage imagining the nuclear bombing of New York City in an essay entitled "If the Bomb Gets Out of Hand" by physicist Philip Morrison, contained in the 1946 anti-nuclear essay collection, *One World or None* (Seed 58). This collection was a central expression of the efforts by scientists in the wake of the bombings of Hiroshima and Nagasaki to ameliorate the potential consequences of the destructive power unleashed by science through the development of the atomic bomb. Among other things, the collection argues that increased nuclear armament might lead to war, rather than ensuring peace, as advocates of increased armament claimed. Several of the contributors to the collection also worry that anticommunist hysteria is in danger of producing a repressive police state in the United States, as does Merril.

They had reason to worry. For example, Morrison himself was called before a congressional investigating committee in 1949 and accused of having communist sympathies. The best-known figure in this sense is J. Robert Oppenheimer, former head of the Los Alamos nuclear project, who became particularly notorious in 1949 for his staunch opposition to the U.S. development of the hydrogen bomb. Oppenheimer was soon ostracized and accused of communist sympathies, then eventually stripped of his security clearance and banned from classified work. His experience no doubt informs Merril's depiction, in *Shadow on the Hearth*, of Dr. Garson Levy, once a respected physicist working at the Oak Ridge National Laboratory. By the time of the attack, however, Levy has been driven from his research job and blacklisted because of his numerous antiwar statements.

Merril makes clear her sympathy for Levy and his antiwar position. When the attack occurs, he is working as a (much beloved) science teacher at the high school attended by Barbara (and previously attended by Barbara's older brother, Tom). In the course of the book, Levy is immediately singled out as a potential saboteur by the repressive security forces, such as those represented by Turner, and is in danger of being shot on sight because of his past record. But Gladys takes him in and hides him from the authorities. In return, he helps fight off the burglars and uses his scientific knowledge to help out around the house and to aid in the treatment of Barbara and Ginny, though he has suffered considerable radiation exposure himself. Levy is not only brilliant, but also kind, caring, and courageous. The clear polar opposition between his characterization and that of Turner leaves little room for uncertainty concerning Merril's position on the issues they represent.

Bernard Wolfe's *Limbo* (1952), described in *The Encyclopedia of Science Fiction* as "perhaps the finest sf novel of ideas to have been published during the 1950s," at times also seems leftist in its sympathies, but is considerably more ambivalent (John and Nicholls 1337).[4] In fact, the novel presents ambivalence as an unavoidable fact of human nature. Wolfe himself was a former Trotskyite who had even served on Trotsky's staff in Mexico. But the politics of *Limbo* are ambiguous, and the book seems to lean to the Left mostly because its depiction of a dystopian post-holocaust future (in the year 1990) is focused primarily on what had been the United States, a fact that Wolfe himself seeks to discount in a post-script, in which he declares his fundamental Americanism and asserts that the very fact that he was allowed to write and publish such a book is a testament to American democracy (437–38).

There is, of course, a clear irony in the fact that Wolfe felt it necessary to protect himself by characterizing his book in this way—a sort of pre-emptive strike that labels any attempts to suppress the book as un-American in advance. In spite of his praise for American freedom of expression, he seems to have assumed that there might be attempts to suppress his work. But it is certainly true that the book never expresses any preference for socialism over capitalism. Indeed, its own position is quite nebulous, and Wolfe's description of the book, in his postscript, as a "grab bag of ideas that were more or less around at the mid-century mark" is accurate (435). Nevertheless, the very scope of this grab bag makes *Limbo* a valuable social document, while at the same time serving as a demonstration of the intellectual ambitiousness of the book relative to most science fiction novels (or most novels, period).

The book is also ambitious in a literary sense. In keeping with the "grab bag" metaphor, Seed notes that "Wolfe deploys a Joycean array of genres and allusions" (107). Joycean may be a bit of an exaggeration, but the book is highly allusive and it does employ a variety of styles and genres. Most obviously, it mixes straight narrative chapters with excerpts from the notebooks of its protagonist, Dr. Martine. It also combines extremely serious subject matter with a playful approach, making extensive use of puns and other wordplay in the midst of an exploration of the baleful aftermath of an all-out nuclear war (in the year 1972), as survivors on both the American and Soviet sides strive to rebuild civilization, while ostensibly taking steps to ensure that such a nuclear holocaust can never again occur.

Within this basic scenario, the plot is simple. As the book begins, Martine, a talented brain surgeon, has been living for eighteen years on a remote Indian Ocean island to which he fled in the midst of World War III. The island is inhabited by the peaceful Mandunji people, who have accepted Martine as a sort of medicine man. There, he has used his skills as a surgeon to refine the traditional Mandunji practice of Mandunga, essentially a lobotomy, forced upon troublemakers to make them tranquil and obedient to the customs of the tribe. In the process, Martine also takes advantage of the availability of all of these human specimens to pursue his own research into brain structure as he attempts to construct a map that will allow him to locate the parts of the brain that are responsible for human aggression. When a group of American athletes arrives on the island, supposedly to train for the upcoming Olympics, Martine realizes that it is time for him to travel back to America to try to determine what is going on there. In particular, these Olympic athletes are all amputees, their physical prowess supplied, not by human muscle, but by high-tech prosthetics that make them capable of feats no ordinary human athlete could achieve. Meanwhile, their activities suggest that the outside world is interested in the island as far more than a pleasant site for athletic training.

Martine travels to New Jamestown, the largest city of the Inland Strip, an area with a population of about 38 million that is the only habitable part of the former United States. Both coasts have been devastated in the 1972 nuclear war, orchestrated on each side by giant computers, called EMSIACs. There, he discovers to his horror that both the Inland Strip and the Eastern Union (the remnants of the Soviet Union) are now dominated by a culture of "Immob," or immobilization. Central to this culture is "vol-amp," or voluntary amputeeism, a sort of literalization of the notion of disarmament. It is widely believed in this culture that amputation of the limbs reduces natural human aggression, thus helping to keep the peace and prevent further nuclear wars. Meanwhile, Immob culture also works to develop substitutes, or moral equivalents (in the words of William James, one of the heroes of this culture) for war, the most important of which is the Olympic games.

What is even more horrifying to Martine is the discovery that Immob culture draws its central inspiration from some of his own writings, particularly the notebooks he kept while serving as a military surgeon in Africa during World War III before his flight to the island of the Mandunji. He himself is regarded as the culture's central martyr, and the president of the Inland Strip is Dr. Helder, Martine's former friend, who draws his authority largely from his former association with Martine. At first, Martine is particularly disturbed because he originally made the comments that have been taken to authorize the self-mutilation of vol-amp in jest, though his particular style of jesting is rather grim. Eventually, however, he realizes that Immob is not as contrary to his real vision as he would like to believe. After all, the surgical removal of limbs as a technique of eliminating aggression is not all that different from the surgery he has been attempting among the Mandunji for the past eighteen years. He thus decides to return to the island to try to end the practice of Mandunga, a move he does not realize has already been spearheaded by his own teenage son, left behind on the island.

In the meantime, Martine's disgust with Immob is increased by the obvious hypocrisy with which both the Inland Strip and the Eastern Union pursue this seemingly radical rejection of violence and warfare. As it turns out, both sides have been stockpiling nuclear weapons for years, mouthing détente, while secretly preparing for war. In particular, both sides are developing techniques for the use of the very prosthetics that are supposed to ensure peace as weapons of destruction. Meanwhile, war breaks out (initiated by the Eastern Union) at the Olympic games themselves, plunging the Inland Strip into widespread destruction, though the text also makes it clear that the Strippers will be able to respond in kind.

Wolfe endows his vision of the prosthetics with a certain verisimilitude by drawing upon Norbert Wiener's pioneering work in cybernetics. However, it should be obvious from this brief summary that *Limbo* is not a serious attempt to envision what life and society might be like in the aftermath of a nuclear holocaust. Rather, it is a purely, somewhat Swiftian, satirical commentary on Wolfe's own contemporary world, employing both its future setting and its outrageous images as techniques of cognitive estrangement.[5] To an extent, of course, the same might be said for virtually all post-apocalypse fictions, but Wolfe's book is particularly overt in its satirical project. The very title of the book is a pun, referring to the emphasis on artificial limbs in Wolfe's future world, and the whole amputation-prosthesis motif is a pun on the notion of disarmament. Through this Swiftian literalization of metaphor, Wolfe makes a number of serious comments on his contemporary world. Indeed, though the book is most directly and obviously engaged with the questions of armament/disarmament, it also includes some of the most extensive interrogation of the twin themes of alienation and routinization in all of the science fiction of the 1950s.

Martine, as the only outsider on the island of the Mandunji, is clearly in an alienated position as the book begins, and Martine's own ruminations make clear the extent to which he feels alone and estranged, even from Ooda, his Mandunji lover. But it is also clear that he had been just as alienated when he lived among Westerners like himself. His memories of his earlier failed marriage, for example, are particularly bitter, and he admits that he had never really known anyone, including Helder, his "closest" friend (28, Wolfe's quotation marks). Meanwhile, the amputee culture of 1990 suggests that individuals in this future society continue to suffer the most fundamental and damaging of all forms of alienation: estrangement from their own bodies and their own selves.

Various forms of routinization are also singled out for Wolfe's dystopian critique. For example, the official anathema of Immob is the "Steamroller," a vaguely defined symbol of the large impersonal forces that drive people helplessly toward aggression. Described as a "flattening of the human spirit" and characterized by "robotized industry, robotized culture, robotized war," the Steamroller is essentially a metaphor for routinization (204, 206). In an obvious recollection of the supposed individualism of American culture in the 1950s, the official slogan of Immob is "Dodge the Steamroller," a phrase derived from Martine's notebooks. But the Steamroller is as powerful as ever: upon first arriving in New Jamestown, Martine is immediately struck by the sterility and excessive symmetry of the gleaming modern city. And he notes that the people seem almost like robots, with "a metronome in every cortex" (99).

To a large extent, Wolfe associates this steamroller-metronome effect with modernity itself. He notes, for example, that the coming of machines inevitably means the coming of clocks and schedules, as people reorient their lives by adapting to the rhythms of the machines, making them "adjuncts of the machine" (97). Further, in an obvious commentary on the industrial-managerial climate of the 1950s, Wolfe notes that "when the Industrial Revolution was completed, life for all but the managers became a nightmare of metronomic monotony, a series of Pavlovian twitches—witness the Ford plant and Taylorism" (97–98). And he emphasizes the universality of this phenomenon by showing that the same process is already beginning to occur on the island of the Mandunji, thanks largely to the technology brought there by Martine.

Despite its seeming critique of modernity, which can be taken as a critique of the Enlightenment, *Limbo* is itself informed by a tendency toward universalization that is a typical characteristic of Enlightenment thought. For example, the Mandunji are described via a variety of problematic Orientalist images. In the favorite image of Hegelian colonialist historiography, they are described as a sleepy people without history, until Martine arrives, jerking the Mandunji out of their timeless tribal malaise and moving them toward modernity. Once this happens, they begin to follow the same historical track as Europe and America, though necessarily lagging behind.

Much of this tendency toward universalization derives from Wolfe's reliance on essentially Freudian notions of human nature. For one thing, he tends to suggest that the arms race is fed, not merely by rivalry between American capitalism and Soviet communism, but by fundamental human drives toward both aggression and masochism. Here, Wolfe draws centrally upon the work not only of Freud, but of Freud's successors, particularly Edmund Bergler. In this way, he suggests that both sides in the Cold War are informed by the same drives, thus eschewing the typical Manicheanism of Cold War rhetoric. In fact, *Limbo* goes so far as to suggest that, by the 1970s, both America and Russia had become dominated by such similar tendencies toward "cybernetic-managerial" routinization that the two opposed nations were "absolutely and irrevocably alike" (140).[6] In addition, Wolfe provides a history of the development of this identity, placing its roots in the rise of "a society in which the technicians, the management engineers, the efficiency experts, the executives and personnel directors, fully equipped with batteries of robot brains, would be in control of the state apparatus, which in turn would preside fully over the activities of its citizens" (139).

This robotized society, of course, is precisely the routinized American society of the 1950s, as described by so many sociologists, and this new group of dominant professionals is a sort of hybrid of the power elite of C. Wright Mills and the "salariat" described by Daniel Bell (*End* 221–23). Wolfe goes a little further than most commentators of the 1950s, however, in suggesting that the Stalinist Soviet Union was informed by many of the same tendencies. Further, Wolfe tracks this tendency into a projected future in which men have not only been enslaved by their machines, but have become machinelike themselves, including the literal substitution of machines for many of their natural body parts. And this projection holds for both East and West: having brought about a cataclysmic war, the Inland Strip and the Eastern Union agree to use the same Immob philosophy to separate themselves superficially from the past, while still maintaining the same fundamental tendencies toward dehumanization. The same self-destructive competition between identical opponents that had informed the original Cold War thus continues unabated.

In this sense, Wolfe's book is extremely pessimistic. Not only does it envision a cyclic repetition of destructive behavior, but it suggests that any attempts to curb this behavior (such as lobotomy or amputation), though deriving from human nature, are nevertheless dehumanizing and thus doomed to failure. Wolfe, realizes this contradiction and attributes it to the contradictoriness of human nature itself. In response, Wolfe to an extent embraces contradiction, continually maintaining that one of the keys to progress for the human race is an understanding and acknowledgment of our own internal contradictions, a recognition that "every blob of protoplasm teems with ambivalence" (28). *Limbo* is, in fact, filled with images of this kind of duality, drawing particularly upon classic cases such as Nietzsche's opposition between the Dionysian and Apollonian in *The Birth of Tragedy* and Freud's opposition between Eros and Thanatos. Wolfe also implies that a basic Aristotelian tendency toward dualism was central to the Cold War and the nuclear holocaust to which it led. Meanwhile, Immob philosophy is supposedly non-Aristotelian, rejecting the dualism of "either-or" logic and embracing the seeming contradiction of "both-and" thinking. They describe their time as the "Age of the Hyphen," in which they are attempting to "work out ways of bringing such polarities together. Through dialectical materialism-idealism" (153).

Unfortunately, Immob is again not what it pretends to be. In it, "all the old, old splits are perpetuated," and its followers have still not learned to accept and be comfortable with the basic ambivalence that Wolfe presents as an intrinsic fact of biology (316). Such acceptance, Wolfe implies, would require above all else a sense of humor, a willingness to accept the fact that God and Dog are part of the same phenomenon, an ability "never to contemplate any divinity without seeing its hilarious canine underside" (409). In short, Wolfe ultimately explains the seemingly silly wordplay with which he addresses fundamental social problems, such as disarmament, by arguing that laughter is the best antidote to the twin human impulses of aggression and masochism. Further, in a mode that anticipates the absurdist tendencies of American literature in the latter part of the long 1950s (the work of Joseph Heller and Kurt Vonnegut is here paradigmatic), Wolfe has Martine, in one of his notebook entries, reject all forms of totalizing theory, all forms of systematic thinking that seek "one all-embracing formula that subsumes and explains everything" (314). Such systems, he concludes, always leave out "the one prime ingredient of reality—what the existentialists used to call the absurd" (315).

Here, Martine specifically evokes the fantastic imagery of Dostoevsky as a major example of what he means by the "absurd," and Martine repeatedly invokes the anti-rationalist philosophy of Dostoevsky's Underground Man as an emblem of his own thought. Martine even wears a tattoo that reads "$2 \times 2 = 5$," in reference to the Underground Man's favorite anti-rationalist slogan (347). On the other hand, it should also be pointed out that *Limbo* is highly dialogic in the manner indicated by Mikhail Bakhtin in his discussion of writers such as Dostoevsky. In particular, the relationship between Wolfe and Martine is highly dialogic, leading to an ultimate interpretive undecidability in which one can never be certain that Martine's remarks should be taken to represent Wolfe's point of view.

Martine's (and, perhaps, Wolfe's) rejection of totalizing systems, like his rejection of dualistic thinking, also recalls the form of logic associated by Bakhtin with the dialogic. Moreover, Wolfe's emphasis on laughter directly recalls Bakhtin's emphasis on the power of carnivalesque laughter in the work of Rabelais. Bakhtin's work is also helpful in identifying the generic tendencies of *Limbo*, which are very similar to those discussed by Bakhtin in relation to the tendency toward Menippean satire in writers such as Rabelais and Dostoevsky, the latter of whom is a major intertextual presence in Wolfe's book. However, it should be noted that, if many of the characteristics of *Limbo* come more sharply into focus by considering the work as Menippean satire, it is also the case that the same characteristics of Wolfe's work can be equally well comprehended simply by identifying his novels as postmodernist. Indeed, a recognition of Wolfe's postmodernism may be even more useful than the association of his work with Menippean satire, though the two insights are not mutually exclusive. William Spanos, for example, has argued, citing Bakhtin, that carnivalesque elements are central to postmodernism as a whole (193–94). For example, the multigeneric nature of *Limbo*, however characteristic of Menippean satire, is equally typical of postmodernism. For Jameson, postmodernist culture is marked by the emergence of a pluralism so radical that the word "fragmentation" is far too weak. And this pluralism is centrally informed by a pluralism in genre that parallels the fragmentation of the postmodern psyche. Postmodernist works thus often involve "radically discontinuous" shifts from one genre to another, a characteristic for which Jameson suggests television channel surfing as an appropriate metaphor. At the same time, Jameson notes that the multiple genres making up a postmodernist work, no matter how discontinuous or even contradictory, tend to begin to bleed into and "interfect" one another, breaking down the boundaries of genre just as categorical boundaries in general tend to collapse in postmodernist art, as well as postmodern society as a whole (*Postmodernism* 373).

In its central use of cybernetic imagery and the gradual replacement of human parts by mechanical-electronic ones, *Limbo* anticipates some of the favorite images of cyberpunk science fiction. Meanwhile, numerous aspects of Wolfe's novel — the comic tone, the deconstruction of polar oppositions, the rejection of totalizing theories, the interpretive undecidability — anticipate some of the central concerns of postmodernism as a whole. *Limbo* thus stands as a major illustration of the way in which the fundamental strategies and attitudes of postmodernism were already in place by the 1950s, even the early 1950s.

If Wolfe's work looks forward to postmodernism, it also looks back to the dystopian classics that appeared in the first half of the twentieth century.[7] David Pringle thus describes *Limbo* as the "closest American equivalent" of the British dystopian masterpieces, *Brave New World* and *Nineteen Eighty-four* (31). *Limbo* is also reminiscent of Evgeny Zamyatin's *We*. Even more reminiscent of *We* is Mordecai Roshwald's *Level 7* (1959), another clear example of the use of the dystopian post-holocaust scenario to comment satirically on the social and political climate of the 1950s. Roshwald's book, like Zamyatin's, consists of the diary of its protagonist, in this case a military officer who has been assigned (permanently) to the seventh and lowest level of a vast underground facility that has been built as a shelter against nuclear attack. The inhabitants of Level 7, like the inhabitants of Zamyatin's One State, are identified only by numbers, the protagonist being X-127. And life in this facility, like life in the One State, is highly regulated: every activity (including conjugal meetings) must be performed according to a strict schedule.

In *Level 7*, as in *Limbo*, ultimate control of nuclear weaponry has been handed over to automated systems. Indeed, anticipating the later scenario of the 1962 novel *Fail-Safe* (basis of the well-known 1964 film), the nuclear war in *Level 7* begins by accident, then quickly gets out of control as the automated response systems kick in. Ultimately, virtually the entire surface of the planet is devastated by nuclear blasts and contaminated by radiation. Indeed, the radiation gradually seeps downward through one level after another, finally ending in the deaths of the inhabitants of Level 7, including X-127 himself.

Level 7 thus warns Americans not to develop a false sense of security that thorough preparations can save them from the effects of nuclear war. Many other aspects of the novel also comment on American society in the 1950s, though the nation for which X-127 works is not actually identified in the book. For example, the structure of this underground facility tells us a great deal about the values of X-127's nation. Level 7, which is designed to control offensive weaponry, has the highest priority and is on the lowest and most protected level. Those in charge of defensive weaponry are headquartered and housed on Level 6, while Level 5 is a refuge that has been prepared for occupation by the society's civilian leaders in the event of war, and Levels 4 and 3 are designated for less important leaders. In a (meaningless) nod toward tolerance, Level 2 is reserved for malcontents and potential subversives, just to keep them quiet. Finally, Level 1 is meant for the general population.

The most potent political commentary in *Level 7* comes from the fact that conditions in the seemingly extreme environment of Level 7 are suspiciously similar to conditions in the America of the 1950s. In addition to the intense routinization that informs life in Level 7, the inhabitants of the facility are all radically alienated. They have, in fact, been specifically chosen for their inability to form and maintain close human attachments. The implication seems clear: the pressures of the arms race threaten to transform American society into a grim, dystopian state, whose primary focus is destruction of the enemy rather than enrichment of the lives of its citizens, who are thereby reduced to living in a machine-dominated hell.

If *Limbo* and *Level 7* both seem bitterly critical of American society in the 1950s, then the same also goes for *Fahrenheit 451* (1951), the first novel of the much-beloved Ray Bradbury. Best known as a short story writer, Bradbury claimed a prominent place among American science fiction writers in 1950 with the publication of his story collection, *The Martian Chronicles,* still widely regarded as his finest work. Much of Bradbury's work leaned more toward fantasy and horror than science fiction proper, indicating a strong desire to escape from the routine of the modern world. Indeed, Bradbury's work is unusual among major science fiction writers in its consistent antitechnology stance. For Bradbury, the principal vision of escape from the alienation and routinization of the modern world is a nostalgic retreat to the conventional world of small-town America — precisely the environment that so often functioned in the culture of the 1950s as the locus of dystopian nightmare.

This sentimental and nostalgic orientation can sometimes be rather puerile, leading Disch to call Bradbury "a lifelong child impersonator of a stature equal to that of Pee-Wee Herman" (81).[8] But Bradbury's nostalgia, like most nostalgia, also has a decidedly dark side, as can be seen quite clearly in *Fahrenheit 451*. And, if this orientation put Bradbury at odds with many of his contemporaries among science fiction writers, it is certainly the case that *Fahrenheit 451* responds to the cultural environment in America in the early 1950s in a way that obviously struck a chord among many of his readers. Bradbury's book relates the story of Guy Montag, a "fireman" in a dystopian America of the future. In this society, however, firemen do not put out fires, but start them. In particular, they burn any books they can find (along with the houses in which those books have been hidden), because books have been strictly forbidden in this society. In lieu of books, the culture of Montag's America consists of an incessant electronic barrage of popular culture that seems designed partly to purvey the official ideology of the society, but mostly to stupefy the populace by saturating their minds with useless information.

Citizens constantly go about with tiny "Seashell Radio" receivers in their ears so this popular culture can follow them wherever they go. And at home they are surrounded by sophisticated three-dimensional television broadcasts that bring the programs alive in their homes to substitute for the lack of any real emotional existence. Montag's wife Mildred, for example, is entirely enthralled by these programs; in fact, she considers the characters in them to be her "family." When Montag comes home after a particularly trying night at work in which an old woman was burned alive with her books, the benumbed Mildred shows no response, instead merely noting that she had a nice evening watching television, despite the fact that the programs she watched were clearly devoid of any real content. When Montag asks what she watched, she says "programs," and when he asks which programs, she says, "Some of the best ever" (52).

Recalling the popular culture depicted in *Brave New World,* the entire culture of Bradbury's future society seems designed precisely to numb the minds of the populace and to prevent them from experiencing any real thought or feeling, à la the Culture Industry of Horkheimer and Adorno. The popular culture of *Fahrenheit 451* also serves to brainwash its audience into conformist behavior of a kind that would have seemed all too familiar to Bradbury's audience in the 1950s. For example, one of Mildred's favorite shows is an interactive one in which she is allowed to play a part. But this potentially promising opportunity for creativity is dulled by the fact that Mildred is limited to reading prescribed responses ("I think that's fine!" "I sure do!") that do little except indicate her agreement with what is being said in the program. In short, these programs are designed merely to extract the audience's agreement with the official ideology of the programs while creating the illusion that the audience has a part in determining that ideology.

Bradbury, however, is no Horkheimer or Adorno, and he pays relatively little attention to the power of popular culture and other means of official propaganda in determining the behavior of individuals. Throughout *Fahrenheit 451* he emphasizes the voluntary participation of the populace in the oppressive policies of the government. For example, when marginal characters (like an old woman burned with her books) suffer violent persecution, they do so with the full agreement of the vast majority of the populace, the anti-intellectualism of which is such that they think it entirely fitting and proper that books should burn, even if their owners must burn with them. Bradbury's book as a whole seems to endorse the claim of Faber (an ex-English professor whom Montag consults after he himself begins to rebel) that the problem is not really with the system, but with the people: "Remember, the firemen are rarely necessary. The public itself stopped reading of its own accord. You firemen provide a circus now and then at which buildings are set off and crowds gather for the pretty blaze, but it's a small sideshow indeed, and hardly necessary to keep things in line" (94).

The book burnings of *Fahrenheit 451* are pure spectacle, just another element of popular culture in Bradbury's dystopian America. In this sense they resemble the public executions that play an important role in the demonstration of official power in dystopian fictions like *We*, *Nineteen Eighty-four*, and, later, Margaret Atwood's *The Handmaid's Tale*. Bradbury, however, seems to view the theatrical demonstrations of power in his book as a commentary not on official power, but on popular taste, suggesting that people simply like spectacles and that the government is merely giving them what they want. His stance ultimately seems to be informed, not only by nostalgia for a time when individuals behaved better, but by a cultural and intellectual elitism; as Zipes notes, "[t]he dystopian constellation of conflict in *Fahrenheit 451* is not really constituted by the individual versus the state, but the intellectual versus the masses" (191).

In a move that anticipates recent debates on "political correctness," Captain Beatty, Montag's superior in the fire department, explains to Montag that the burning of books had its roots in the original movement of various minorities to demand that certain works they found offensive be banned. Because of this pressure, authors began to turn out more and more insipid works, seeking to avoid controversy and thereby reach a larger audience. Eventually, real books ceased to be written altogether, replaced by comic books, sex magazines, and television, because (says Beatty) that was what the public really wanted (61). Beatty is not presented by Bradbury as an exemplary figure, but in point of fact Bradbury indicates in a 1979 "Author's Afterword" to the book his own agreement with Beatty's analysis. Appealing to icons of the Western literary tradition like Shakespeare, Dante, and Milton, Bradbury demands that we not "allow the minorities, be they dwarf or giant, orangutan or dolphin, nuclear-head or water-conservationist, pro-computerologist or neo-Luddite, simpleton or sage, to interfere with aesthetics" (183). If minorities do not like his books, Bradbury haughtily proclaims, let them write their own. The real source of all the trouble, in good 1950s fashion, is the Other, which, according to Bradbury, seems to include everybody except artists.

In addition to aesthetics, Bradbury presents Christianity as a positive alternative to the oppressive conditions of the dystopian America of *Fahrenheit 451*. In this thoroughly commercialized society everything, including people, has been reduced to the status of commodities. Faber explains that even Jesus Christ now functions as a sort of celebrity endorser of commercial products on television: "I often wonder if God recognizes His own son the way we've dressed him up, or is it dressed him down? He's a regular peppermint stick now, all sugar crystal and saccharine when he isn't making veiled references to certain commercial products that every worshipper *absolutely* needs" (88).

This commercialization of Christ functions for Bradbury as an image of the spiritual sterility of his dystopian America. The Bible itself has been banned in this bookless society, and when Montag joins a group of rebels who oppose the burning of books by memorizing entire texts he himself is assigned to memorize the Book of Ecclesiastes. Eventually, Bradbury's dystopian society is destroyed in a massive nuclear war that surely draws upon the widespread nuclear fears of the early 1950s. In this case, however, the nuclear holocaust is pictured as a sort of cleansing that brings the potential of new birth. Indeed, this holocaust clearly figures as an image of the Christian apocalypse, with a new society (to be led by Montag and the book-people) arising from the ashes of the old as a sort of literate New Jerusalem. The book ends as Montag and his new friends trudge back from their exile in the wilderness toward the devastated city, with Montag recalling to himself a passage from the Book of Revelations.

Bradbury's vision of a "salvation" that will require the destruction of most of humanity parallels Christian projections of the future quite closely, but it is certainly a questionable solution to the problems he saw in his contemporary America. Even Bradbury is not entirely optimistic about the prospects for a New Jerusalem at the end of his book. For one thing, the history of Bradbury's dystopian America has been rewritten much in the manner of *Nineteen Eighty-four*, and most of the populace in the book believe that things have pretty much always been the way they are. For example, the official history books of this society claim that fire departments have always been organized for the burning of books, attributing the formation of the first book-burning fire department in America to Benjamin Franklin in 1790 (37). As a result, most of the survivors of the nuclear holocaust might be expected to attempt to rebuild a society much like the one that was just destroyed. After all, the death and rebirth myth that provides a structural model for Bradbury's plot itself implies a cyclic history, and the rebel Granger suggests at the book's close that the rise of civilization phoenixlike from its own ashes is unlikely to result in any improvement over the disasters of the past unless people can somehow learn from their past mistakes:

And it looks like we're doing the same thing, over and over, but we've got one damn thing the phoenix never had. We know the damn silly thing we just did. We know all the damn silly things we've done for a thousand years and as long as we know that and always have it around where we can see it, someday we'll stop making the goddamn funeral pyres and jumping into the middle of them. We pick up a few more people that remember every generation. (177)

Granger's conclusion is ultimately a hopeful one, but, like much of Bradbury's book, it appears rather questionable. Learning from the past, especially the distant past, requires more than individual memory, and Bradbury's individualist approach fails to account for the ability of those in power to distort official history, even though his own book—like many dystopian fictions—describes this ability quite well.

An even darker scenario informs Richard Matheson's *I Am Legend* (1954), which combines Stewart's bio-catastrophe with the fictions of nuclear holocaust that are conventionally associated with the fears of the 1950s. Matheson's novel, like Wolfe's *Limbo*, is a hybrid text in a number of ways, including the fact that it combines science fiction with gothic horror to produce one of the most frightening last-man-on-earth visions to be published during the decade.[9] In the book, nuclear war, through some process that is never explained, spurs the growth of bacteria that turn everyone on earth (except protagonist Robert Neville) into vampires. Neville spends his life alone, barricaded in his house at night, then carrying out guerrilla raids in the daytime, when the vampires sleep. He is thus the ultimate alienated individual, somewhat in the mode of Scott Carey in Matheson's 1956 novel, *The Shrinking Man* (and the 1957 film, *The Incredible Shrinking Man*, scripted by Matheson). Indeed, though far less known than the works of science fiction superstars such as Asimov, Pohl, Bradbury, and Heinlein, Matheson's books of the 1950s contain some of the most representative science fiction expressions of the concerns of the decade. *I Am Legend* also deals with the theme of routinization, as when Neville, grown weary from battling the vampires, realizes that his biggest enemy is not terror, but "monotony" (411). Still, much of this monotony is really a matter of loneliness, as can be seen in the poignant segment in which Neville, desperate for companionship, attempts to adopt a stray dog, only to have it die within a week (408–409).

I Am Legend again contains numerous echoes of *Robinson Crusoe* in its depiction of the dogged attempts of Neville to build a life for himself, drawing upon whatever resources happen to be at his command. Meanwhile, the nightly siege of Neville's house by the enraged vampires has more than a little in common with Crusoe's feelings of being besieged by savage cannibals. However, Matheson's treatment of the Us vs. Them opposition between Neville and the vampires turns out to be far more interesting than any quick summary of the scenario might lead one to suspect. At the very beginning of the book, Neville recognizes the conformism of the vampires, realizing that they cannot tolerate his difference. He thus concludes that the only sure way to be free of them is to "be one of them" (29). Soon afterward, Neville realizes the irony of the fact that the vampires are now on top, having been, throughout history, an outcast minority against whom the majority has shown extreme prejudice. Yet, despite his own embattled predicament, Neville realizes that the historical hatred of vampires might have been unfair. He wonders, for example, if the vampire is "worse than the manufacturer who set up belated foundations with the money he made by handing bombs and guns to suicidal nationalists?" (32).

Here, of course, Matheson comes very close to tapping into a long Marxist tradition of using figures such as vampires and cannibals as metaphors for capitalism. As Marx notes in the first volume of *Capital,* "Capital is dead labour, that, vampire-like, only lives by sucking living labour, and lives the more the more labour it sucks" (362–63). Matheson does not follow up on this notion that capitalism sucks. He does, however, follow up on his association of the vampires with underprivileged minorities. At the end, when Neville is finally overwhelmed by the vampires as they seek to set up a new vampire society, the book takes a startling turn when he realizes that the poles of normality and abnormality have now been reversed. As the majority, the vampires are now normal; as a one-of-a-kind freak (who has, among other things, been going about committing mass murder by driving stakes through the hearts of sleeping vampires), he is the abnormal one, the one who is a danger to organized society. "I'm the abnormal one now. Normalcy was a majority concept, the standard of many and not the standard of just one man" (169). Thus, in a final passage that gives the book its title, Neville realizes that he will go down in the history of the new vampire society as a legendary terror, playing the role that Dracula had played in the former human society (170).

The social criticism embedded in this turn at the end of *I Am Legend,* which clearly associates the conformist drive for normality in America of the 1950s with vampirism, may be one reason why the novel was not adapted to film in that decade. But Matheson, in ending the book the way he does, avoids the tendency toward romanticization that informs so many of the post-holocaust works of the decade. Such romanticization is particularly overt in Pat Frank's *Alas, Babylon* (1959), which may be precisely why Frank's book was one of the most popular post-holocaust works of the long 1950s. *Alas, Babylon* deals overtly with war between the United States and the Soviet Union, though it provides relatively few de-tails of the war itself, concentrating instead on the struggles of the inhabi-tants of a small Florida community, Fort Repose, to survive in the wake of the cataclysmic conflict. Nevertheless, Frank's book (like much of his work) is extremely representative of a certain style of conservative thought in the 1950s in that it treats nuclear war (triggered by Soviet ag-gression, of course) as inevitable, while warning that the United States is sorely prepared for such a war. In this sense, Frank's book can be read as a cautionary tale, urging greater vigilance and greater preparedness. For example, the book complains at several points that governmental au-thorities have failed to prepare the populace for this crisis, simply be-cause they did not want to cause undue anxiety: "The chaos did not re-sult from a breakdown in Civil Defense. It was simply that Civil Defense, as a realistic buffer against thermonuclear war, did not exist" (118).

Frank, in the long 1950s, had virtually made a career of complaints about government ineptitude in the face of the coming nuclear crisis, satirizing bureaucratic inefficiency in *Mr. Adam* (1946) and warning more grimly of the laxness of the American defense system in *Forbidden Area* (1956). Frank also addressed similar topics in his journalistic writings, culminating in the 1962 bestseller, *How to Survive the H-Bomb, and Why*, a sort of nonfiction version of *Alas, Babylon*. Given Frank's (right-wing) conviction of the inability of the federal government to deal adequately with the kind of crisis that would arise in the wake of nuclear conflict, it is not surprising that, in *Alas, Babylon*, virtually all official systems fail, leaving the resourceful inhabitants of Fort Repose to fend for themselves. Nor is it surprising that Frank sprinkles this story of the destruction of the United States as a world power with references to the fall of Rome, making the typical right-wing point that Americans, in the midst of the affluent 1950s, had grown complacent and decadent, enjoying their wealth and privilege, but failing to live up to their responsibility to de-fend this way of life against the evil Soviets, who, for some reason un-stated by Frank, are determined to start a mutually destructive nuclear war.

What is surprising, given Frank's apparent devotion to preventing ex-actly the kind of disaster he describes in the novel, is that he seems al-most to revel in the destruction of the modern American system, depict-ing post-holocaust Fort Repose as a kind of laissez faire utopia, where strong individuals can work out the solutions to their problems without the interference of government regulations and bean-counting bureau-crats. Indeed, Frank seems relatively unconcerned about the massive de-struction and loss of life associated with the nuclear attack, which he is in fact careful not to depict—an odd choice in a book that is supposed to warn readers about the horrors of nuclear war. As Jeffrey Porter points out, what does seem to concern Frank is the "possible disappearance of such middle-class durables as electricity, gasoline, whisky, steak, honey, salt, first aid, and razor blades" (42). Perhaps there is even a sort of I-told-you-so satisfaction in Frank's fantasy of what will happen to the United States as a result of not heeding his warnings. Never fear, however. Frank's heroes manage to find ways to replace most of these commodities, doing so well, in fact, that Porter concludes that *Alas, Babylon* "is essentially sympathetic to the idea of nuclear war" (46).

But there is also a sense that the destruction of the country returns the "good old days" of the American frontier, when men were men and women were women, and the bureaucracy of the modern welfare state did not interfere with the ability of strong individuals to carry out their plans and fulfill their desires. In this sense, *Alas, Babylon* is a story of escape from routinization, nuclear bombs having cleansed Fort Repose of its pre-holocaust regimen. As a result, protagonist Randy Bragg is able to take matters into his own hands, make a few simple rules of his own, and essentially run the town according to his own common-sense principles. Thus, when a gang of highwaymen waylay Dr. Dan Gunn, one of Bragg's confederates, Bragg reacts swiftly, organizing a group of armed vigilantes, who go after the culprits, find them, and kill them. In this fantasy of swift, right-wing justice, good triumphs and evil is punished, without courts, lawyers, or any other legalistic complications. Bragg runs the entire town as a sort of military strongman, declaring his authority on the basis of the fact that martial law has been declared nationwide, making him, as a lieutenant in the army reserves, the de facto ruler of Fort Repose, but also rationalizing his actions via a sort of neo-Darwinian argument about the survival of the fittest, which presumably means Bragg himself.

The breakdown of conventional authority in Fort Repose thus leads, not to anarchy, but to a military dictatorship, a situation that most of the locals, yearning for strong leadership in a crisis, welcome warmly. Bragg, of course, is a benevolent dictator, treating everyone who follows his rules kindly, regardless of race, creed, or color. Indeed, the book makes a point of arguing that racism has been rendered absurd in the midst of such a crisis, when all right-thinking people need to work together. On the other hand, it is also telling that Bragg, gathering a personal cadre around him, invites his white supporters to move into the big house with him, while his black supporters, the extremely subservient Henry family, remain in their own humble dwelling, which has grown out of nineteenth-century slave quarters. Meanwhile, Bragg, who had been something of a womanizer before the holocaust, rejects his Latina girlfriend, Rita Hernandez, as a grasping slut, but invites his wholesome white girlfriend, Elizabeth McGovern, to move into his compound and eventually to marry him so that they can propagate the species.

Frank's utopian vision also involves an escape from alienation. Though Bragg is the scion of a long-prominent local family, he begins the book regarded as something of an outsider by the locals, who do not appreciate his bachelor lifestyle. He is, in fact, regarded as being a bit strange. For example, his neighbor, Florence Wechek, suspects that Bragg is using his telescope not for bird watching, as he claims, but for trying to get a closer look at her middle-aged body. But such distrust of neighbors has no place in the post-holocaust world, where neighbors must work together. When the tragedy strikes, Bragg shows his true leadership qualities and is immediately accepted by the locals as just the sort of strong leader they need. Meanwhile, he gathers his closest supporters about him, where they live together as a harmonious community of the kind that would have been impossible before "The Day." They live off the land, fishing, hunting, and growing their own food (the Henrys do most of the actual farm work, of course), establishing an efficient communion, not only among themselves, but also with nature.

As the book ends, a helicopter lands on Bragg's lawn, bringing the first contact with the outside world since the war. They learn that the United States has won the war, reducing the Soviet Union to rubble. Unfortunately, America has been reduced to the status of a second-rate power itself and is actually accepting foreign aid from South America. But parts of the United States are relatively uncontaminated by radiation, and the crew of the chopper offer to take Bragg and his cadre out to a clear area. Not surprisingly, they refuse, preferring to stay where they are, in their own little utopia, even though they know it may be generations before they can venture forth from Fort Repose, which luckily happens to be in the middle of virtually the only area of Florida that has not been rendered uninhabitable by radiation.

Perhaps the best known and most critically respected post-holocaust novel of the 1950s is Walter Miller's *A Canticle for Leibowitz* (1959). Actually a series of three novellas, Miller's book employs a Viconian vision of cyclic history to trace the course of civilization from the year 2570 (six hundred years after a nuclear holocaust has plunged humanity into a second Dark Ages), to the year 3174 (when a second Renaissance announces a rebirth of science and culture), to the year 3781 (when civilization has recovered its former heights, only again to destroy itself via nuclear war). The book, though informed by considerable ironic humor, suggests an extremely dark and pessimistic vision of human civilization, arguing that humans need to use science and technology in order to fulfill their potential, but that they will inevitably misuse these tools, leading to their own destruction. As one character asks (rhetorically) in the third novella, "Are we helpless? Are we doomed to do it again and again and again? Have we no choice but to play the Phoenix, in an unending sequence of rise and fall?" (245).

A Canticle for Leibowitz deals primarily with the role played by the Catholic Church in this cyclic history, focusing in particular on a single abbey somewhere in what had been Utah, occupied by the monastic Order of St. Leibowitz. The Leibowitz Abbey is named for Isaac Edward Leibowitz, a twentieth-century Jewish technician, who became a priest and joined the Church in order to escape the "Simplification," in which mobs, blaming science for the recent holocaust, murdered scientists and technicians and destroyed their equipment and books. In the Church, Leibowitz founded his order, which is dedicated to the preservation of certain "memorabilia" that are stored in the abbey. By the time of the first novella (by far the most successful and richly realized of the three), six hundred years after the time of Leibowitz, the monks of the order have only a vague understanding of these memorabilia, which consist primarily of miscellaneous technical documents. Nevertheless, devoted to their founder (who is canonized near the end of the first novella), the monks steadfastly protect the memorabilia and even make copies of them, convinced that the documents contain information that will be invaluable once the Dark Ages pass and civilization begins to rebuild itself.

In the second novella, the burgeoning growth of civilization is accompanied by widespread conflict, foreshadowing the end to which this civilization will lead. In the realm of knowledge, the Church begins to take a back seat to secular scholars, who use the documents preserved in refuges such as the Leibowitz Abbey as a starting point for their own researches. These scholars are able to extend and develop scientific knowledge, rather than merely preserve it. At the same time, they lack the reverence of the monks and soon begin to put their new knowledge to practical use, leading quickly to misuse. By the third novella, the rebirth of nuclear technology leads quickly to a second nuclear holocaust. The monks of the Order of Leibowitz, fearing that life on earth might be destroyed altogether, load up a starship with memorabilia and head for the stars, accompanied by the ominous suggestion that the destructive cycles of human history will continue to repeat themselves even there.

A Canticle for Leibowitz is unabashedly pro-Catholic, despite the fact that the monks of the Leibowitz Order make an important contribution to the (ultimately destructive) second rise of science by preserving the memorabilia in their care. Miller, who converted to Catholicism at the age of twenty-five, presents the Church as an entirely positive force devoted to the humane preservation of knowledge. There is no mention of the actual historical role of the Church in destroying and suppressing knowledge during its heyday in the Middle Ages. Nor does Miller show any recognition of the fierce opposition of the Church to the growth of scientific knowledge during the Enlightenment. Similarly, making the

Jewish Leibowitz such a central figure ignores the historical anti-Semitism of the Catholic Church, as does the motif of the Wandering Jew, who circulates through all three novellas. As a result, Miller's vision of the future seems seriously compromised by a fundamental misunderstanding (or at least misrepresentation) of the past. More importantly, Miller's suggestion that the fallen nature of humankind ensures that the species will never be able to prosper is so pessimistic that it seems to make all secular human effort meaningless—which might be why he felt the need, in the third novella, to include an extended (and not very convincing) argument against suicide.

Miller's vision of a cyclic repetition of nuclear holocaust is reminiscent of *Limbo*, while his notion of a second coming of the Middle Ages resembles the historical model that underlies Asimov's *Foundation* trilogy in some obvious ways. However, Asimov in no way implies that his historical vision of decline and fall is part of an endless series of inevitable repetitions. Further, Asimov presents science as a benevolent force that can greatly improve the condition of humankind over time, with religion (for Asimov, a synonym for superstition) being the most important negative force that science must overcome (or at least co-opt) in order to do its good work.[10]

Miller's book is unusual among Golden Age science fiction books for a number of reasons, including its strongly positive treatment of organized religion, though organized religion itself experienced a sort of golden age in the 1950s.[11] In particular, its vision of coming nuclear war is in no way a cautionary tale. For Miller, the threat of nuclear holocaust does not arise from the specific global political situation of the Cold War. Instead, such holocaust is simply inevitable, so there is no particular reason to warn against it. Thus, there is no suggestion in *A Canticle for Leibowitz* that we should work for nuclear disarmament or that, alternatively, we should rev up our weapons development in order to stay ahead of the evil Soviets.

A Canticle for Leibowitz may be the single most prominent example of post-holocaust novels of the long 1950s. However, the true poet of post-holocaust visions during the period is probably Philip K. Dick, who wrote a whole series of such fictions, including *The World Jones Made* (1956), *The Man Who Japed* (1956), *Vulcan's Hammer* (1960), *The Penultimate Truth* (1964), and *Dr. Bloodmoney* (1965). Of these, only the last (which echoes Stewart's *Earth Abides* in a number of ways) makes any serious attempt realistically to depict conditions that might prevail after a nuclear war. Most of them are, instead, satirical fictions that use their post-holocaust settings merely to provide a fresh perspective from which to critique the already dystopian character of contemporary American capitalist society. In fact, even *Dr. Bloodmoney* is intended largely as a de-familiarizing commentary on America at the end of the long 1950s, as

Dick suggests in his 1980 afterword to the book. Indeed, many motifs in the book function overtly in this way, as when black TV salesman Stuart McConchie (the character with whom Dick claims, in his afterword, to identify most) only becomes fully aware of his lifelong alienation as he lies in a collapsing basement after nuclear bombs fall on Berkeley. With plenty of time to think, "he had realized that it had always been hard for him to make out what other people were doing; it had only been by the greatest effort that he had managed to act as they acted, appear like them" (97).

Still, *Dr. Bloodmoney* is unique among Dick's post-holocaust novels in a number of ways. Most importantly, it is the only one of Dick's post-holocaust novels of the long 1950s that includes important utopian elements, as numerous critics have noted. In particular, as Kim Stanley Robinson emphasizes, *Dr. Bloodmoney* is the only one of these novels in which nuclear destruction is extensive enough to destroy corporate capitalism, thus opening up new possibilities for social and economic organization: "In Dick's view, the triumph of capitalism results in a dystopian state; it follows, then, that the defeat of capitalism opens up utopian possibilities" (Robinson 77). In a similar mode, Fredric Jameson argues that the nuclear holocaust in *Dr. Bloodmoney* effects a sort of renewal of the commodified universe of capitalism, leading to the development of a "genuinely Jeffersonian commonwealth beyond the bomb" ("After Armageddon" 42). Meanwhile, Darko Suvin goes so far as to describe the book as informed by a Rousseauist utopianism ("Artifice" 83). Other critics have been less certain of the book's utopianism. Douglas A. Mackey does not see the book as utopian at all, but merely as less dystopian than Dick's other post-holocaust novels (59). Hazel Pierce, meanwhile, sees the world of *Dr. Bloodmoney* as a "quasi-utopian" one, in which the utopian aspects are "undercut by a sense of perverseness" (132).

In point of fact, *Dr. Bloodmoney* is a complex combination of utopian and dystopian elements. It is a highly multifaceted work, informed throughout by a particularly complex version of the doubleness and ambivalence that are typical of much of the science fiction of the long 1950s. One of the most interesting motifs in *Dr. Bloodmoney* involves the depiction of Walt Dangerfield, an astronaut stranded in orbit by the war, left endlessly circling the globe and acting as a sort of glorified disc jockey, broadcasting music and commentary to the population below, which listens with rapt attention, starved for entertainment in the wake of the collapse of American media culture. Dangerfield himself is clearly presented as a virtuous, even heroic, figure, and there is clearly a utopian aspect in the way he is able to help the survivors of the holocaust in their struggle to maintain some sense of cultural identity after the collapse of the culture they had previously known. At the same time, the extent to which the population hangs on Dangerfield's every word serves as a tell-

ing commentary on the extent to which the American population is held
in thrall to media culture, desperate to receive any tidbit at all as long as
it is broadcast over the airwaves. Dick also suggests that the considerable
power of the media can easily be abused; late in the book, Dangerfield's
broadcasts are taken over by an impostor, seeking personal power.

In a clearly satirical vein, Dick's book presents a number of exaggerated images of the effects of nuclear war, such as the growth, through
radiation-induced mutation, of talking dogs and "brilliant" rats, with
considerable technological capability. Meanwhile, in the person of young
Bill Keller, Dick creates one of the most unusual human mutants in all of
science fiction. Conceived on the day of the bombing, Bill lives inside an
inchoate hull, his body having never really formed; this hull is lodged
inside the body of his twin sister, Edie. Bill can communicate with Edie
telepathically, and he has other unusual mental powers as well, but he
can live only as a parasite inside his sister or another host.

Bill's counterpart in the text is Hoppy Harrington, a phocomelus,
whose lack of limbs is caused, not by the book's 1981 nuclear war, but by
the effects of thalidomide on his pregnant mother in the 1960s. In Dick's
universe, if it is not one thing it is another: human beings seem to have a
genius for creating freaks, even if they do not always know how to deal
with them. Like Bill (and like many of the physical and psychological
"sports" in Dick's fiction), Hoppy's physical shortcomings are accompanied by compensatory powers, in this case the ability to exert force at a
distance through sheer mental projection. Using these powers, Harrington manages to hijack Dangerfield's broadcasts, nearly killing Dangerfield. There is a third freak in the text as well, in the person of Dr. Bruno
Bluthgeld, the "Dr. Bloodmoney" of the title. Bluthgeld was centrally involved in a 1972 nuclear test that went awry, exposing large numbers of
civilians to damaging radiation. Though many others were involved in
the test, the somewhat megalomaniacal (and fanatically anticommunist)
Bluthgeld feels personally responsible, and that opinion seems to have
lodged in the popular imagination as well, making him a notorious figure. On the day of the 1981 nuclear attacks, the troubled Bluthgeld is
consulting Dr. Stockstill, a psychiatrist; subsequently, Bluthgeld concludes that he has somehow caused the war. This belief seems to be an
element of his mental instability, yet there is evidence later in the text
that he may be right.

The depiction of Bill Keller, Hoppy Harrington, and Bluthgeld participates in the concern with "abnormal" characters that runs through all
of Dick's fiction, which treats these characters in complex ways that tend
to call into question any simple definition of the boundary between the
normal and the abnormal. Indeed, after the nuclear war, weird mutations
become the norm, leading Stockstill, now working as a general practitio-
ner in rural West Marin County, California, to realize that "there is noth-

ing ... outside of nature; that is a logical impossibility" (162). Despite the extreme and seemingly unrealistic nature of many of the book's characters, Dick manages to endow all of them with a genuine humanity and to make all of them unusually compelling. Readers are thus subtly encouraged not to accept a simple distinction between realistic and absurd characters, just as the book itself combines realistic and absurdist depictions of the effects of nuclear holocaust. The characters are morally complex, as well. Bluthgeld, for example, may not be insane at all; he may merely be evil. Meanwhile, Harrington, physically crippled by circumstances beyond his control, is far from a helpless victim. Not only does he have considerable psychic powers, but he is ultimately willing to use them in problematic ways, including the killing of two men, one of whom is Bluthgeld. Meanwhile, Bill, the most seemingly helpless character of all, turns out to be even more powerful than Harrington, ultimately ousting him from his mechanically enhanced body, which Bill himself subsequently occupies as his own.

In his 1980 afterword, Dick announces that he views Bluthgeld and Harrington as evil and the other major characters as essentially virtuous. However, he also states that he intentionally gave the villains some positive qualities and the other characters some villainous qualities. Harrington, in particular, has developed his lust for power as a reaction to a life of humiliation. In *Dr. Bloodmoney*, in fact, the difference between the victims and the villains is extremely unclear. Similarly, the line between the utopian and the dystopian is quite vague. It is true, as Robinson, Jameson, and Suvin have emphasized, that the nuclear war of the book wipes out many of the negative characteristics of modern corporate capitalism. On the other hand, the conditions that prevail after the war are hardly ideal. In fact, despite its satirical and fantastic elements, the book provides some of the most realistic (and horrifying) visions of all of the post-holocaust fictions of the long 1950s. In one scene, for example, McConchie is forced to eat a dead, raw rat in order to survive.

Dr. Bloodmoney does suggest that the post-holocaust societies that arise over the seven years following the bombing have many utopian aspects. This is especially true in the West Marin County community, where the citizens gather in public meetings to make genuinely democratic decisions, presumably in the interest of the public good. However, these decisions sometimes have a sinister aspect, as when they decide, in a demonstration of their suspicion toward strangers, to kill Mr. Austurias, their community teacher, for the highly questionable reason that he has not been entirely honest with them about his background before coming to the community. In addition, when McConchie, still living in the urban San Francisco Bay area, fantasizes about fleeing the difficult conditions there for a better life out in Marin County, his partner and mentor, Mr. Hardy, warns him about idealizing conditions in the country, suggesting that such idealizations are "one of the greatest myths that ever existed" (154). Among other things, he warns Stuart that a black man like himself is likely to encounter far more racial prejudice in the country than in the city. By the end of the text, not only has Stuart decided to stay in Berkeley, but Andrew Gill and Bonnie Keller, two of the leading members of the West Marin community, have decided to move there as well. And they move there in order to pursue a business partnership with Hardy and McConchie, a partnership that clearly takes them a step closer to the reestablishment of corporate capitalism, which proves not to be so easy to kill off after all.

Ultimately, *Dr. Bloodmoney* is powerful as social commentary because the negative aspects of its post-holocaust world are the ones that most resemble the characteristics of Dick's contemporary America, while the positive aspects of his post-holocaust world are those that differ most dramatically from conditions in America at the end of the long 1950s. Still, the radical ambivalence of the book defies any simple interpretation, moving instead into an undecideability that can only be described as postmodern. In this sense, the book, which was published with the full title *Dr. Bloodmoney, or How We Got Along after the Bomb* (1965), resembles Stanley Kubrick's 1963 film, *Dr. Strangelove, or, How I Learned to Stop Worrying and Love the Bomb*. Actually, the writing of book was essentially complete before the release of Kubrick's film, and there are few direct links between the two works, but the clear reference to Kubrick's film in the published title calls attention to the fact that Dick's novel shares with Kubrick's film a postmodernist sense of the absurdity of the Cold War arms race.[12]

Kubrick's film, of course, is an unusual one that is hardly typical of the post-holocaust films of the long 1950s. Actually, relatively few of the science fiction films of the 1950s were specifically post-holocaust films, perhaps because the material was considered too disturbing by mainstream filmmakers. The post-holocaust films that did appear often seemed designed to calm the nuclear fears of the decade, displacing their vision of nuclear holocaust into the far future and often providing happy endings to assure audiences that everything would be fine, nuclear holocaust or no. The post-holocaust films of the decade generally present far less troubling images than do the novels, both in their representation of nuclear devastation and in their commentary on contemporary American society. Still, these films do attempt to make certain political points, ranging from the vaguely left-wing anti-racist perspective of Arch Oboler's early effort, *Five* (1951), to the almost deranged anticommunism of William Asher's *The 27th Day* (1957).

Five takes it title from its focus on five survivors of a nuclear war and thus has some claim to be the first film to deal with such a scenario. The film's survivors somehow make their ways from various points around the world to the California coast, taking refuge in a modernistic house perched on a hilltop. The five brawl among themselves, largely due to the disruptive influence of one of them, who is depicted as a sort of neo-Nazi. This neo-Nazi is clearly the villain of the piece, thus providing much of the film's political commentary, as when his animosity toward (and eventually killing of) the only black survivor serves as a demonstration of the evil and stupidity of racism. Most of the brawling among the survivors is verbal, however, and *Five* depends heavily on dialogue to make its antiwar and antiracist points. Eventually, though, only one man and one woman survive, going forth to repopulate the world (and hopefully to avoid repeating the militaristic mistakes of the past).[13]

Five has its limitations, many of which can be attributed to its minuscule budget. Nevertheless, critics have agreed that it was historically important in its groundbreaking depiction of a post–nuclear holocaust world. However, many, such as Ernest Martin, have complained that the film is overly pessimistic in its vision of the extent of the death that would result from a nuclear war (12). Meanwhile, Martin is also concerned about the film's seemingly romantic ending, which runs counter to the basic pessimism of the rest of the film (14). Such romanticized endings, however, would become almost a convention of the genre in the coming decade. Indeed, the post-holocaust films are far more consistent than the post-holocaust novels of the long 1950s in their tendency to end hopefully. Even when the films do not suggest the coming rebirth of human civilization, they tend to present the death of the old civilization in a highly romantic way.

Roger Corman, never one to shy away from potentially shocking subject matter, still tacked a comforting ending onto his entry into the post-holocaust genre, *The Day the World Ended* (1955), his first science fiction film. Like most of the films directed (or produced) by Corman, *The Day the World Ended* seems a bit silly at times, but turns out to have its interesting moments. Like most post–nuclear holocaust films of the period, it concentrates on the survivors of a nuclear war rather than on the destruction of the war itself. Indeed, all of the film's action occurs in a sheltered valley that just happens to be protected by lead-filled hills on all sides. A total of seven survivors of the war gather in the valley at the home of rancher Jim Maddison (Paul Birch), who has laid in supplies for just such an eventuality.

Unfortunately, Maddison had not planned on feeding this many people, so supplies are short and it is not at all clear that they will be sufficient to see the survivors through until radiation levels die down in the outside world. Meanwhile, tensions flare within the group, partly because gangster type Tony Lamont (a pre-Mannix Mike Connors) begins to ignore his stripper girlfriend, Ruby (Adele Jergens), in favor of Maddison's beautiful daughter, Louise (Lori Nelson). Louise is not pleased by the attention, which is also resented by both Maddison and Louise's newfound beau, the upright Rick (Richard Denning). In addition, one of the group, Radek (Paul Dubov), is suffering from severe radiation poisoning and is gradually transforming into a monstrous mutant who, among other things, feeds on human flesh. Thus, the mutant, though described as the product of "a million years of evolution with one bomb," is actually the product of devolution, representing a reversion to the primitivist stereotypes (such as cannibalism) that degeneration fantasies are made on. Meanwhile, there is also a full-blown mutant roaming the valley and menacing the survivors. At one point, this three-eyed, rubber-skinned mutant, in good King Kong fashion, makes off with Louise, with Rick in hot pursuit. At this moment, it begins to rain, an event that all of the survivors have dreaded, assuming the rainwater would be contaminated with radiation. But the water is pure, bringing new hope for survival. In addition, it turns out that uncontaminated water is poison to this mutant—and presumably to any other nearby mutants as well. The mutant dies in the downpour, leaving the valley to the humans. By this time, however, only Rick, Louise, Tony, and Maddison are left alive, and Maddison quickly kills Tony, who is about to kill Rick. Maddison then dies of radiation poisoning, leaving only Rick and Louise to face the future. They pack up and leave the valley, going forth to seek other survivors, assuming that the cleansing rains have made the surrounding countryside safe for human habitation.

Hackneyed plot, stock characters, and really cheesy-looking monster aside, *The Day the World Ended* is still notable as one of the few films of the 1950s that actually showed the effects of radiation on humans, however unrealistic its depiction of those effects might have been. It thus differs from the most popular post-holocaust film of the 1950s, Stanley Kramer's *On the Beach* (1959), which shows no such effects. In this film, set in 1964 and based on the bestselling post-holocaust novel of the 1950s, Nevil Shute's 1957 Australian novel of the same title, a global nuclear war has apparently destroyed all human life everywhere on earth, except Australia, which has been spared because of its remote location. Unfortunately, the clouds of deadly radiation that cover the rest of the globe are headed for Australia as well, so the Australians themselves have only a few months before what seems to be inevitable death.

To an extent, *On the Beach* is more human drama than science fiction, detailing as it does the attempts of the various characters to cope with their impending doom. Indeed, while the how-could-we-be-so-stupid senselessness of the nuclear war looms in the margin as a message throughout, Kramer also seems to have wanted to make the film a sort of universal commentary on how human beings come to grips with the realization of their own certain mortality. This same comment might be made about the book, whose author, incidentally, was a dying man at the time he wrote it. Among other things, as Spencer Weart notes, both the book and the film concentrate more on love stories involving "steadfast military men" and "blindly sentimental women" than on nuclear disaster. Further, the film, "by showing none of the physical agony and demolition that a real war would bring, made world extinction a romantic condition" (Weart 219). The film is entirely sanitized. There are no corpses, no radiation burns, not even property damage. While we do see shots of post-holocaust San Francisco and San Diego, the cities are entirely undamaged. The only change is that all the people seem to have disappeared. As such, the film's anti–arms race message is a bit muted, though still clear.

Other post-holocaust films of the long 1950s were even more indirect in their representation of nuclear war and its aftermath. For example, in Edward Bernds's *World without End* (1956), the nuclear holocaust is projected hundreds of years into the future, and the film itself is set hundreds of years after that, when radiation levels have essentially returned to normal. In this film, a team of astronauts on earth's first mission to Mars (in 1957) encounters strange turbulence in space; they are hurtled forward in time into the early twenty-sixth century as they return to earth. They find that the surface of the earth is now dominated by primitive, mutant, one-eyed cavemen, while the remaining "normal" humans on the surface are slaves of the mutants. There is, however, a technologically advanced community of humans living beneath the surface. These humans live in peace and comfort, but they have become so passive and effete that they are gradually dying out. Or at least the men are passive: the scantily-clad women are all beautiful, full of life, and sexually excited by the power and energy of the newcomers.

The film never quite follows through on this titillating sexual premise, but the obvious attraction of all these women to the newcomers is indicative of the overall atmosphere of the film. The depiction of the mutant cavemen, meanwhile, draws upon typical 1950s fears of radiation-induced degeneration. Ultimately, however, *World without End* is less a cautionary tale than an adventure story that simply uses the possibility of nuclear holocaust as an avenue of escape from the routinization of life in the 1950s. Indeed, for a post-holocaust film, it is an oddly pro-militaristic work, in which the newcomers (clearly presented as being in the right) struggle to convince the underground humans to build weapons and return to the surface to battle the mutants for supremacy. Meanwhile, one of the astronauts notes that the passivity of the underground people is merely an extension of trends toward a yearning for safety and comfort that were already at work back in the 1950s, so that the film's invocation to armament has a certain relevance to its contemporary world. In the end, of course, the more vital and energetic astronauts win out, the mutants are defeated, and the humans establish a new colony on the surface. "What we're looking at," says the astronaut leader, proudly, "may well be the rebirth of the human race."

Many aspects of *World without End* seem derived from H. G. Wells's classic 1895 novel, *The Time Machine*, which would be adapted more directly to film a few years later in George Pal's *The Time Machine* (1960). Indeed, *World without End* and Pal's film have at least one obvious intertextual link: Pal's time traveler is played by Rod Taylor, who had played one of the astronauts in *World without End*. The film version of *The Time Machine* is a reasonably faithful adaptation of Wells's novel and therefore seems to have little to do with the genre of the post–nuclear holocaust film. On the other hand, Pal (who had produced many of the leading science fiction films of the previous decade) does at one point have his time traveler (who begins his journey on New Year's Eve, 1899) stop off in 1966, where he is nearly killed in a nuclear assault on London. Therefore, when he subsequently travels into the far future (he ends up in the year 802,701, just as in Wells's book), the depiction of the dystopian environment of that future is given a post-holocaust cast. As in Wells's book, the time traveler discovers that the human race has evolved (actually, devolved) into two separate species. The passive Eloi live on the gardenlike surface of the planet, enjoying lives of mindless leisure. They are completely indolent, illiterate, and incapable of creative thought or action. Meanwhile, the aggressive and animalistic Morlocks live beneath the surface, where they still have at least some operating technology. It turns out, meanwhile, that they are raising the Eloi essentially as cattle, taking them, at full maturity, beneath the surface to be slaughtered for food.

The Morlocks function in the film, as they do in Wells's novel, as typical images of humanity in a degenerate state. As the time traveler says, upon discovering the true relation between the Morlocks and the Eloi, the Morlocks have "degenerated into the lowest form of human life—cannibalism." The novel, meanwhile, makes more clear than the film that the passivity of the Eloi has come about primarily because they achieved a level of technological domination of nature that left them no further challenges, leading to a degeneration of a different kind. The film, showing its roots in the 1950s, seems to imply that both the Eloi and Morlocks may have reached their state as a result of nuclear war, an implication that is entirely missing in the novel. Audiences in 1960 could probably also not have helped seeing at least a vague connection between the passivity of the Eloi and contemporary concerns that America had become too soft and spoiled to resist the dogged onslaught of the determined Soviets. In this sense, the Morlocks might be associated with the Soviets themselves, though their description in terms of classic racist-colonialist stereotypes tends to associate the blue-skinned Morlocks with the threat posed by the Third World, with its supposedly savage energies, to an effete America, represented by the pale, blond Eloi.[14]

Perhaps because it did draw upon this paranoid fear of the Other, the film also differs from the novel in that it attempts to tack on a happy ending (reminiscent of the ending of *World without End*), as the time traveler stirs the Eloi to revolt, destroying the Morlocks. Meanwhile, as the film ends, he returns to 802,701 to help lead the Eloi in their attempt to build a new world and regenerate their ability for creative action. In this sense, *The Time Machine* is typical of the science fiction films of the 1950s in its attempt ultimately to calm the very fears that it draws upon for its central energies. One need only note *The 27th Day*, in which alien invaders distribute devastating antipersonnel weapons among several humans, who subsequently learn how to use the weapons so that they will only kill off "every enemy of peace and freedom." It turns out, fortunately, that there are only a few thousand such enemies, most of them found among the leaders of the Soviet Union. Thus, the doomsday weapon wipes out the bad guys and ushers forth a new era of peace and prosperity for the vast majority of the earth's population, which in this film is virtually everyone who is not a Soviet apparatchik.

By 1962, science fiction films began to deal a bit more directly (and less optimistically) with nuclear holocaust, though a film such as Ray Milland's *Panic in Year Zero* still resembles *On the Beach* in its focus on the human drama of the survivors of the disaster, not the human tragedy of the victims. There are again no actual signs of nuclear destruction, though the film does depict certain negative consequences, such as the looting, rape, and murder that occur in the wake of a nuclear attack. By and large, however, *Panic in Year Zero* is essentially a survivalist adventure, in which the resourceful Baldwin family meet all challenges and ultimately survive the nuclear war unscathed. A British film, Val Guest's *The Day the Earth Caught Fire*, also released in 1962, is less romantic in its dramatization of nuclear-related destruction, but it displaces this destruction from nuclear war to nuclear testing, which inadvertently sends the earth careening off course and hurtling toward the sun. Meanwhile, it ends as the Russians and Americans work together to try to save the earth, but eschews the easy solution of a happy ending, closing with the outcome of these efforts still in doubt.[15]

Finally, the nuclear-holocaust films of the long 1950s were topped off, in 1963 and 1964, by an important series of what might be called preholocaust films. No doubt influenced by the perceived close call of the 1962 Cuban missile crisis, each of these films in its own way deals, not with the aftermath of a nuclear holocaust, but with a proposed scenario that might be envisioned as leading to such a holocaust. Actually, John Frankenheimer's *Seven Days in May* (1964, written by *Twilight Zone* maven Rod Serling) deals only indirectly with the prospect of nuclear holocaust. In this taut political thriller, Air Force General James Mattoon Scott (Burt Lancaster), the chairman of the Joint Chiefs of Staff, leads an effort of the U.S. military to take control of the federal government to prevent President Jordan Lyman (Fredric March) from pursuing a course of détente with the Soviets. Fortunately, Scott's aide, Colonel Martin "Jiggs" Casey (Kirk Douglas), learns of the plot and tips off the president, who is thereby able (just barely) to avert the coup.

Seven Days in May deals with nuclear holocaust in the sense that Scott justifies his coup attempt on the basis of his conviction that the Soviets, once the Americans are weakened by a policy of disarmament, are bound to launch a sneak nuclear attack on the United States. Lyman, on the other hand, counters with the theory that the coup itself might lead the Soviets to attempt a preemptive strike in order to defend themselves from the threat posed by an American regime headed by a zealot such as Scott. Meanwhile, the fanatic Scott is unambiguously identified as the villain of the piece, so that the film is quite clear in its critique of the hawkish military mentality that he represents. It is also clear in its suggestion that overzealous attempts to defend American democracy from outside foes might themselves lead to the downfall of the democracy that these attempts are supposedly designed to prevent. Scott, however, is more a symptom of a larger phenomenon than a cause. Thus, Lyman explains that the real enemy is not Scott and his supporters, but "an age, the nuclear age. It happens to have killed man's faith in his ability to influence what happens to him." It is this feeling of helplessness that makes the general population vulnerable to a demagogue like Scott, whom Lyman, in this sense, compares to Senator Joseph McCarthy.

Seven Days in May thus joins Frankenheimer's earlier *The Manchurian Candidate* (1962), which lampoons McCarthy even more directly, as two of American film's central explorations of the mentality of the Cold War. Meanwhile, Sidney Lumet's tense thriller, *Fail-Safe* (1964), explores the dangers of the Cold War arms race in a different way. Here, it is not crazed ideologues, but simply overly complex machinery that gets out of hand, sending American nuclear bombers toward Moscow by accident. The elaborate security measures that are built into the system make it impossible to recall the bombers and, in the end, Moscow is bombed, despite the best efforts of the President (Henry Fonda) and the American military to avert the bombing. Moreover, as a gesture of good faith, the president orders New York bombed as well, thus preventing Soviet retaliation, which might have led to the total destruction of both the United States and the Soviet Union.

The primary message of *Fail-Safe* is that our current course of developing more and more sophisticated defense systems will almost certainly lead to a catastrophe of this sort, even if intentional nuclear war never comes. Meanwhile, the film addresses a general anxiety over the growing importance of machines in American life, expressing the widespread fear that we are becoming the servants of our technology, rather than the other way around. At the same time, the film, scripted by formerly black-listed screenwriter Walter Bernstein, also criticizes the militant anticommunist hysteria that informed American attitudes during the Cold War. For one thing, the Soviets, and especially the Soviet premier, are presented in an extremely positive light, responding rationally and humanely to the crisis. But the same cannot be said for one of the major American characters, the civilian political scientist Professor Groeteschele (Walter Matthau), who serves as a top advisor to the Pentagon. Groeteschele, though a civilian, is an ideological counterpart to General Scott of *Seven Days in May*. A virulent anticommunist, Groeteschele urges the Pentagon to take advantage of the accidental bombing of Moscow to launch an all-out first-strike assault, destroying the evil Soviets once and for all. Luckily, cooler heads prevail, and no one takes his advice, though he is still at work at the end of the film, urging authorities to make no attempt to rescue human survivors of the bombing of New York and to concentrate instead on the recovery of corporate records, which are vital to our economy.

Groeteschele's attitudes are thus linked to corporate capitalism, though he himself admits that he learned his ruthless attitudes from the German Nazis. This background makes him a counterpart to the title character of the brilliant *Dr. Strangelove* (1963), which, more than any other single film, captured the lunacy of the Cold War mentality, while at the same time suggesting that certain American attitudes in the Cold War might have been inherited from the Nazis. *Dr. Strangelove*, in its parodic focus on the comic absurdity of the arms race, also signals a turn to postmodern strategies in dealing with the tensions of the Cold War. Based (loosely) on the novel *Red Alert* (1958) by Peter George, *Dr. Strangelove* goes well beyond the novel in its absurdist satire of the ideology of the Cold War arms race. *Dr. Strangelove* became a cult favorite of the 1960s youth movement and was one of the classics of American culture of the 1960s, even though, strictly speaking, it is a British film, produced at London's Hawk Studios. The film is so representative, in fact, that historian Margot Henriksen entitled her own study of the ideology of Cold War America *Dr. Strangelove's America*.

The premise of the film is simple: both the United States and the Soviet Union are so caught up in the arms race that they pursue insane courses that make nuclear holocaust almost inevitable. Indeed, the film's crisis is triggered by literal insanity, that of General Jack D. Ripper (played with appropriately grim lunacy by Sterling Hayden), commander of Burpelson Air Force Base and of a wing of the Strategic Air Command's fleet of B-52 nuclear bombers. Unhinged by his extreme anticommunist paranoia (which leads him to believe that communist conspiracies are seeking to "sap and impurify all of our precious bodily fluids" through techniques such as fluoridation of water), Ripper orders his bombers to attack the Soviet Union, thereby triggering the labyrinthine security procedures that make it almost impossible to recall such an order.

Most of the film involves the efforts of the American government to recall the attack and thus avert the inevitable Russian retaliation. Much of it is set in the memorable war room, where President Merkin Muffley (played by Peter Sellers, who also plays Dr. Strangelove and Group Captain Lionel Mandrake, a British exchange officer serving as Ripper's aide) convenes a meeting of his chief strategic advisors in an attempt to deal with the crisis. Chief among these advisors are General Buck Turgidson (played by George C. Scott and so named for both his phallic exploits and his penchant for inflated rhetorical posturing) and the zanily sinister Strangelove, whose continuing loyalty to his former Nazi bosses becomes increasingly obvious in the course of the film. When all attempts to avert the attack seem to be failing, Turgidson suggests an all-out assault while the United States still has the element of surprise on its side. Muffley, however, opts to warn the Russians, apologetically explaining the situation to Soviet Premier Dimitri Kissov in terms that make launching a nuclear strike seem like nothing more than a sort of social faux pas. The Americans then learn to their horror that the Russians, as a deterrent to precisely such attacks, have installed a Doomsday Machine that will be automatically triggered by any nuclear blast over the Soviet Union, enveloping the planet in a cloud of radioactive dust and destroying all life.

Ripper, the only man who knows the code that can cancel the attack order, commits suicide to avoid revealing it. Fortunately, however, Mandrake manages to deduce the code, but before he can deliver it to the president, he is taken captive by Army Colonel "Bat" Guano (Keenan Wynn), who suspects that Mandrake, as a foreigner, is a commie "prevert." Finally, after a comic scene in which he has to convince Guano to break open a Coke machine (despite concerns of potential retribution from the Coca Cola Company) to get change to use a pay phone, Mandrake calls the president and gives him the information so the attack can be averted. In the meantime, one of the bombers, commanded by Major J. T. "King" Kong (Slim Pickens), has been damaged by antiaircraft missiles and is unable to receive the command to avert the attack. The crew struggles to keep the plane aloft and manages to reach a potential target, only to find that the damage from the missile has also caused the bomb doors to jam. Kong crawls down into the bomb bay and manages to open the doors and release the weapon, dropping out of the plane astride the bomb and, in one of the most memorable scenes in modern film, riding it bronco-style, waving his cowboy hat and whooping it up as the bomb falls to earth.

The screen then goes white as the bomb hits, which might have been the best ending, dramatically, for the film. However, Kubrick tacks on an additional scene that makes some important thematic points. In the scene, Strangelove, while involved in a comic wrestling match with his bionic right arm, which seems intent on shooting upward in a Nazi salute, concocts a plan for preserving civilization by founding colonies at the bottom of mine shafts, safe from the radioactive cloud. This plan is a burlesque of virtually all of the post-holocaust fictions of the long 1950s, revealing the fantasy elements that lie behind so many of them. For example, Strangelove suggests that, in order to facilitate repopulation of the earth, the new colonies should include ten women for every man and that, in order to encourage the men to do their reproductive duty, these women should be chosen for their "stimulating sexual characteristics." Meanwhile, Turgidson's gleeful reaction to this plan reveals the true nature of his personality. The scene ends as both the Americans and the Russian ambassador, called to the war room as part of the effort to avert the crisis, begin to get concerned about a possible "mine shaft gap," suggesting that the two sides have still failed to learn their lesson about the folly of such competition. The film then ends with a sequence of shots of nuclear explosions and mushroom clouds, with sentimental music (Vera Lynn's "We'll Meet Again") playing in the background.

In many ways, *Dr. Strangelove* is weak as a political film. It does nothing to examine the historical and political background of the Cold War, depicting it essentially as an ego contest between American madmen and Russian madmen. In the kind of association between violence and sexuality that is central to much of Kubrick's work, the film characterizes the Cold War as a phallic competition driven by erotic energies, with macho generals on both sides trying to establish their greater manhood by proving that they have the bigger and more effective weapons. Strangelove (so memorable in Sellers's portrayal, despite the fact that he is actually onscreen a surprisingly short time) may be the film's most potent political image. His crucial presence as the president's chief strategic advisor in the Cold War (emphasized through the titling of the film) tends to align the American position with that of the German Nazis, suggesting that Cold War America has followed in Hitler's footsteps in attempting to exterminate the Soviet Union and all it represents. If nothing else, this motif calls attention to the willingness of the United States to align itself with repressive right-wing regimes around the world in the effort to win support in the battle against communism. In addition, the film can, as Charles Maland notes, be read as a powerful critique of the "Ideology of Liberal Consensus" that was the dominant paradigm of American political life in the late 1950s and early 1960s. Still, the primary political orientation of the film is not procommunist, or even anti-American, but antimilitary, with the Soviet military leaders being at least as insane as the Americans in their blind pursuit of nuclear superiority.

The explosions at the end of *Dr. Strangelove* presumably mean the end of human civilization, and perhaps human life, on earth. But, in another sense, they signal the end of an era in post-holocaust fiction and film. They also signal the arrival of a full-blown postmodernism, as does the near-contemporary fiction of Dick. After the postmodern turn of *Dr. Strangelove*, it would become increasingly difficult to produce post-holocaust films (and, to an extent, novels) with a straight face. In particular, after Kubrick's definitive statement on the absurdity of the arms race, film could no longer effectively perform its established function of soothing and softening nuclear fear. Indeed, Disch argues that *Dr. Strangelove* itself was partly responsible for the dramatic downturn in nuclear fear among the American population from 1964 onward. Meanwhile, American society became more and more concerned with the war in Vietnam and with the domestic politics of the civil rights and women's movements. The Golden Era of nuclear fear was at an end, though the Cold War (and the tensions that went along with it) would persist for another quarter of a century, infecting American attitudes about everything from literature to liberation, from cinema to sexuality, in ways that we have only just begun to understand.

3

We're There and They're Here!: Space Exploration and Alien Invasion Films of the Long 1950s

In an important early essay written right at the end of the long 1950s, Susan Sontag set the tone for most subsequent criticism of the science fiction films of the 1950s, arguing that these films reflect (and, to an extent, deflect) the various fears of the decade, which she collectively refers to as "the imagination of disaster." These films, she notes, are not about science, but about disasters, generally disasters wrought by the irresponsible use of science, though science, used responsibly, can also be the key to dealing with the disasters. "The standard message," she notes, "is the one about the proper, or humane, use of science, versus the mad, obsessional use of science" (216). She goes on, reading specific films, to provide a brief catalog of themes, including mistrust of intellectuals, fear of nuclear destruction, anxieties over the state of the contemporary psyche, fear of the dehumanizing consequences of life in the modern world, and a fear of moral decline in a modern world so complex that even the most black-and-white moral choices no longer seem clear. Sontag notes, however, that these films tend not only to invoke these fears, but to attempt to allay them. By their very nature, they provide fantasy content that can help to "lift us out of the unbearable humdrum and distract us from terrors" (225). She argues, in fact, that these films, by allaying our fears, are ultimately "in complicity with the abhorrent" (225). By providing fantasy solutions to real-world problems, they discourage action to solve those problems in reality. The films, she concludes, "inculcate a strange apathy concerning the processes of radiation, contamination, and destruction. ... The naïve level of the films neatly tempers the sense of otherness of alien-ness, with the grossly familiar. ... The films perpetuate clichés about identity, volition, power, knowledge, happiness, social consensus, guilt, responsibility which are, to say the least, not serviceable in our present extremity" (225).

In fact, the attempt in 1950s film to allay fears of nuclear destruction and associated issues (particularly radiation) even went so far as to produce comedies centering on the effects of radiation poisoning, including the Mickey Rooney vehicle *The Atomic Kid* and the Dean Martin and Jerry Lewis vehicle *Living It Up*, both released in 1954. Neither film was successful, but both illustrate the lengths to which Hollywood was willing to go both to try to take advantage of nuclear fear to increase attendance and to play along with official government attempts to assure a nervous populace that nuclear weapons were the key to safety and prosperity for themselves and their children. Of course, Hollywood—besieged by HUAC on the one hand and by declining attendance on the other—had its own problems in the 1950s, which might account for some of its conservatism in addressing the troubling issues that faced Americans in the decade.[1]

However, it is not so easy to put the genie back in the bottle, and the science fiction films of the 1950s, having conjured up the fears and anxieties of the decade, were not necessarily so effective at putting those fears to rest. Almost any parent knows that it would be a bad idea indeed to tuck a small child into bed with the admonition that, whatever they do, they should not worry about the boogie man or other things that go bump in the night. Yet, to some extent, this admonition was precisely the one contained in the science fiction films of the 1950s, almost all of which seemed to want to calm the anxieties of the period by calling attention to them. Even the most cataclysmic of 1950s science fiction films tend to turn out well, with the ever-present threat of global destruction averted, usually by the efforts of either the staunch American individual or the virtuous American military-industrial complex, depending on the ideology of the film. But such statements nevertheless called attention to the anxieties of the decade, potentially making them worse, however reassuring they tried to be. In addition, success in these films generally means restoration of the status quo: science and technology might be able to help avert disaster, but there is little sense in the decade that they might be able to lead to any sort of utopian transformation of society.

Sontag's insightful essay has proved extremely influential. Peter Biskind, in a broader survey of 1950s film, pays considerable attention to science fiction films and to the anxieties they addressed, specifically identifying Sontag as an important predecessor. Biskind, attempting to sort out the politics of the films of the decade, divides them into "centrist" films (which support the powers that be in American society of the time) and "radical" films (which attack the center and the Left from the Right, or the center and the Right from the Left). Biskind's realization that different films had different agendas provides an important correction to Sontag's analysis (in which all of them sound the same), though it is also the case that Biskind uses the term "radical" in a very relative sense. None of the science fiction films of the decade were radical in any absolute sense, certainly not from the Left, though a few rightest films— like *Red Planet Mars* (1952) and *Invasion U.S.A.* (1952) could be pretty extreme.

Other critics have provided variations on the basic theme sounded by Sontag. Cyndy Hendershot provides detailed readings of a number of specific films to illustrate their participation in the general paranoia of the 1950s, though she tends to attribute that paranoia almost entirely to worries over the atomic bomb, when in fact the decade was troubled by a much larger variety of anxieties and concerns. The science fiction films of the decade, like all of the decade's cultural products, were in one way or another influenced by those broader concerns. Hendershot may also try a bit too hard to relate the anxieties of the 1950s to literal, clinical paranoia, frequently comparing attitudes of the decade to those espoused by Freud's famous patient, Daniel Paul Schreber. It is true, however, that science fiction films were particularly well suited to reflect the specifically technological anxieties of the decade, and that a metaphorically (if not clinically) paranoid fear of nuclear holocaust was the most obvious of those anxieties.

The doubleness with which science fiction films of the 1950s called attention to the era's anxieties while trying simultaneously to reassure their audiences that it would all work out in the end was part of a larger tendency toward doubleness in the treatment of numerous issues. Telotte thus notes that science fiction films of the 1950s showed an "increasing tendency" toward the "double vision" that he sees as "inherent in the science fiction genre" (113). And such doubleness may be one factor contributing to the oddly double reputation enjoyed by these films. There are good reasons why the decade is often thought of as a sort of Golden Age of science fiction film. In terms of sheer numbers, there were more science fiction films produced in the 1950s than in any decade before or since. In addition, the science fiction films, however conservative, often explored the anxieties of the decade in ways that more mainstream films were not able to do within the paranoid political climate of the period.

On the other hand, the science fiction films of the decade are now remembered by many as simplistic, low-budget efforts, marked by bad scripts, worse acting, and special effects that seem laughably cheap and hokey, especially to a *Star Wars* generation accustomed to spectacular computer-generated effects that would have been impossible in the 1950s at any cost. This latter reputation, of course, was enhanced by later parodies, such as *Attack of the Killer Tomatoes* (1977) or *Killer Klowns from Outer Space* (1988), which gained cult followings by poking fun at 1950s science fiction films, creating the impression among younger filmgoers that the earlier films were worse than they really were—and also creating a sort of cult revival that made the worst films of the 1950s more popular than the best. Similarly, in the 1990s, films such as *Ed Wood* (1994) helped to make cult classics of some of the truly awful films from the 1950s, including Wood's notorious *Plan 9 from Outer Space* (1956). This sort of phenomenon was also furthered by events such as the television series "Mystery Science Theater 3000" (known among its fans simply as MST3000), which had a great deal of fun at the expense of 1950s science fiction films, even some relatively good ones.

Part of the reason why 1950s science fiction films have sometimes seemed so dreadful to later generations of viewers is that many of them, especially late in the decade, were intentionally dreadful in the first place, thereby actually increasing their appeal to teenage audiences, who, according to Mark Jancovich, identified with "the ludicrousness and artificial aspects of these films." Jancovich notes in this regard that many critics have praised the films of Roger Corman in this regard, because they are "so clearly self-conscious and self-parodic" (201). In this sense, Corman's films of the late 1950s are among the most clearly postmodernist of the science fiction films of the decade.

Jancovich further notes that young audiences in the late 1950s, plagued by a self-conscious sense of alienation, often identified with the "pathetic and monstrous outsiders" who were central characters in the films (201). But 1950s science fiction films may now strike us as even more ludicrous because they were so centrally situated within the concerns of the decade and thus now appear dated. For example, the early classic *Donovan's Brain* (1953) features the typical scientist who doesn't know when to quit, leading him into experiments that result in his mind being taken over by the brain of a dead millionaire (the scientist, treading where no man should, is keeping the brain alive in an aquarium after the millionaire's death). Thus, the film addresses the decade's fear of both science run amok and mind control, though the mind control is performed by an evil capitalist (who hopes to "dominate the international financial scene" through his newfound powers of mind control), rather than an evil communist. But, from the perspective of nearly a half-century later, *Donovan's Brain*, a serious film in 1953, seems approximately as ridiculous as *The Brain That Wouldn't Die* (1963), made a decade later and with considerable tongue in cheek, as an over-the-top scientist cruises bars and strip joints seeking a suitably voluptuous female body onto which to transplant the preserved head of his fiancée, whose original body was destroyed in an auto accident. He finds the perfect choice (a figure model with a badly scarred face), but then his plans are disrupted when the monster he keeps in his closet gets loose and runs amok.

The anticommunist paranoia that informs so many science fiction films of the 1950s must also surely have seemed more serious as a theme at the time than it does now. One might consider here a film such as Lee

Sholem's *Tobor the Great* (1954), which featured evil communist agents trying to steal our technology (à la the Rosenbergs). Other films, including *Invasion U.S.A.* (1952), *Red Planet Mars* (1952), and *The 27th Day* (1957) overtly thematized the 1950s paranoid fear (and hatred) of communism. Still others were slightly more subtle, combining the decade's fascination with science and technology with a variety of paranoid fears to produce a memorable series of films dealing with space travel, alien invasion, and attacks by exotic monsters, all in ways that managed to address the day-to-day concerns of ordinary Americans, however outlandish their premises.

Given the excitement felt by many Americans in the 1950s over the impending possibility of space travel, films depicting the exploration of outer space were surprisingly rare in the decade. Thus, even a film such as *20 Million Miles to Earth* (1957) is set entirely on earth, despite the title. The paucity of films set in outer space can be attributed to a number of factors, the most important of which are technical and budgetary. In particular, outer-space films required relatively sophisticated special effects in order to appear convincing, in the depiction of either space flight itself or the exploration of foreign worlds. Thus, even when such worlds are explored, they tend to be extremely earthlike, allowing the films to be made with relatively little in the way of special sets or scenery, but also limiting the imagination (and cognitive estrangement) with which filmmakers could depict foreign worlds. Nevertheless, some of the most interesting and important science fiction films of the decade did deal either directly or indirectly with travel to outer space and to other worlds.

One of the earliest of such films was *Destination Moon*, released in 1950. Presented in an almost documentary fashion, the film seriously treats space flight as a practical possibility, supporting its portrayal of a mission to establish a base on the moon with a variety of realistic details, including some surprisingly convincing special effects. As one might expect from a film scripted by Robert A. Heinlein (based on his 1947 novel, *Rocket Ship Galileo*), the film also clearly shows its Cold War context, while strikingly anticipating the coming space race. In particular, the American mission is propelled by the perceived urgency in reaching the moon before some less scrupulous nation (we know which one) can establish a base there.[2] And the success of the American effort is a distinct victory for free-market capitalism, not only over communism, but also over government in general. The mission is a purely private affair, funded and carried out by enlightened capitalists, who in fact are forced to overcome opposition from the United States government in order to complete the mission.

Destination Moon ends with the vaguely utopian message "THIS IS THE END OF THE BEGINNING" displayed on the screen, suggesting that this mission has initiated a new era in human endeavor. In retrospect, the message also announces the way in which the success of the film would usher in the 1950s craze for science fiction films, many of which seemed to go out of their way to reproduce various elements of *Destination Moon*. One film that actually had to go out of its way *not* to resemble that film in too much detail was *Rocketship X-M*, also released in 1950. This film was rushed through production and released slightly before *Destination Moon*, while still attempting to ride on the coattails of the advance publicity of the latter film. This attempt was so blatant that *Rocketship X-M*, originally conceived as a story about a trip to the moon, was reformulated as the story of a trip to Mars after a threatened lawsuit from Pal.

The plot of *Rocketship X-M* reflects this history quite directly. In the film, a rocket is launched for the moon, but veers off course and toward Mars after it encounters a meteor shower in space. Approaching the red planet by accident, the crew decides to land here. While exploring the barren landscape, the earthlings find evidence of a once-advanced civilization, now in ruins, apparently due to a nuclear war. The film was thus among the first to dramatize the potential destruction of an entire civilization by nuclear weaponry, drawing directly upon the nuclear fears of the early Cold War years. The potential biological effects of radiation are indicated in the film as well: the only remaining Martians are a race of deranged caveman-like primitives, driven from the atomic age to the stone age through the effects of radiation-induced mutations. *Rocketship X-M* was thus among the first films to dramatize the notion that atomic radiation might somehow lead to degeneration of the human species to a primitive state. The savage Martians kill two of the earthlings, but the others, led by Colonel Floyd Graham (played by a young Lloyd Bridges), manage to take off and fly back to earth. Then, in one of the most downbeat finishes of all of the science fiction films of the 1950s, their rocket runs out of fuel and crashes on earth, killing everyone on board—but not deterring the scientists on earth from immediately starting construction of Rocketship X-M II.

The special effects in *Rocketship X-M* are not particularly good, but the scenes on Mars (filmed mostly in California's Mojave Desert, at Red Rock Canyon, and using black-and-white film that was later tinted pink) are surprisingly effective at creating the feel of an alien environment. The odd-looking Martian mutants are effectively alien as well, yet not enough to interfere with the warning that we earthlings, but for the grace of God (or wise mediation of the arms race), might soon be in the same boat. In fact, to reinforce this effect, the Martians look very much like mutated humans, not like members of an entirely alien species, producing one of the decade's first ruminations on the similarity of Us and Them in the complicated environment of the modern world (or universe).

Pal's followup to *Destination Moon* was *When Worlds Collide* (1951), based on the 1932 serial novel by Philip Wylie and Edwin Balmer. Perhaps because of its basis in a novel from the early 1930s, *When Worlds Collide* seems less obviously situated in the Cold War than do most science fiction films of the early 1950s. Nevertheless, in this film, the worst fears of the 1950s come true, and the entire earth is destroyed. However, it is destroyed, not by nuclear war or the stupidity of humankind, but by a purely accidental (and highly implausible) collision with a runaway "star." Meanwhile, the film picks up on the space-race theme, though this time the race is against time rather than the Soviets, as a team of scientists scrambles to develop a spacecraft that will allow at least a few humans to escape to the planet Zyra, which is also, rather conveniently, passing near earth at the time. Supported by private funding, mostly acquired from the rather sinister industrialist, Sydney Stanton (John Hoyt), Dr. Cole Hendron (Larry Keating) and his team do in fact develop the ship, which escapes to Zyra, though Hendron (willingly) and Stanton (unwillingly) are forced to stay behind to make room for younger passengers.

Thus, this story of global destruction somehow manages to have a happy ending, assuring audiences that even total destruction cannot keep the indomitable human race down for long. Global calamity or no, the shipload of technologists (plus a cute kid and a pregnant female dog) manages to escape to another planet to begin life anew. Indeed, the dog gives birth to a fine litter of puppies just as the ship lands on Zyra, while the lovers Dave Randall (Richard Derr) and Joyce Hendron (Barbara Rush) are together as well and will no doubt soon produce a litter of their own, thus reinforcing the note of rebirth and renewal with which the film ends. There is even a utopian (if somewhat sinister) suggestion that the outcome is all for the best; these handpicked young, educated, intelligent, clean-cut, white Americans (looking suspiciously like Nazi youth) will no doubt build a better world than the one they left, with its heavy baggage of multiracial riffraff.[3] The message is clear: no matter what happens, American scientific know-how can handle it.

Nevertheless, a film that depicts the destruction of the entire earth could not have seemed entirely reassuring in the context of a 1950s America in which people were already paranoid about the possibility of global destruction. In fact, many of the science fiction films of the era tended to leave nagging questions hanging in the air, despite their generally happy endings. This is true even of the children's film, *Tobor the Great*, which avoids the problem of depicting space exploration altogether, focusing instead on the space race on earth, as the Americans and Soviets struggle to get the upper hand in the Cold War by being the first to reach space. In fact, *Tobor the Great* is really more a spy story than science fiction. In this pre-Sputnik, Rosenberg-era film, the Americans hold the technological edge, of course, while the Russians concentrate primarily on trying to steal American secrets. The Americans, meanwhile, seem to have solved virtually all problems except "the oldest obstacle in the history of mankind: the human factor." In particular, there is still a great deal that is not known about conditions in space, so that the human pilots of the first spacecraft will be in considerable danger. Interestingly, officials of the Civil Interplanetary Flight Commission, the government organization that is heading the research effort, seem perfectly willing to take this risk. However, virtuous scientists Dr. Ralph Harrison (Charles Drake) and Professor Arnold Nordstrom (Taylor Holmes) balk at the prospect of risking human pilots. Harrison, in fact, protests even against experiments with human subjects, noting that "under other forms of government, men are deliberately killed or crippled every day in experiments like this," but insisting that the Americans should be more respectful of human life.

Those "other forms of government" are, of course, the Soviets. Thus, it comes as no real surprise that, when Nordstrom asks Harrison to help him in his private effort to develop a robot space pilot, the two immediately find themselves besieged by Soviet spies. However, Nordstrom's high-tech security system proves to be too difficult to penetrate, so the evil (but somewhat inept) spies are forced to kidnap Nordstrom and his whiz-kid grandson, Gadge (Billy Chapin), then to try to force the professor to reveal his secrets. Never fear, though. Nordstrom uses a transmitter hidden inside his pen to summon the remarkable robot, Tobor (which, as the film for some reason reminds us repeatedly, is "robot" spelled backward), to the rescue. The spies discover and destroy the transmitter, but young Gadge then takes over, calling the robot through telepathy. Tobor routs the commies, saves the Nordstroms, and then goes on to become the pilot of the first space mission, as we learn from a quick cut to a rocket blasting off with Tobor at the controls. Human pilots are thus spared, though Tobor himself is far more than a machine. Described as a thinking, feeling "sentient being" in his own right, he is "an electronic simulacrum of a man." The film thus asks us to accept the virtual humanity of the lovable robot, but also the fact that he is blasted off into space, very possibly never to return. However sentient he may be, he is different from us, and thus expendable. But then *Tobor the Great*, apparently designed mostly for little boys, does not pretend to tangle with difficult questions. On the other hand, it is particularly telling that a children's film, apparently designed as light entertainment, would be so laced with anti-Soviet propaganda. The word "brainwashing" comes to mind.

Other space exploration films of the era tried for a bit more artistic respectability. Thus, Byron Haskin's *Conquest of Space* (1955), another George Pal production, employs some of the most ambitious special effects in all of 1950s science fiction film to produce one of the decade's most extensive depictions of life in space. Unfortunately, the budget was not quite up to the ambition, and, though some of the film's scenes of life in and around an orbiting space station are impressive, most of the effects are somewhat disappointing. Even more disappointing is the plodding script, which helps to make *Conquest of Space* one of the slowest-moving of all of the science fiction films of the 1950s. In the film, a special international crew (no Russians, of course) trains for a year on the space station, expecting soon to be assigned to fly to the moon aboard a ship that is being constructed at the station. At the last minute, however, the plans are changed, and the mission is redirected to Mars. The crew flies there, experiences difficulties (which they rather easily overcome), then returns to earth, having determined that Mars is, in fact, able to support life and thus is a good candidate for future colonization.

Haskin attempted to spice up this banal plot with humor, introducing characters such as the comically vulgar electronics expert from Brooklyn, Sergeant Jackie Siegle (Phil Foster), a reincarnation of Joe Sweeney (Dick Wesson), the comic Brooklyner of *Destination Moon*. Unfortunately, in *Conquest of Space*, these comic elements are more annoying than amusing. About the only thing that does make the film interesting is the depiction of General Samuel T. Merritt (Walter Brooke), the original builder of the space station and now the mission's commander. On the way to Mars, Merritt is overcome by an attack of religiosity. First, he begins to read the Bible incessantly. Then, he begins to shout religious platitudes, declaring that, according to the Bible, humans were created to people the earth but were never intended to go beyond it. Eventually, Merritt concludes that the mission to Mars is sheer blasphemy, apparently seeing it as similar to the building of the Tower of Babel. Finally, he becomes completely unhinged and attempts to sabotage the mission, resulting in his accidental death in a scuffle with his own son, Captain Barney Merritt (Eric Fleming). The mission is thus saved, and science triumphs over religion.

General Merritt's attitude may reflect genuine concerns of certain religious groups in the 1950s, but he is clearly depicted as insane in the film, which thus becomes one of the few science fiction films of the 1950s that even comes close to a critical treatment of religion by presenting it as an irrational alternative to scientific rationality. More commonly, such films were nervous about science itself. For example, a film such as Fred Wilcox's *Forbidden Planet* (1956) warns against scientific excess, meanwhile basing its plot on Shakespeare's *The Tempest*, thus asking to be taken seriously as art.[4] This film also dispenses with overt anticommunist propaganda, displacing its warnings about the dangers of technology run wild onto the distant planet of Altair and its once mighty rulers, the Krel. The Krel, it seems, were so advanced that they freed themselves of any dependence on machinery, performing whatever tasks that needed to be done through sheer mind-power. Unfortunately, they did not anticipate that this supercharging of their minds would unleash monstrous subconscious forces that would eventually destroy them.

This monsters-from-the-id theme resonates with degeneration-related fear that our worst enemy is our own primitive past. Thus, the source of the monsters unleashed by the Krel is specifically identified as "the murderous primitive" that still lurks within even their ultra-sophisticated minds. More specifically, this particular version of the degeneration motif suggests anxieties over psychoanalysis and the savage forces it might find while poking around too deeply in the primitive recesses of the human mind. The film also draws upon the decade's anti-intellectual concerns by showing the potential pitfalls of too much intellect. Dr. Morbius (Walter Pidgeon), the film's Prospero figure, is an earthling philologist, who uses his language skills to decode some of the Krel texts and begin to learn their secrets of mind power. These secrets unleash the monsters that lurk within his unconscious mind, destroying all of the members of the initial expedition to Altair, except Morbius and his daughter Altaira (Anne Francis). They also nearly destroy the earthlings who come to Altair to check on the fate of the earlier mission. Luckily, however, the earthlings escape, along with Altaira, and the remarkable Robby the Robot, constructed by Morbius using Krel technology. Altair is demolished and with it the secret knowledge of the Krels, but the earthlings return to earth with a valuable lesson, summarized by their leader, Commander John Adams (Leslie Nielsen in his pre-*Naked Gun* days), who notes that all this should serve "to remind us that we are not God."

This Frankensteinian lesson about the limitations of scientific inquiry could not, in the 1950s, have failed to suggest to audiences the dangers of the nuclear arms race, however indirectly the film approached that issue. At the same time, the film, by locating the real danger in the primitive mind, is in no way an unequivocal rejection of technology. It is significant, for example, that Robby, probably the film's most memorable technological artifact, is saved from the destruction of Altair. Presumably, he will return to earth to be studied and thus to spur spectacular advances in robot technology.[5] (He would also go on to have something of a show-business career, guest starring in the 1957 film *The Invisible Boy* and in several episodes of *The Twilight Zone*, which also frequently used the spacecraft from *Forbidden Planet* whenever it needed one.)

The most common 1950s film warnings about the dangers of nuclear war were alien invasion films, though even these films sometimes seemed unable to decide whether our most dangerous enemies were Soviets and other foreigners or American society itself. The popularity of alien invasion films in the 1950s was no doubt due partly to the fact that such films could be set in a perfectly normal earth environment, thus saving the expense and technical difficulty of depicting alien settings. But the popularity of such films was no doubt also due in great measure to the embattled sense that many Americans felt during the decade. Given their embeddedness in the concerns of the 1950s, it is probably not surprising that many of these films often now seem a bit bizarre. Perhaps the weirdest of all such films was Harry Horner's *Red Planet Mars*, in which the earth is metaphorically invaded and taken over by Martians, who are led by no less than Jesus Christ himself. One of the worst and most implausible films of the decade, *Red Planet Mars* is (accurately) described by Bill Warren as "one of the most preposterous films of all time" and as interesting only for its very weirdness, because it is "so far the only hysterically anticommunist religious science fiction picture" (I, 87).[6]

In the film, American scientists, using technology first developed by a Nazi superscientist, apparently make contact with Mars, learning that an extremely advanced civilization has established a utopia there via advanced technology. This technology, in fact, makes earth's technology seem obsolete, a fact that immediately leads to the collapse of the world's capitalist economies, while the evil Soviets look on and gloat. Then, suddenly, the Martian messages turn spiritual, announcing that the real secret to their success has been their faith in God and their adherence to the message of Christ. This announcement triggers a global outburst of religious hysteria, though the film does not really explain why most of the earth's inhabitants, who are not Christians, would be so enthusiastic over this announcement, which seems to derive directly from the Sermon on the Mount. In fact, most earthlings unaccountably conclude that the messages are coming from Christ himself, and the film takes it for granted that the earth's population, even the non-Christian majority, would immediately and unequivocally accept the bizarre notion that Christ is alive and well and living on Mars. Russian peasants return to religion with a particular vengeance, despite the scenes of pure Cold War propaganda in which dozens of them are mowed down by Soviet machine guns as they kneel to pray. In fact, they manage to overturn the Soviet government and to install the patriarch of the Russian Orthodox church as the new leader of the Russian government, a fact that is treated as a positive movement toward world peace in the film, which apparently does not know very much about the Russian Orthodox Church or its contempt for the West.

In fact, the world seems headed for a new era of Christian utopia, led by the president of the United States (Willis Bouchey, who looks a lot like Eisenhower, even though the film was made during the Truman administration). There is no hint, of course, that such a development might be greeted by the majority of the world's inhabitants as decidedly dystopian, nor is there any explanation of how the world is going to recover from the economic collapse that has just been triggered by the "Christian" messages from Mars. Indeed, by this point, the film has completely forgotten (and therefore does not explore the implications of) the fact that the wave of religious hysteria that it depicts so positively has already destroyed, not only communism, but capitalism as well.

Then, the plot thickens. Franz Calder (Herbert Berghof), the original Nazi superscientist, suddenly appears in the laboratory of Chris Cronyn (Peter Graves), the virtuous American scientist who has used Calder's "hydrogen valve" to construct a device for communicating with Mars.[7] Calder announces that the first messages from Mars were actually hoaxes perpetrated by himself in order to cause the collapse of the Western economies. Calder, however, admits that he did not send the later religious messages, but then Cronyn offers the intriguing theory (never followed up in the film) that these might have been fabricated by the U.S. government. Whatever the source of those messages, Calder realizes that his revelation of the original hoaxes will cast doubt on the later messages as well, causing the new (Christian) world order to collapse overnight. And so much the better, as far as he is concerned—Calder is no fan of Christ. In fact, he admiringly quotes Milton's Satan and announces: "That's my god: Satan. Lucifer is my hero."

Hoax or no hoax, Cronyn and his perfect 1950s wife, Mrs. Cronyn (Andrea King), are determined to keep the new order in place, so their children can live in a safe and happy world. They prepare to blow up the lab with themselves and Calder in it to prevent him from revealing the truth to the public. Then, suddenly, a new message begins to come in, this time presumably really from Mars. Calder shoots the receiving device before the message can be completed, setting off an explosion that destroys the lab and reduces himself and the Cronyns to smithereens. So all is well. The world never finds out about Calder, the Cronyns become worldwide martyrs, and the president goes on the airwaves worldwide, quoting the Bible and cashing in on the new mood of religiosity for all it is worth—like any good demagogue, except that the film treats him as a positive figure.

Invasion U.S.A. is a sort of companion piece to *Red Planet Mars*. Neither film is really science fiction in the usual sense; both are fantasies driven by Cold War-inspired anti-Soviet paranoia. *Invasion U.S.A.* begins as several individuals, including TV newsman Vince Potter (Gerald Mohr) and an attractive woman, Carla (Peggie Castle), hang out in a New York bar. There is also a strange figure in the bar known only as Mr. Ohman (read, omen). Suddenly word comes that the enemy has attacked, and the rest of the film shows evil communist invaders murdering, raping and pillaging their way across the United States, aided by a liberal dose of atomic bombs dropped by their air force. These invaders, though identified in the film as communists, are never specifically identified as Soviets, though the actors playing them occasionally make vague efforts at effecting Russian accents. Actually, the invaders look and sound a lot like German Nazis; indeed much of the film consists of old combat footage from World War II.

In the course of the film, most of the people who had been in the bar are killed as a result of the invasion and of the "bitter struggle against the forces of evil." Meanwhile, romance ludicrously blooms between Carla and Vince, though he is eventually shot down by a fat communist soldier, and Carla has to throw herself out the window to avoid being raped by the same soldier. All is again well, however. As Carla hurtles earthward, the people in the bar suddenly regain consciousness: it has all been a mere illusion produced by Ohman, who has hypnotized everyone in the bar to teach them a lesson about preparedness. They learn the lesson well, and all agree to change their ways, devoting themselves henceforth to preparing Americans for all-out war against communism.

Invasion U.S.A. joins anticommunist films such as *I Was a Communist for the FBI* (1951) and the John Wayne vehicle *Big Jim McLain* (1952) to show the depths to which Hollywood was willing to sink in the early 1950s to demonstrate its ideological orthodoxy in the midst of the communist witch-hunts of the period, which had already identified the film industry as a convenient target. The production of such films would thus be a dark episode in the history of Hollywood, except for the fact that all of them are so incredibly bad that they tend, in retrospect, to do more to discredit anticommunism than to promote it. Of course, we should not forget the hysteria that reigned during the period, producing a climate in which many found these films absolutely convincing. *Invasion U.S.A.*, however, is perhaps the least convincing of the lot, its conception and execution being so silly that one is tempted to wonder if the filmmakers were producing a sly spoof. After all, the film was produced by Albert Zugsmith, who later produced Orson Welles's diabolically clever *Touch of Evil* (1958), a masterpiece of film art masquerading as lurid drivel. But *Invasion U.S.A.* director Alfred E. Green was no Orson Welles, and, alas, the film is probably just what it pretends to be. Even at that, of course, it leaves an awkward question hanging at the end. If the film's hysterical warnings about the dangers of communist aggression turn out to be hallucinations produced by hypnosis, does this really mean that we should take such warnings seriously, or does it mean just the opposite?

Other alien invasion films of the 1950s were a bit more straightforward as works of science fiction. In those films, the invasion clearly comes from the Other, even if the Other is often extremely hard to identify or to distinguish from ourselves. Of course, the alien from outer space was the classic Other of the 1950s, an object of particular fascination among Americans in the decade both because space flight was rapidly becoming a reality and because Americans felt an unprecedented sense of connection with (or vulnerability to) the alien populations of the rest of the world. The earth, surrounded by a potentially threatening universe, became in 1950s science fiction films a consistent metaphor for the United States, surrounded by a potentially threatening world. Emerging from World War II the most powerful and richest people on earth, Americans suddenly found themselves supplanting the British as the central bearers of the banner of Western democracy worldwide. Thus, Americans were confronted not only with the red menace of the Russians (and the opposed red, white, and blue menace of McCarthyism), but with the red and brown and yellow and black menace of all those Third-World hordes who had formerly been held in check by the global power of the British Empire. Little wonder that Americans felt so paranoid in the decade, and little wonder that this paranoia often found expression in films dealing with alien invasions, which so neatly captured the American sense of being surrounding by foreigners who just do not act and think like we do. This phenomenon accounts for the remarkable frequency with which the earth (read America) turns out, in 1950s science fiction films, to be a superb source of resources for alien civilizations (read the Third World, or the jealous Soviets, or both), which often seem poor and desperate, despite their advanced technologies.

In Christian Nyby's *The Thing from Another World* (1951), in many ways a prototype of the alien invasion films, there is at least the suspicion that the eponymous Thing has come to earth to colonize the planet for itself and its fellow vegetable creatures, planning to use the human race as a source of its favorite plant food, blood.[8] Given that the Thing is not even a member of the animal kingdom (it is described at one point in the film as "some form of super carrot"), it would seem to be an extremely alien Other.[9] On the other hand, it is actually one of the most humanoid of the space creatures of the 1950s; it looks a lot, in fact, like James Arness, who plays the Thing in his pre-*Gunsmoke* days. But the rather silly appearance of the Thing itself may be the least impressive thing about this film, one of the most respected science fiction films of this or any decade.[10]

The Thing is powerful, highly intelligent, and literally bloodthirsty. And it is especially dangerous because it belongs to a plant species that is able to multiply rapidly. As the film begins, the Thing crash-lands its flying saucer near the North Pole and is taken into captivity by the Air Force men who are dispatched to the area to check out the situation. They take it, frozen in a chunk of ice, back to a nearby scientific base, where they accidentally allow it to thaw out and escape. The first thing it does after gaining its freedom is take over the base greenhouse, in which it begins to raise lots of little Things, picking off the base personnel one by one in order to use their blood to feed the babies. The personnel are thus forced to defend themselves, luring the Thing into an electrical trap and zapping it into vapor, after which they burn the babies, ending the alien threat.

If the Thing is thus defeated fairly easily, it is also the case that the most important and interesting battle in the film is not that between the Thing and the humans, but the squabbles that erupt among the humans concerning the proper way to deal with the Thing. In this sense, the primary opposition is between Captain Patrick Hendry (Kenneth Tobey), leader of the air force contingent, and Dr. Arthur Carrington (Robert Cornthwaite), a famous scientist (described as "the fellow who was at Bikini"), who heads the research team at the base. Carrington wants to preserve the creature at all costs, seeing it as an unprecedented source of scientific knowledge. Moreover, he also admires the creature, seeing it as the ideal advanced being, on the assumption (never really explained in the film) that, as a vegetable, it must operate on pure logic, with no interference from human emotions, especially sexual ones. Carrington concludes that the Thing and its civilization have been able to develop flying saucers because they have evolved further than emotional humans ever could. "Its development," Carrington proclaims, "was not handicapped by emotional or sexual factors."

Hendry serves as a counterpoint to Carrington because of his human compassion for his men and because of his own strongly sexual feelings for Nikki Nicholson (Margaret Sheridan), Carrington's beautiful secretary. But Hendry and Carrington are not shown as opposed extremes. On the contrary, Hendry is presented as a figure of moderation. As an air force officer he is devoted to his duty. When he refuses to allow a journalist who accompanies the expedition to report the existence of the Thing, despite its potential importance to the world, Hendry replies, "I'm not working for the world. I'm working for the Air Force." Yet Hendry is not so devoted to his duties that he is inflexible. In fact, he disobeys direct orders from the top when he decides to kill the Thing at all costs, thus saving the human race. Carrington, on the other hand, is the ultimate extremist. So devoted to science and reason that he becomes entirely unreasonable, he repeatedly endangers all the humans on the base (and perhaps on the planet) through his sympathetic treatment of the Thing.

If the film thus makes clear its preference for Hendry over Carrington, the precise implications of that preference may be less clear. Numerous commentators have noted that Carrington, in some scenes, wears a Russian-style fur hat, thus associating the logic-loving villain of the piece with the evil Soviets. In a broader sense, Biskind concludes that *The Thing from Another World*, in its positive depiction of Hendry and negative depiction of Carrington, is a conservative, individualist film, critical not only of the cold rationalism of Carrington's science, but also of the military bureaucracy that Hendry must defy in order to defeat the Thing. At the same time, he argues that the Thing itself is far more complex in its signification than it first appears. On the one hand, it, like Carrington, is a force aligned with heartless rationality and the communism of which that rationality is supposedly characteristic. On the other hand, it represents an assault of nature on culture, as well as suggesting the possible consequences of uncontrolled desire: "Although the blood-sucking carrot from another world is a head-over heart veggie Red monster from the superego one minute, it is an extremist heart-over-head monster from the id the next" (Biskind 135). In short, the Thing seems simultaneously to embody the threat posed to America by both the ultra-scientific Soviet Union and the irrational hordes of the Third World.

Jancovich, on the other hand, challenges Biskind's reading of *The Thing from Another World* as conservative, seeing the film as a complaint against the growing rationalization of American society that is in many ways reminiscent of the work of 1950s leftist thinkers such as Dwight MacDonald and C. Wright Mills (34–41). I think Jancovich oversimplifies Biskind's argument, which is not as thoroughly opposed to his own as he seems to think. Nevertheless, such debates, plus Biskind's own description of the complexity of the film's system of signification, suggest the multiple meanings that tend to emanate from the science fiction films of the 1950s, however simplistic many of those films might appear at first glance. Part of this complexity might be generic, arising from the doubleness I have noted. But the science fiction films of the 1950s are *particularly* multiple and ambivalent in their production of meaning, perhaps due to the fundamental (early postmodern) ambivalence of American society toward so many issues in that decade.

Still, if the monster of *The Thing from Another World* is more complex than it first appears, it is clear that it is *bad*. The same goes for the Martians of the much-admired *Invaders from Mars* (1953), even though there is a vague suggestion that the invasion of that film is really a defensive measure designed as a preemptive strike against the U.S. space program to prevent the earthlings from reaching Mars. The focus here is on young David Maclean (Jimmy Hunt), whose youthful innocence helps to identify the earthlings as the good guys, opposed to the ultra-sophisticated (and thus evil) Martians.[11] In the film, young David sees the Martian saucer land, but can get no one to believe him when he reports the landing, especially as the saucer has taken refuge underground, doing its work there by sucking anyone who approaches down through the sand that covers it. Then David watches in horror as his parents, two policemen, and various other adult authority figures turn into robot-like zombies, controlled by the Martians. David thus becomes the prototype of the alienated individual, all alone in his knowledge of an alien invasion, crying out fruitless warnings to an unheeding world.

Such figures would, of course, become central to the alien invasion films of the 1950s. But, as a child, David is particularly vulnerable, and his situation appears especially terrifying. Science fiction film was also quick to realize that aliens who can disguise themselves as humans were particularly terrifying as well. As Vivian Sobchack notes, the traditional defamiliarization effect associated with the depiction of aliens in such films becomes particularly "devastating and disturbing" when the difference between the aliens and humans is extremely small (121). Of course, this was particularly true in the 1950s, when America's most frightening enemies were communists, who did not necessarily look any different from "normal" Americans and who, according to such sources as Senator Joseph McCarthy, had already infiltrated American society to an astounding extent.

Fortunately, David's isolation, however terrifying, is relatively short-lived. He discovers rather early on two adult authority figures, medical doctor Pat Blake (Helena Carter) and astronomer Stuart Kelston (Arthur Franz), who accept his story with surprising ease. Kelston's credibility is especially high, and he has no trouble getting the military to accept his warnings, even though General Mayberry (William Forrest), the highest ranking officer in the area, has been taken over by the Martians. From this point on, *Invaders from Mars* is a relatively straightforward combat film. The invaders and their human robots attempt to blow up the local rocket plant and, along with it, a new advanced rocket that is capable of reaching Mars. The military responds by surrounding the landing site with tanks and artillery; soldiers then invade the system of underground tunnels in which the Martians have taken refuge by digging their way through the earth with "some kind of ray." The medical authorities cooperate as well, quickly discovering that the affected locals are being controlled by electronic devices implanted in their brains by the aliens. After a few close calls and tense moments, the army, led by Colonel Fielding (Morris Ankrum), manages to plant a "demolition charge" in the Martian saucer, at the same time rescuing David and Dr. Blake, who have just been taken captive. As the saucer attempts to take off, it explodes into smithereens, awaking David, who, it turns out, has apparently been dreaming the whole thing. Yet, as the film ends, David looks out the window and sees still another saucer landing off in the distance.

Invaders from Mars, with its vision of high police and military officials taken over by alien mind control devices, would seem to participate in a particularly obvious way in the McCarthyite paranoia of the early 1950s. Thus, David Seed finds this film the "most politically explicit" of the alien "conspiracy" films of the period, relating the mind control motif to contemporary revelations over the supposed brainwashing of Korean POWs by their communist captors (133).[12] In some ways, however, the film, directed by art designer William Cameron Menzies, puts more emphasis on style than substance, and its set designs are probably the most impressive thing about it. Further, the film, described by Warren as a "cockeyed classic," does not seem entirely sure of its own ideology (1,

116). For one thing, in opposition to McCarthy's charges against the U.S. Army, most of the police and military in the film are perfectly reliable, and they deal with the emergency in good order, so that the film ultimately seems reassuring in its representation of authority. Scientists and intellectuals, such as Kelston and Blake, also come off relatively well. However, the film's famous Martian can himself be taken as a figure of the period's anxiety over intellectuals. The head Martian (literally) is a metallic-looking creature that is essentially all brain, living in a glass globe, waving its weird tentacles, and controlling, through telepathy, a troop of drone-like mutant slaves, who do all of its physical work. Described as the ultimate product of evolution, this Martian thus becomes a figure of the dangers of excessive intellectual development, which threatens to produce super brains who might lose touch with their true humanity, then heartlessly take over and control the rest of us.

Brains, in fact, seem to have been regarded as especially sinister throughout the long 1950s, from *Donovan's Brain* to the intentionally campy *The Brain That Wouldn't Die*, which does not actually feature a brain per se, but tries, with its somewhat misleading title, to cash in on the horror appeal of the brain image. Then there was the semi-campy *The Brain from Planet Arous* (1957), in which a sex-crazed criminal alien brain occupies the body of a nuclear scientist (played by John Agar) and attempts to take over the world. The latter film is particularly interesting in the doubleness in its presentation of the criminal brain, which recalls the Thing in the way that it wields the power of pure intellect, yet is simultaneously driven by animalistic sexual impulses. As the scientist's besieged girlfriend (played by Joyce Meadows) puts it, he seems to have "turned into a regular caveman." The film thus combines fears of advanced intellect with fears of degeneration, recalling the conclusion of Max Nordau that the line between genius and degeneration was a fine one, indeed.

In the same vein, the brainiac alien of *Invaders from Mars*, with its bulging head and atrophied body, physically resembles the genius type as described by Nordau. That alien also symbolically resembles the Martians of Byron Haskin's *The War of the Worlds*, released in the same year. This film, probably the slickest and most technically impressive of all of the science fiction films produced by George Pal during the 1950s, was based on H. G. Wells's classic 1898 novel, but updated and Americanized, reflecting concerns of the early 1950s. In Wells's novel, the Martians are intellectually and technologically advanced, but physically weak, tapping into a number of turn-of-the-century discourses related to anxieties about various forms of degeneration. In particular, Wells's novel is reminiscent of the work of social Darwinist Herbert Spencer, who argued that human societies advance through a process of natural selection analogous to that attributed to plants and animals by Darwin, presumably assuring that society will gradually progress to more and more efficient and sophisticated states. For Spencer, human societies begin as primitive, or "militant," societies that support themselves primarily through conquest and subjugation of their neighbors; however, such societies, if successful, tend to evolve into advanced, or "industrial," societies that support themselves through productive labor and efficient administration.

Unfortunately, in Spencer's vision, industrial societies tend to lack the raw energy and physical vigor of militant societies, implying that societies, as they advance, have a tendency to become decadent and effete.[13] Of course, in Spencer's social Darwinist vision, the evolution of these societies is mirrored in the biological evolution of their citizenry, a fact that Wells drew upon most directly in his depiction of the opposition between the primitive, but strong, Morlocks and the cerebral, but passive and effete, Eloi of *The Time Machine* (1895). But this same Spencerian model also informs Wells's depiction, in *The War of the Worlds*, of Martians who are vastly more advanced than humans intellectually, but so weak that, when they come to earth, they are quickly killed off by germs that are harmless to humans, because of the humans' more primitive resistance to infection. Indeed, their whole reason for coming to colonize earth is that Mars is old and worn out, while earth, as a planet, is younger and more vital.

This degeneration motif, in the updated context of the 1950s, is indicated in the film as well. Of course, in an American context, the film is probably more reminiscent of Orson Welles than H. G. Wells, recalling the 1938 live CBS radio broadcast of Welles's "Mercury Theatre on the Air," a broadcast that many took as an actual news report of an alien invasion, famously causing widespread panic. According to Hadley Cantril's study of this phenomenon, approximately six million people listened to the broadcast; of those, more than a million took it for a serious news report. As a result, the radio broadcast serves, retrospectively, as an anticipation of the anticommunist paranoia of the 1950s, as an announcement of the willingness of the American populace to submit to panic and paranoia in the face of alien assaults.

Meanwhile, Wells's novel also draws upon British fears of the growing military power of Germany, anticipating later American fears of Soviet power and again making the book perfect material for a science fiction film of the 1950s. And the film makes good use of this material, making it one of the most successful of such films, especially in its special effects. In the film, the Martian invaders are quickly opposed by conventional military forces after scientist Clayton Forrester (Gene Barry), a famous "astro- and nuclear physicist," learns of their existence and alerts the authorities, who quickly mobilize. Unfortunately, the Martians prove invulnerable to conventional attack, surrounding their hovercraft with force fields that are impermeable to the bombs and bullets that are launched against them. Desperate, the top American brass order an atomic attack, but the Martians prove impervious even to a bomb that is "ten times more powerful than anything used before." All seems lost, when the Martians suddenly die off due to their lack of resistance to the germs that inhabit earth's atmosphere.

Forrester has no difficulty getting the authorities to believe him, so this film lacks the lone-individual-against-the-establishment motif that informs so many alien invasion films of the period, especially those with the conservative orientation of *The War of the Worlds*. On the other hand, the film does attempt to draw upon the individualist inclination of American film audiences by isolating Forrester in much of the film, taking every opportunity to show him alone, pursued by the invaders. The film also includes the usual romantic subplot, involving Forrester and Sylvia Van Buren (Ann Robinson), a former physics student who did her M.S. thesis on the work of Forrester. However, Sylvia's educational background should not be taken as a sign of the film's progressive attitude toward gender. Despite her scientific background, Sylvia is an entirely conventional female character: weak, helpless, and dependent upon Forrester (whom she idolizes as a hero) for her survival. Granted, Robinson's baleful acting inadvertently contributes to this characterization, but the film openly endorses this view of its lead female character. Thus, despite her training in physics, she now works, for some unexplained reason, as a teacher of the suitably feminine subject of "library science." And when Forrester and a group of soldiers prepare to do battle with the Martians, Sylvia does her part by loyally serving coffee and doughnuts.

Despite its scientist protagonist, *The War of the Worlds* is typical of the early 1950s, not only in its conventional portrayal of gender roles, but also in its expressed fears over the possible drawbacks of scientific advancement. The Martians are far more scientifically advanced than their earthling opponents, but their technology cannot protect them from their own physical weakness. Meanwhile, the earthlings defeat the invaders, not through the use of technology, but through sheer luck (and sheer physical vigor in their resistance to the germs that kill the Martians). What's more, the film asks us to believe that this "luck" was largely a matter of religious faith, the Martians having been destroyed by what is essentially presented as divine intervention. Indeed, the whole film takes on a strongly religious tone at the end as the Martians attack a Los Angeles now peopled only by a few stragglers, who gather in churches, praying for protection, as God presumably favors humans over Martians, despite the suggestion in *Red Planet Mars* the year before that Christ himself is a Martian. Forrester, having become separated from Sylvia, finally locates her in one of these churches, where they embrace, preparing to die as the Martians approach. Science has failed, and Forrester can protect

Sylvia no more, his helplessness signaled in the film by the fact that he has lost his glasses in an altercation with looters. Then, with perfect timing, the Martian craft, having made the mistake of attacking churches (thus showing that the Martians are weak spiritually as well as physically), begin to drop from the sky when their pilots succumb to earth's atmospheric bacteria. As the film closes, church bells ring and a chorus sings "amen," while the narrator informs us that the Martians have been killed by "the littlest of things, which God in His wisdom had put upon this earth."[14]

The alien invaders of *This Island Earth* (1955) are overtly identified as scientists, but this film is far more positive in its figuration of science. These aliens, from the besieged planet of Metaluna, have come to earth, not to colonize the planet or to prevent the evolution of earth technology, but to recruit earth scientists to help them develop better sources of nuclear power so they can fight off their enemies on the neighboring planet of Zahgon. We are told that this recruitment is necessary because most of the Metalunan scientists have already been killed in the war, but it is fairly clear that the depiction of the Metalunans picking the brains of American scientists in this film heavily partakes of the same mindset that convinced Americans in the 1950s that the primitive Soviets could not possibly have developed nuclear weapons without somehow stealing the technology from their more advanced American rivals. Nevertheless, the depiction of the Metalunans also partakes of the 1950s ambivalence in attitudes toward the Other. After all, the Metalunans are not really evil, just desperate, and the film hints that the Zahgonians (who are never actually seen in the film) are probably far worse. Though a comparatively high-budget effort, *This Island Earth* contains a number of particularly cheesy-looking visuals, which is one reason why it was the featured object of parody in the 1996 theatrical film version of *Mystery Science Theater 3000*, though the commentary there (the film is described as a "stinky cinematic suppository") makes *This Island Earth* seem a good deal sillier than it really is. In any case, he-man scientist Cal Meacham (Rex Reason) and beautiful female scientist Ruth Adams (Faith Domergue) are able to triumph, escaping from the Metalunans, defeating a bug creature who makes a cameo appearance (presumably to add action and suspense), and returning to earth, where they will no doubt get married and breed several beautiful and intelligent American children.

Scientist Russell Marvin (Hugh Marlowe) and new wife Carol (Joan Taylor) have a similarly bright future at the end of *Earth vs. the Flying Saucers* (1956), but only after helping to mobilize the American military-industrial complex to defeat an invasion of aliens, who again do not seem all that evil, other than the fact that they hope to come to earth to live, their own planet having been rendered uninhabitable. But, of course, this in itself is a frightening prospect, just as Americans of the 1950s were widely hostile to the idea of all those Third World masses moving here to take our jobs and use up our resources. So the relatively peaceful aliens are greeted with military force, resulting in an all-out war. The earthlings win, again assuring audiences that good-old American know-how can handle anything the aliens can throw at us, but the film also features some of the most disturbingly paranoid footage in all of the science fiction films of the 1950s. In the decisive battle in which the alien fleet of flying saucers is defeated via a new sonic weapon developed by Marvin and his research team, the aliens also manage practically to level Washington, D.C., destroying such beloved American national treasures as the White House; the Capitol Building; and the Washington, Jefferson, and Lincoln monuments.

If the aliens of *Earth vs. the Flying Saucers* are forced to turn to violence largely because of the belligerence of the earthlings who greet them, there is no such ambivalence in the depiction of the aliens of *Invasion of the Body Snatchers* (1956). In this classic the-aliens-are-already-among-us statement (based on Jack Finney's 1954 novel of the same title but also reminiscent in many ways of Heinlein's *The Puppet Masters*), Dr. Miles Bennell (Kevin McCarthy) returns home to the small California town of Santa Mira after a trip to a medical convention. At first, the once peaceful town seems very much as it has always been, but Miles quickly begins to encounter signs that something sinister and strange is afoot. When numerous local citizens (all of whom, interestingly, are women or children) begin to report that their friends and loved ones have been replaced by impostors, psychiatrist Dan Kaufman assures Miles that they are suffering from an "epidemic" of "mass hysteria." But Miles begins to think otherwise when one of his friends discovers a strange body that seems not to be a corpse, but a sort of blank that has yet to assume its individual identity. Soon the blank body begins to assume the characteristics of the friend, and Miles realizes that the local citizens really are being replaced.

The film features the usual romantic subplot, in this case the renewal of a former courtship between the divorced Miles and his old girlfriend, Becky Driscoll (Dana Wynter), who has just returned to town after her own divorce. When Miles realizes that the replacements are real, he rushes off to the home of Becky, whose father has been acting strangely. He discovers another blank body in the basement, this one beginning to assume the identity of Becky. He rushes to her bed and carries her out of the house to his car and drives her back to his home. Through most of the rest of the film, Miles and Becky struggle to escape from the town so that they can go for help, meanwhile watching everyone in town, especially the town's authority figures, gradually being replaced. In the process, Miles and Becky learn that the replacement bodies are being grown from seed pods that originate from seeds that have blown in from outer space.

Surrounded by an army of emotionless replacements, Miles and Becky become images of remarkable individuals who fight to maintain their own distinctive identities and their ability to experience human emotion. Scenes in which masses of townspeople pursue the two lone surviving individuals make the film's privileging of the individual over the community quite clear. Eventually, even Becky is replaced, leaving Miles as a lone (and alienated) Jeremiah, crying out in the California desert. He finally manages to escape to a neighboring town, where he is initially thought insane and hospitalized. Indeed, director Don Siegel originally envisioned the film ending with Miles's warnings still being ignored, so that he turns to the audience and warns them they will be next. However, the studio insisted on tacking on a more upbeat ending, so, as the released version of the film comes to a close, an accident victim is brought into the hospital, having been struck by a truck containing giant seed pods. The psychiatrist who has been interviewing Miles suddenly realizes that Miles's story is authentic. He quickly calls the federal and state authorities, who send out an urgent alert that will presumably lead to the defeat of the pod people. The ending is thus doubly reassuring in that it allows Us to overcome Them, while at the same time identifying such sometimes suspect figures as psychiatrists, the military, and the federal government as the principal agents of that victory.

But *Invasion of the Body Snatchers* is ultimately more troubling than reassuring. The replacements, who look the same as everyone else, but feel no emotion and have no individuality, directly echo the era's most prevalent stereotypes about communists. Thus, the repeated assurances given Miles by the replacements that his life will be far more pleasant if he simply goes along with the crowd and learns to live without emotion can be taken as echoes of the supposed seductions offered by communist utopianism. On the other hand, the film also draws upon the decade's more general concern about the difficulty of telling the difference between Us and Them. It demonstrates a typical 1950s doubleness by offering multiple interpretations of the significance of the pod people. Thus, the obvious interpretation that the pod people represent communism is certainly available. But it is also perfectly consistent with the content of the film to read the interchangeable pod people as representative of conformist forces within American society itself. Biskind, in fact, concludes that the film is ultimately a right-wing assault on the political center that largely uses its apparent attacks on communism as cover to avoid being labeled as extremist. The film's critique of an enforced placidity, in which the emotional aberrations of individuals have been suppressed, can also be taken as a critique of the era's fascination with psychoanalysis and other forms of psychotherapy, especially given that Kaufman, the evil Jewish psychiatrist, is one of the leaders of the pod people.

Hendershot describes Gene Fowler's *I Married a Monster from Outer Space* (1958) as a "feminine analogue" of *Invasion of the Body Snatchers* (56). Indeed, Fowler's film is very much like Siegel's, but with the genders often reversed. These two films together thus represent not only the extent of 1950s paranoia about unrecognizable aliens, but also the extent to which anxieties over gender roles were central to the decade. In fact, science fiction films often address such anxieties. Thus, one of the reasons Jancovich finds *The Thing* more progressive than many critics do is that he feels Nikki Nicholson is an interesting character, who "embodies both masculine and feminine virtues" (40). Of course, in the context of the 1950s, Nikki's "masculinity" might have seemed a bit threatening to many — except that she really plays an entirely secondary role in the film, not only taking a back seat to Hendry in the battle against the Thing, but showing an almost reverential respect (and maybe even a bit of sexual desire) for her imposing boss, Carrington. Her main contributions lie in bringing coffee to the men (though they do not usually seem to want it) and in the fact that she provides the clue to the use of heat to kill the Thing when she suggests, drawing upon her womanly experience in the kitchen, that the best way to deal with an unruly vegetable is to boil it.

Anxieties over gender roles are also at the center of *I Married a Monster from Outer Space*, which directly addresses a number of concerns surrounding the centrality of marriage and family to American life in the 1950s. In this film, aliens from the "Andromeda constellation" are scouring the universe trying to find females with whom they can mate in order to preserve their species, all of their own females (presumably being weaker than males) having been killed when their sun became unstable. Thus, *I Married a Monster* would, at first glance, appear to be a relatively simple alien invasion film, just another story of Others coming to America to take our stuff. In this case, the stuff in question is our women, who are thereby treated as just another valuable commodity that we need to protect from outsiders. Meanwhile, this motif surely partakes of the common racist fear among white American men in the 1950s that non-white men were uncontrollably attracted to white women (and perhaps even had the primitive sexual power to ensure that white women, having gone black, would never go back).[15] At the same time, this film also draws on the fear of American women of being enclosed in the domestic sphere while their husbands went out into the world of the military-industrial complex, doing mysterious things that clearly made their lives fundamentally different from those of the wives.[16]

I Married a Monster is one of a number of alien invasion films from the 1950s in which the aliens are particularly problematic because they can assume human shape, making Them indistinguishable from Us. In this case, the aliens pursue their quest by duplicating the bodies of human men, producing replicants that then replace these men in their relationships with human women. Unfortunately, these replicants have not yet been able successfully to breed with human women, but their scientists are hard at work on that little problem in genetics. Meanwhile, the aliens replace most of the male inhabitants of the small town of Norrisville and seem well on their way to a successful colonization of the earth. However, as is usually the case in such invasion films, a lone human, in this case Marge Farrell (Gloria Talbott), learns of their scheme and tries to warn the town. After more than a year of marriage to her husband, Bill (Tom Tryon), Marge finally discovers that his weird behavior comes from the fact that he has been replaced by an alien. But, when she tries to warn the town, she finds that her cries fall on deaf ears: the locals think she's nuts—except for the ones who are already aliens themselves. Finally, the town doctor (played by Ken Lynch) heeds her warning. He then comes up with the idea of recruiting all the new fathers from the local maternity ward to help him fight the aliens, on the theory that these fathers must be human or they would not have been able to impregnate their wives. Luckily, there seems to have been a lot of recent births for such a small town, so the doctor is able to round up a sizeable posse, go to the alien ship, and liberate the original human bodies, which are stored there, hooked up to electrical devices that power the substitutes. When these devices are disconnected, the substitutes dissolve into goo, but not before they warn their fleet not to mess with earth people. As the film ends, the fleet is shown in space, heading elsewhere.

In many ways, *I Married a Monster* is one of the most representative science fiction films of the 1950s. As in *The Thing*, the aliens are completely lacking in emotion: they are interested in human females strictly as breeding stock, which is, apparently, the way they had regarded their own women back home. This lack of emotion again recalls 1950s depictions of communists, who are thus vaguely implicated in this threat of alien subversion. However, this film stands out in its particular focus on gender issues and in its special horror at the notion that our women might be having sex with aliens. It is also unusual in the fact that the lone individual who warns of the alien invasion is a woman, who thereby finds herself aligned against Norrisville's masculine authorities, most of whom are already aliens. Nevertheless, the film, despite its apparent suggestion that you never know when your spouse might be an alien, or a communist, or something similarly sinister, ultimately makes a statement in favor of the conventional nuclear family, symbolized by the fact that the aliens are ultimately routed by a group of responsible males who have recently done their familial duties by producing offspring.

Nevertheless, this film again has its complications, leading John Baxter to conclude that, despite its "unappetizing" title, it is "a work of more than usual brilliance" (142). In particular, the film gains considerable interest from the fact that the aliens, however emotionless they may be and however strange they look when not in human disguise, are actually treated with relative sympathy. There is, after all, a certain poignancy to their plight, a whole fleet of men wandering the universe without women, a whole species on the verge of extinction. This sympathy is particularly clear in the film's treatment of Bill. He starts out as a heartless monster, symbolized by his unromantic treatment of Marge and by the fact that he brutally strangles a puppy that she buys him for their first anniversary. Later, he also kills a cat. As the film proceeds, however, Bill gradually begins to take on human characteristics. It turns out that the human bodies (however poorly designed, as one of the aliens complains) have an effect on their hosts, making them more and more human the longer they stay in human form. Thus, the film comes close to being a sort of allegory of the assimilation of immigrants into America: however many aliens show up, they will eventually be absorbed into the human melting pot, because they will eventually become human themselves. Alternatively, this motif can be read as an allegory of the assimilation of men into marriage. However much they resist and however out of touch with their emotions they may be, they can eventually be domesticated and made into suitable, loving mates, if only their wives will be patient. Thus, Bill, late in the film, begins to understand emotions such as love, and even to fall genuinely in love with Marge, despite the fact that, once she realizes he is an alien, she gives him the cold shoulder and consigns him to the guest room, which is 1950s code for refusing sex. Thus, ironically, the passionless alien Bill experiences love and genuine desire for Marge, while the human Marge, less able to overlook their difference in species, is unable to return the emotion. In short, the easy distinction between humans and aliens begins to break down altogether. Audiences were no doubt meant to feel relief when the aliens were defeated and sent on their way and to be pleased when Marge was reunited with the real Bill. Still, the demise of the alien Bill (who complains, as he dissolves, that he was only just learning to love) is clearly designed to generate a certain amount of pathos.[17]

If *I Married a Monster* differs from *Invasion of the Body Snatchers* in showing some genuine sympathy for its aliens, it is still the case that the two films together constitute a paired set of statements of 1950s paranoia concerning invasion and occupation by a subtle and invisible Other. One might oppose such films to ones, such as *The Thing* or *Them!*, in which the alien invaders are monsters, frightening and destructive, but easily identifiable. If these are the two basic types of 1950s alien-invasion films, Kurt Neumann's *Kronos* (1957) tries to have it both ways. This film really has two separate plot lines, though it attempts (unsuccessfully) to integrate them. In one plot line, an alien intelligence (represented by a sort of energy ball) inhabits the brain of high-ranking scientist Hubbell Eliot (John Emery), controlling his actions. In the other plot line, a huge (more than a hundred-feet-high) mechanical robot (the Kronos of the title, named for one of the Titans of Greek mythology) lands in a spaceship off the coast of Mexico, then moves across the landscape of Mexico and California, absorbing all of the energy resources in its path.

Unfortunately, the plot surrounding Eliot is not well developed. It evokes some of the same fears as alien-possession films such as *Invasion of the Body Snatchers*, but seems much less frightening because there is only one alien energy ball, which cannot multiply. Thus, this motif lacks the usual element of such stories, in which the alien intelligences threaten to propagate rapidly, taking over the whole population. This possession is fairly dangerous because Eliot is in such an influential position, but in point of fact, he does little to damage the earth's defenses against Kronos. Meanwhile, the alien intelligence seems, at times, to be controlling Kronos, but when Eliot finally dies, subsequently killing the alien, the event seems to have little or no effect on the robot.

It is, in fact, only the robot that is interesting in this film. For one thing, the highly schematic design of the robot (two cubes connected by columns, with a dome on top) is surprisingly effective. It allows Kronos to look vaguely anthropomorphic, but nevertheless entirely alien and mechanical. In addition, the energy absorption motif has considerable promise as a theme. As astronomer Leslie Gaskell (Jeff Morrow), aided by his sidekick, Dr. Arnold Culver (George O'Hanlon), and his technician/girlfriend, Vera Hunter (Barbara Lawrence), leads the fight against the invader, he learns that the aliens have come to earth in search of energy resources, having depleted all such resources on their own planet. At first glance, this motif makes the film merely another example of the story of the alien invader who has come to earth to appropriate our resources. In this case, however, the film explicitly warns against such depletion on our own planet, thus becoming one of the few science fiction films of the 1950s with a conservation theme. The film also includes a more subtle antinuclear theme surrounding the robot. In one sequence, the American military attempts to drop a hydrogen bomb on the monster, only to have it simply absorb the energy of the bomb, becoming larger and more powerful than ever. Kronos thus becomes a metaphor for the arms race, in which similar bombs cannot stop other bombs, but merely feed them in an acceleration toward Armageddon.

Some of the special effects involving Kronos are impressive as well, especially for such a low-budget film. Particularly good is the scene of the destruction of the robot after Gaskell devises a method to make it short-circuit and consume itself, converting its mass back into released energy. If we read Kronos as a metaphor for the nuclear arms race, the message seems clear: our best course is to dismantle our nuclear armaments, not to build bigger and more powerful ones. But the film also includes some highly problematic effects, the worst of which are the bizarre early scenes in which Gaskell and his team pick up what is obviously a flying saucer on their observation screen, but insist on identifying the object as an asteroid. The lack of integration of the two plot lines is also a problem, but, overall, the potential thematic richness of the plot line surrounding the robot makes the film worth watching and pondering.

The same can also be said for *The Man from Planet X* (1951), directed by the semi-legendary Edgar G. Ulmer, famous for his ability to turn ultra-low-budget films—such as *The Black Cat* (1934) and *Detour* (1945)—into minor classics.[18] However, if most of the alien-invasion films of the 1950s seem to express, and feed on, the decade's paranoia, Ulmer's film can be taken as an anti-paranoia statement. Here, the mysterious Planet X wanders into earth's solar system, propelled by "scientific degravitation" as the inhabitants of the dying planet seek a new home. One of the Planet Xers comes to earth (on a remote Scottish island), encountering paranoia and hostility, despite his seemingly peaceful intentions, though the film leaves open the question of whether a large-scale immigration from Planet X would be good or bad for earth. Unfortunately, the man from Planet X encounters violent opposition and is eventually blown to smithereens by the British military. The approaching planet then veers away and decides to give earth a wide berth. Meanwhile, this seemingly rather typical alien-invasion plot is enhanced by the atmosphere and look of the film, which features continual scenes of fog and darkness on the Scottish moors. Indeed, the film looks more like a gothic horror movie than science fiction, leading Warren to call it "the first science fiction gothic horror film" (1, 42).

In a somewhat similar way, the aliens of *It Came from Outer Space* (1953) are dangerous to us only because we are insufficiently advanced (and too paranoid) to be able to understand them. Here, however, the aliens are somewhat better able to defend themselves. When their flying saucer crash-lands on earth (purely by accident, with no intention of conquest or colonization), they quickly set out to repair their ship and get on with their travels. Unfortunately, their landing is spotted by writer John Putnam (Richard Carlson), a free spirit who lives alone out in the desert and is thus the perfect candidate for the film's image of the lone alienated individual. Putnam, up to this point, seems to play much the same role as Miles Bennell; he tries to warn the nearby small town of Sand Rock, Arizona, that the aliens have landed. At first, the super-conformist townspeople (who, we are told, are afraid of anything they do not understand, including outsiders like Putnam) merely think he's crazy. Then, townspeople begin to disappear, only to reappear as zombie-like replicas. Putnam, however, learns that the aliens mean no harm, that they intend to restore the original earthlings once they are finished with the repairs on their ship, and that they have only assumed human form out of fear that their strange appearance (which is only hinted at in fleeting shots) will frighten the xenophobic earthlings.

They're right, of course. Now that the townspeople have been aroused, Putnam is unable to convince them that the aliens mean well. The locals quickly become a mob, reminiscent of the murderous mob of peasants that pursues the hapless monster in the original *Frankenstein* film, then go out to the abandoned mine in which the aliens are repairing their craft. Luckily, Putnam is able to delay the mob just long enough to allow the aliens to complete their repairs and blast off back into space. Putnam, however, warns (or maybe promises) the townspeople that the aliens will no doubt return some day, but only after earthlings have evolved far enough to be able to greet them properly.

This suggestion that earthlings have a bit to go before they can achieve the sophistication of the most advanced alien civilizations is taken even further in Jack Arnold's *The Day the Earth Stood Still* (1951), an early Cold War film that is essentially a plea for global peace and understanding. As such, the film was rather daring for its time. Not only does it suggest that we had better learn to get along with the Soviets, but it does so by making reference to a number of contemporary figures and issues, the most obvious of which is its inclusion of an admirable scientist figure, Professor Barnhardt (Sam Jaffe), who is quite transparently based on Albert Einstein, at that time a rather controversial figure through his pleas for détente.

Biskind describes *The Day the Earth Stood Still* as "left-wing sci-fi" (150). Indeed, he anticipates the recent work of Alan Wald by arguing that, in the difficult climate of the 1950s, the genre of science fiction provided "freedom for uncompromising left-wing statement" because it was "so thoroughly removed from reality" (159). That may be a bit of a stretch. Biskind is surely right that *The Day the Earth Stood Still* is left-wing in comparison to films such as *Invasion of the Body Snatchers*, but the film is hardly "uncompromising" in its leftist sympathies.[19] For example, the film is in no way pro-Soviet or procommunist. Jancovich, however, may go too far in seeing the film as an intensely authoritarian film that supports and defends "the scientific-technical rationality of the American state" (42). After all, *The Day the Earth Stood Still* is clearly internationalist and pro-intellectual, which were themselves controversial stances at the time. Not only do Barnhardt and other international intellectuals provide leadership to the earth in the crisis, but the film's alien, Klaatu (Michael Rennie), is himself an intellectual of sorts. There is, however, no suggestion here that Klaatu might be identified with either the Russians or the Americans. Though Klaatu looks reassuringly human, he transcends such human oppositions altogether, making the Cold War look rather petty in the galactic order of things. In fact, in a bit of somewhat hokey symbolism, Klaatu is repeatedly identified in the film, not only as superhuman, but as a figure of Christ, though this time a Christ with the backing of Gort, a giant and seemingly invincible robot.

Unlike all those films that seem determined to assure earthlings of their ultimate superiority over any alien invaders that might come along, *The Day the Earth Stood Still* counsels humility. Klaatu arrives in peace, but is immediately shot down by an American solider. Gort revives him, of course, but the experience merely confirms the original reason for Klaatu's mission: earthlings are so warlike and so irresponsible in their development and use of destructive technologies that they might soon become a threat, not only to themselves, but to the rest of the galaxy. Barnhardt and the intellectuals are willing to listen seriously to Klaatu's message, but, with the exception of Helen Benson (Patricia Neal) and her young son, Bobby (Billy Gray), the hardheaded earthlings, especially those in positions of authority, continue to meet Klaatu's message of peace with stubbornness, stupidity, and violence, just as they had initially greeted Christ.

Eventually, Klaatu is again shot down, then again revived, Christlike, from the dead. This time he's had enough, however. He delivers a final stern warning to the puny earthlings, then flies away into space with Gort. That warning is simple: the earth will be destroyed if it seeks to extend its violent ways beyond earth. Translation: the Americans and the Soviets had better learn to get along or their animosity will eventually destroy the planet. Meanwhile, Klaatu even extends a bit of advice as to how the earth's violent ways might be curbed. His own civilization, he explains, has invented a race of invincible robot supercops (of whom Gort is one), programming those robots to enforce peace by any means necessary.

Technology used irresponsibly can destroy us; technology used wisely can be our salvation. *The Day the Earth Stood Still* thus addresses directly, if ambivalently, many of the decade's anxieties about technology. And that ambivalence perfectly captured the spirit of the time, which generally admired technology and the scientists who enabled it as never before, but which also worried that this technology was becoming so complex that ordinary people could not understand it. As film after film taught us in the 1950s, ordinary people tend to hate and fear anything they do not understand, even if it is actually good for them. To make matters worse, ordinary people felt, in the 1950s, that they were at the mercy of the scientists who did understand the decade's new technology. Meanwhile, a suspicious number of those scientists were foreigners (with funny accents and funny hair) and therefore suspect themselves. *The Day the Earth Stood Still* tries to reassure its audience that those scientists can, in fact, be trusted, and thus still seeks to allay certain basic fears of the decade, despite its sternly cautionary tone.

Other invasion-from-outer-space films were not so cerebral, using the motif merely as an excuse to introduce fairly conventional monsters. The classic case here is the notorious *Plan 9 from Outer Space*, really a vampire-zombie movie, which introduces alien invaders who decide to raise the dead to serve as foot soldiers in their plan to colonize earth, on the premise that living earthlings are just too difficult to deal with. Another well known example of this genre is *The Blob* (1958), in which the eponymous jello-creature rides in on an asteroid and then starts to ingest the inhabitants of the obligatory small town, one by one.[20] The blob bears certain metaphorical resemblances to Cold War visions of communism, creeping along and devouring everything in its path. Such devouring blobs were popular in the international science fiction films of the 1950s, suggesting that they also responded to a general sense of helplessness and of being swallowed up by overwhelming, but nebulous (and perhaps mindless), forces beyond understanding.[21] However, this particular blob has no specific political agenda, so its actions raise social, political, or philosophical issues only in this indirect and figurative sense. The only social issues raised directly by the film have to do with the opposition between protagonist Steve Andrews (Steve McQueen, in his first starring role) and the local authorities. Once again, Andrews is the lone witness to the existence of the invader, and once again he has trouble convincing the local authorities of the authenticity of his claims. In this case, however, the real problem is the generation gap: Andrews is a teenager (though McQueen was twenty-eight at the time and looked at least that), and the police doubt his story on the grounds of his age, suspecting that his report of the blob sighting is a prank.

The Blob is, in many ways, related more closely to teen problem films like *Rebel without a Cause* (1955) than to science fiction films like *The Day the Earth Stood Still*. It thus draws both upon the adult 1950s fear of juvenile delinquents and the juvenile 1950s fear that parents and figures of authority were so compromised by their drive for conformist success that they could not be trusted to do the right thing in a crisis. At the same time, *The Blob* grows out of the recognition by many in the film industry of the 1950s that their best hope for survival in the face of competition from television lay in teenage audiences, who would presumably come out to theaters and drive-ins for dating purposes, even if they could see much of the same fare on television. Independents such as American International Pictures (AIP) were at the forefront of this recognition, producing a variety of low-budget films (many of them in the science fiction and horror genres) that were clearly designed to appeal to teen audiences. Indeed, as Thomas Doherty notes in tracing this turn in American film history, horror movies were a perfect choice for this project, partly because teens, with their rapidly changing and increasingly alien-feeling bodies, had "better reason than most to feel a kinship" with the outcast monsters of such films (146–47). Thus, the "teen" figures in 1950s monster movies were often the monsters themselves, including such overt examples as the central figure in Gene Fowler's *I Was a Teenage Werewolf* (1957), one of AIP's biggest hits. Indeed, the teenage werewolf film (which introduced Michael Landon as the title character and is still a cult favorite) was so successful that it was predictably followed by Herbert Strock's *I Was a Teenage Frankenstein* (1958). The AIP teenage-monster trilogy was then topped off by Strock's *How to Make a Monster* (1958), an intensely self-parodic (and vaguely postmodernist) commentary on such films in general.[22]

The Blob was released by Paramount, rather than one of the low-budget independents, but it is quite self-conscious about its participation in this phenomenon. Thus, one of the film's most memorable scenes involves an attack by the blob, now grown huge, on a theater in which a primarily teenage audience is attending a "Midnight Spook Show" featuring the lurid (and incredibly low-budget, even by 1950s standards) 1955 film, *Daughter of Horror*, an Oedipal generation-gap tale (initially banned by the New York State Board of Censors), in which a teenage girl is assaulted by a monster that looks suspiciously like a cross between a mummified pig and her dead father, whom she helped to kill.[23]

But *The Blob* is a relatively conservative film in which the teenagers are aligned against the monster, not with it. And, while *Rebel without a Cause* treats the gap in values between generations seriously, *The Blob* assures us that there is nothing to fear. The not-all-that-rebellious Andrews is perfectly clean-cut, and he definitely has a cause: he is trying to help save his community (and his best girl). Meanwhile the town parents and police, despite the bitterness of teen-hating Sergeant Jim Bert (John Benson), turn out to be benevolent as well, thanks to the leadership of kindly Lieutenant Dave (Earl Rowe). The local teens and police (and, ultimately, the national military) end up working smoothly together to defeat the monster, which, luckily, is fairly easy to do: all they have to do is freeze it by spraying it with fire extinguishers, then call the air force to fly it up to the North Pole so it will stay frozen. *The Blob* is thus unusually overt in its attempt to allay the fears of its audience, but then it is meant to be a fun film, its real orientation indicated by the hip, upbeat opening theme music. Nevertheless, even this film ends with a giant question mark on the screen as the blob parachutes onto the polar ice cap, thus suggesting a note of possible future danger. After all, even at the North Pole, the blob might not stay frozen forever, as viewers would have known if any of them were old enough to remember *The Beast from 20,000 Fathoms* (1953), in which scientists work with the military to use radiation to destroy a prehistoric rhedosaurus, which had earlier been freed from frozen entrapment in the Arctic ice cap by an atomic bomb test.

   The Blob also resembles films like *The Beast from 20,000 Fathoms* in that it is less an alien invasion film than a straightforward monster movie, the outer space source of its monster being beside the point. Of course, alien invasion films and monster movies were, in the 1950s, closely related and overlapping genres, both growing out of the special anxieties of the decade and each reinforcing the other as cultural phenomena. Nevertheless, home-grown monsters tended to have slightly different implications than monsters who invaded the earth from outer space, so that monster movies deserve to be treated as a separate phenomenon, as will be seen in the next chapter.

4

The Creature from the Cold War: Science Fiction Monster Movies of the Long 1950s

As Carlos Clarens notes in his chapter on the science fiction films of the 1950s, these films show the anxieties of a period when "human annihilation became a possibility when not a certainty" (118). Further, he notes that these anxieties were often played out in attacks of monsters on human beings, especially attacks of monsters from outer space, because "things from other worlds offer unlimited variety as creatures of horror, untied as they are to anthropocentric codes" (122). Clarens is right, of course. However, one might also argue that the large number of science fiction films that featured anthropomorphic monsters of a terrestrial origin demonstrates that some of the fears of the decade arise, not because Americans are afraid of living in a world where everyone is different from them, but because they are afraid it will turn out that all those inhabitants of the dark places of the earth do not, in the final analysis, turn out to be very different from Americans, after all. If this is the case, the huge difference in standard of living between America and the Third World becomes indefensible and the new international division of labor is simply an extension of the exploitative structures of colonialism. Meanwhile, the polar distinction between the United States (as the champion of global liberty) and the Soviet Union (as the champion of global oppression) collapses in a heap.

Radically nonhuman monsters from outer space such as the blob provided especially vivid examples of Otherness, yet one of the important television phenomena of the decade was the reintroduction of the old Universal monster flicks from the 1930s (all featuring anthropomorphic monsters, such as Frankenstein, Dracula, the Mummy) as late-night television fare. Meanwhile, a whole series of remakes and sequels to these films began to come out in the 1950s themselves, the most important of which were produced by the British studio, Hammer Films. Such classically gothic horror films dominated the monster-movie scene in America by the late 1950s. However, as Bill Warren points out, the phenomenal success of *King Kong*, reintroduced in theaters in 1952, helped to trigger a spate of big-monster films in the early- to mid-1950s, films that tended less toward the gothic and more toward science fiction. For example, the giantism of the monsters was typically produced by radiation or some other sort of scientific experiment; or, if the monsters were naturally huge, they tended to live in remote Third-World places that kept them away from civilization, until they were released by human interference, such as nuclear testing.

One of the earliest of these films was Sam Newfield's *Lost Continent* (1951), in which a team of scientists and soldiers goes to a remote Pacific island to try to retrieve some crucial data from an experimental rocket that accidentally crashes there. In many ways, the film is a routine adventure. The scientists and soldiers have to climb a mountain to reach the rocket. At the top of the mountain, they discover a strange prehistoric world, populated by dinosaurs. Though one scientist and one soldier are killed in the process, the team manages to retrieve the data and leave the island, just as it breaks up from volcanic pressures and sinks into the sea. Within this simple plot, however, the film addresses a number of issues. For one thing, it is an early expression of 1950s degeneration fears, particularly fear that nuclear war might somehow trigger a reversion to primitive savagery in human life. Not only is this "lost continent" described as a throwback to prehistoric times, but there are indications that the primitive conditions on the mountaintop are somehow related to the fact that the mountain is filled with what are apparently the world's richest deposits of uranium. Thus, one of the scientists, Michael Rostov (John Hoyt), warns the group that the forces on the island may be similar to those produced by the atom bomb, then goes on to postulate that the very rocket they are seeking (and the nuclear arsenal of which if could eventually be a part) "may have us someday all living back in a world like this one."

Lost Continent also directly expresses the anxieties of the Cold War. For one thing, the retrieval of the data from the rocket is depicted as being crucial because the very existence of the United States might be threatened if unnamed enemies (obviously the Soviets) were to retrieve the information first. For another, Rostov's Russian background becomes a major issue in the film as the military leader of the mission, Major Joe Nolan (Cesar Romero), increasingly suspects, based on no real evidence, that Rostov is really working for the other side. In one crucial scene, Nolan apologizes for his suspicions, having realized that Rostov is, in fact, trustworthy after he rescues the American scientist Phillips (played by Hugh Beaumont, who was featured in several science fiction films before settling into his signature role as Ward Cleaver in 1957). Rostov tells Nolan not to feel badly about his suspicions. "I'm a Russian," he says.

"I'm used to it. Almost my whole life has been a witch-hunt one way or another." Coming in 1951, when the McCarthyite anticommunist (and anti-Soviet) witch-hunts were at their peak, this moment seems stunning, a rare instance of courage in the face of the purges then underway in Hollywood. However, Rostov quickly goes on to suggest that the witch-hunts he means are the ones conducted, first by Hitler, then by Stalin. In fact, he reveals that his wife and unborn baby died in a Stalinist prison camp and that he himself hopes someday to return to Russia to liberate his fellow Russians from communist rule. Don't worry, Nolan tells him, you will, and we'll be right there with you, even if it has to be with nuclear missiles. The potential anti-McCarthy moment thus quickly becomes an anti-Stalinist one, complete with a full-scale endorsement of nuclear aggression against the Soviet Union.

The Beast from 20,000 Fathoms (1953) is another fairly straightforward monster film that nevertheless addresses the nuclear tensions of the early 1950s, while also drawing upon fears that nuclear weapons might somehow activate primitive forces. The giant, germ-infested rhedosaurus of that film has been frozen in the Arctic ice cap for 100 million years, only to be thawed and released when a nearby hydrogen bomb test melts the ice in which it is trapped.[1] The beast of the film was created by Ray Harryhausen, who had earlier assisted Willis O'Brien on the special effects for the 1949 *King Kong* wannabe, *Mighty Joe Young*. *The Beast from 20,000 Fathoms* thus ushered in the career of the greatest special-effects master of 1950s science fiction film. Indeed, the film seems promising, especially as the rhedosaurus is a sort of triple-threat monster, drawing upon the decade's fears of radiation, germs, and all things primitive. And the beast is indeed far more technically impressive than the dinosaurs of *Lost Continent*. Unfortunately, the film itself is rather unimaginative, and it does not really develop any of the issues that are potentially at stake in its premise. The mindless beast, which is not only physically destructive, but also riddled with germs that are infectious to humans, makes its way to Manhattan and starts both wrecking and infecting the city. It therefore must be killed, and scientists and the military work together smoothly to do the deed. There is a certain pathos in the death of the monster amid the flaming wreck of a roller coaster it has been demolishing, but otherwise the creature evokes little sympathy and the film raises few questions, other than the suggestion that we should use a certain caution in nuclear testing.

Of course, it should be pretty obvious that exploding H-bombs at the North Pole is not a good idea. Subsequent warnings about the possible effects of nuclear testing were a bit more subtle, however. For example, *Them!* (1954) warns about tests that are not only thinkable, but have actually occurred. In this film, the Manhattan Project testing of nuclear bombs in the New Mexico desert results in a nest of gigantic, man-eating

ants that seem to threaten the entire nation until they are dispatched by
an alliance of scientists, police, and the military, ultimately reassuring
audiences that the military-industrial complex was there to protect them
from such dangers, even if the dangers had, in fact, been produced by
that complex in the first place.

A similar dynamic operates in *It Came from beneath the Sea* (1955), in
which nuclear tests disturb a gigantic octopus (also created by Harryhausen), driving it out of its normal habitat and to the Pacific coast of the
United States in search of food. The creature is again killed by an alliance
of scientists and the military, who develop a special atomic torpedo,
which explodes in the monster's brain, killing it, but only after it has destroyed the Golden Gate Bridge and ravaged much of San Francisco.
Harryhausen's monster is impressive for the time, but the most interesting thing about *It Came from beneath the Sea* is the romantic triangle that
arises among naval submarine commander Pete Mathews (Kenneth Tobey) and two scientists, the businesslike Professor John Carter (Donald
Curtis) and the sultry Professor Lesley Joyce (Faith Domergue).

Joyce, though she looks a bit young for such status, is identified as the
world's leading marine biologist, which makes her perhaps the most important woman scientist in all of 1950s science fiction film, which usually
restricts women "scientists" to second-class status as graduate students
or technicians. She is also an unusually strong and independent woman,
though she occasionally seems on the verge of melting beneath the onslaught of Mathews's masculine charm. Mathews has never met such a
woman, so Carter has to explain to him that Joyce is one of a "new
breed" of women "who feel they're just as smart and just as courageous
as men—and they are. They don't like to be overprotected. They don't
like to have their initiative taken away."

By the end of the film, Mathews and Carter have proved equally heroic, each at one point saving the other in the battle against the monster.
They also both appear still interested in Joyce, who has similarly acquit-
ted herself well in the battle against the monster. But Joyce remains independent. Though she seems more physically drawn to Mathews (he is
the only one of the two she kisses during the film), she is clearly more intellectually attracted to Carter. Mostly, though, she remains committed to
her work. Thus, when Mathews suggests to her that they might marry
and settle down, she counters with the suggestion that they collaborate
on a book about the giant octopus instead. Then she prepares to go off to
the Red Sea on a scientific expedition with Carter. Mathews, seeming
amazed that she is able to resist his macho magnetism, simply shrugs,
turns to Carter, and says, "Say, doctor, you were right about this new
breed of woman."

It was standard practice to have one beautiful young woman scientist
among the cast of characters in the science fiction films of the 1950s,

though they usually played a secondary role and lacked the firm independence of Lesley Joyce. Still, even this minor gesture suggested a growing destabilization of gender roles in American society. In this sense, it was not just aliens and monsters who were among the mysterious Others of science fiction film, and Pete Mathews was not alone in having a great deal of trouble learning to cope with women in such new roles. Generally, however, these women were safely contained in a romantic relationship by the end of the film, just as the monsters and aliens were generally killed or sent back where they came from.

In *Them!* the female scientist, Dr. Pat Medford (Joan Weldon), is doubly contained. First, she is the daughter of Dr. Harold Medford (Edmund Gwenn), a more prestigious scientist, to whom she serves as a sort of assistant. Second, she becomes the love interest of FBI agent Robert Graham (James Arness), who is attracted enough by her beauty to overcome whatever vague anxieties he feels about her status as a scientist. Meanwhile, even more than the octopus of *It Came from beneath the Sea* or the reptilian (and diseased) rhedosaurus of *The Beast from 20,000 Fathoms*, the ants of *Them!*, as the title indicates, are unremittingly Other, and there is never a suggestion that moviegoers might consider having any sort of sympathy for them. Ants, of course, were an ideal choice for this project. As insects, they seem to have little in common with human beings. As matriarchal insects, they are even more foreign and threatening. And, as highly organized, communal insects whose every activity is orchestrated by central planning, they served as a perfect metaphor for the 1950s fear of regimentation, either communist or capitalist.[2]

In fact, insects were widely used as a symbol of the dehumanizing consequences of life in the 1950s. For example, Bernard Wolfe's *Limbo* (1952), citing Kafka's "The Metamorphosis" as a predecessor text, projects a 1972 nuclear war controlled, not by people, but by machines, while the people themselves feel more and more like insects, because "the insect's life is all compulsion ... propelled by vast impersonal forces, agencies beyond their reach. That's a characteristic of modern life in general" (211).[3] However, within the context of the 1950s, the use of ants as images of regimentation was already double voiced. On the one hand, the ants would seem to provide the perfect metaphor for Soviet communism, at least as represented in the anti-Soviet rhetoric of the decade, which tended to depict the Soviet citizenry as mindless drones, terrorized and/or brainwashed into submission by Stalin and his henchmen.[4] On the other hand, the ants might also be taken as metaphors for the 1950s fear of corporate regimentation, the matriarchal nature of their society in this sense suggesting the fear of the 1950s male of being feminized because of his powerlessness in the face of the large corporate forces that dominated his life.

In this vein, some viewers of *Them!* in the 1950s must have been bothered by the role played by the consortium of soldiers, scientists, policemen, and bureaucrats that mobilizes to seize control of the situation and
defeat the ants. Granted, the chief scientist, Dr. Harold Medford, is presented as a benign figure indeed, seeming throughout most of the film
more like one's favorite comic uncle than a figure of power. But the police and military in the film, roughly represented by the alliance between
federal cop Graham and local cop Sergeant Ben Peterson (James Whitmore), are not quite so unequivocally positive. Granted, they are humanized to an extent, delaying their attack on the ants in the storm drains of
Los Angeles in order to save two children who are trapped in the drains
with the ants. But they show no hesitation in suspending civil liberties in
order to deal with the ants in an unencumbered manner. Realizing that
the ants are in Los Angeles, they quickly declare martial law to prevent
interference from the citizenry, presenting a potential suggestion that,
when faced with a serious outside threat (like, perhaps, Soviet communism), the forces of authority in America were more than willing to dis-
pense with democracy in order to meet the threat. Meanwhile, if this aspect of the film makes its figures of authority look a little like Joseph
McCarthy, other aspects of the film make them look like stereotypical
Stalinist hacks. Attempting to avert a public panic, the authorities carefully suppress news of the existence of the ants through most of the film,
suggesting a willingness to do away with freedom of speech, freedom of
the press, and free flow of information whenever the need arises. In one
scene, an individualistic pilot (Fess Parker) spots one of the queen ants
flying toward Los Angeles and seems anxious to announce his sighting
to the world. In response, the authorities, echoing Cold War rumors
about the Soviet use of mental asylums as political prisons, order the pilot detained in a psychiatric ward in order to keep him quiet, even
though they know perfectly well that he is sane.

Them! seems to address the decade's ambivalence toward Otherness
by repressing it, making the giant ants clearly Other and clearly evil,
even though this repression merely displaces its ambivalence onto the
film's images of authority. The success of *Them!* meanwhile encouraged
other films to use the same big-bugs-created-by-radiation strategy. In
Bert I. Gordon's *Beginning of the End* (1957), ordinary locusts eat some
huge vegetables created by radiation experiments. The locusts in turn
grow huge and soon take over Chicago, which the feds decide to nuke to
get rid of them. Fortunately, this radical bit of pesticide proves unneces-
sary when entomologist Dr. Ed Wainwright (Peter Graves), with the full
cooperation of the authorities, manages to synthesize the sounds that the
locusts use as signals, luring them into Lake Michigan, where they
drown.

Here, the monsters are unequivocally bad and the authorities are un-equivocally good, making for a pretty dull film except for the way in which it addresses the decade's anxieties over experiments with irradi-ated food. After all, it was Wainwright who grew the tainted vegetables in the first place.[5] Meanwhile, in the oddly interesting (because of its To-bacco-Road-meets-Peyton-Place subplot) *Attack of the Giant Leeches* (1960), radiation emanating from atomic rocket tests at Cape Canaveral contaminates a Florida swamp, causing ordinary leeches to grow larger, sprout arms, and generally begin to look a lot like men in cheap plastic leech suits. The leeches begin to suck the blood out of the local white trash, but are quickly dispatched by a charge of dynamite from the local game warden.

In a slight variation on this motif (with bugs replaced by crustaceans), the title creatures of Roger Corman's *Attack of the Crab Monsters* (1957) are made huge (and aggressive) by fallout from American atomic bomb tests in the Pacific. In a film that is far creepier and more campily entertaining than any quick summary can make it sound, these giant crabs also have a form of extrasensory perception, drawing upon the decade's fascination with telepathy and other parapsychological phenomena. In particular, they have the ability to eat people's brains, absorbing their minds and memories, which they can then use to contact other humans telepathi-cally, luring them to their doom. This power, in fact, is so impressive that the crabs (though there are only two of them and one of those is quickly killed) conceive a plan to conquer the world. Luckily the crabs cannot stand electricity, so the last one is quickly zapped, ending the threat.

Other big bugs were produced not by radiation, but by primitive an-tiquity, drawing upon the decade's fear of all things ancient and primi-tive. Thus, the giant bugs of both *The Black Scorpion* (1957) and *The Deadly Mantis* (1957) are primeval creatures released into the present by volcanic eruptions. Both of these films, of course, draw upon the fact that their in-sects have scary reputations even when they are of normal size. Jack Ar-nold's *Tarantula* (1955) draws upon a similar fear. In this film, the mon-ster is again unequivocally evil and the authorities who battle it are un-equivocally competent and good, while the central issue is again radia-tion experiments. This time, however, the film includes other complexi-ties, managing to encapsulate many of the decade's anxieties about, not only radiation, but also degeneration, population growth, the hostility of nature to humankind, the suspicious activities of scientists, and changing gender roles. In *Tarantula*, Leo G. Carroll plays Professor Gerald Deemer, a well-meaning biologist who hopes to use his research to produce new sources of food for the earth's burgeoning population. This project is re-lated to the nuclear fears of the 1950s in that Deemer uses a radioactive isotope to "bind and trigger" his experimental nutrients, which cause normal baby animals to grow abnormally large within a matter of days, or even hours. Moreover, we find out in the course of the film that Deemer began his research while working at Oak Ridge years earlier, which, in the context of the mid-1950s, was meant to indicate to audiences that he had worked on the Manhattan Project. And the entire film is set in the desert Southwest, which could not help but recall the White Sands nuclear tests, as well as allowing the desert itself (which is at one point in the film described as "evil") to stand in for the dangers posed to man by a sometimes inhospitable nature.

The monster of the film is relatively uninteresting: it is merely a tarantula that escapes from Deemer's lab after receiving injections of his nutrient. Loose in the sinister environment of the desert, the spider becomes gigantic and begins to menace the locals, though it is quickly, and rather easily, killed by the air force before it reaches the local town. However, like most Jack Arnold films, this one does have its interesting aspects. It is not for nothing that John Baxter calls Arnold "the great genius of American fantasy film" (116). One thing that is interesting in this case is that the monster is killed by napalm bombs, oddly anticipating the role such bombs would play in the (unsuccessful) attempts of the American military to subdue the combined forces of inhospitable nature and incorrigible natives during the Vietnam War.

What is even more interesting about *Tarantula* is the way its treatment of the science-without-restraint theme resonates with the theme of degeneration. The title creature of *Tarantula* is described as arising from a "primitive world," suggesting the way in which so many film monsters of the 1950s were equated with the primitive. As Biskind notes, in the science fiction films of the 1950s, "the American, European, Asian, or African past is equated with 'primitive,' 'barbarous' nature," while nature itself, as the opposite of civilization, often comes out as sinister in such films as well (108). More importantly, the film's depiction of Deemer and his experiments is largely a reinscription of Robert Louis Stevenson's *The Strange Case of Dr. Jekyll and Mr. Hyde* (1886), the all-time classic of degeneration induced by unbridled scientific inquiry. Thus, Deemer is predictably injected with his own formula (as two of his associates had been before him), then spends the rest of the film gradually degenerating, becoming more and more simian and beastlike. Given that the formula is radioactive (and that Deemer has already been linked to the Manhattan Project in the film), the message is clear: modern science, having unleashed the atom, may also be in danger of unleashing the primitive beast that lies dormant within us all.

Meanwhile, the obligatory romantic subplot of this film seeks to allay fears about changing gender roles by showing us that they need not interfere with normal sexual relations. This subplot features the budding courtship of Matt Hastings (John Agar), the local country doctor, and girl scientist Stephanie Clayton (Mara Corday), whose pursuit of a normally masculine occupation is signaled by the fact that she prefers to be called "Steve." Never fear, though, she is only a graduate student and thus no competition for a world-renowned scientist like Deemer, for whom she works as a lowly lab assistant. Moreover, she is pretty much putty in Hastings's hands, even remaining perfectly sweet tempered when he complains (jokingly, but a bit insecurely) that the advent of women scientists is a logical, but unhealthy, consequence of "our" ill-considered decision to give women the vote. "Steve" behaves in a suitably feminine manner in other ways as well. When Deemer notices that she keeps taking time off from her lab work to go to the beauty parlor, she good-naturedly explains that "science is science, but a girl must get her hair done." She is also suitably feminine when the tarantula finally attacks, falling limply into the arms of the virile Hastings, who comes to the rescue in the nick of time, saving her just as the air force will soon save the town.

Other women in 1950s monster films were not so cooperative. In fact, sometimes women played the role of the monster. One of the most interesting of these films was *The Leech Woman* (1960), partly because the monstrous woman of the title is such a sympathetic figure, more a victim of the male focus on feminine youth and beauty than a true monster. Made to accompany the British Hammer Films import, *The Brides of Dracula*, on double bills, *The Leech Woman* is itself related to the vampire genre, as the title reference to blood-sucking worms indicates. However, the leech metaphor is only vaguely apt, since the title character never actually sucks blood from anyone. In the film, an American endocrinologist, Dr. Paul Talbot (Phillip Terry), travels to darkest Africa with his aging wife, June (Coleen Gray), seeking a legendary potion that can reverse the aging process in women. The potion, as it turns out, consists of two ingredients, both difficult to obtain. One ingredient is derived from the pollen of a rare orchid that grows in an area of Tanganyika inhabited by the savage Nandou tribe. As if that were not enough of an obstacle, the other ingredient is a hormone that can be extracted only from the pineal glands of young men — and only at the expense of killing the men.

Somewhat predictably, the expedition runs into trouble in Africa, and both Talbots, along with their guide, David Garvay (John Van Dreelen), are captured by the Nandous, who, oddly enough, live in a state of primitive savagery in the midst of a Tanganyika that was, at the time, moving rapidly toward independence under the modern and enlightened leadership of Julius Nyere and his leftist Tanganyika African National Union (TANU). In short, the film, like so many Western representations of Africa in the 1950s, ignores historical reality and instead appeals to primitivist stereotypes of the kind that had made so many Tarzan and Jungle Jim movies successful in the American market during the decade. We are mercifully spared the standard scene in which the Africans try to cook the white people in a big pot, but otherwise the film is largely a collection of African-adventure clichés.

While held captive, Garvay and the Talbots learn the secret of the Nandou anti-aging process and even observe as an old Nandou woman is made young again. As a bonus, the process also seems to make women beautiful and irresistible to men. Unfortunately, having learned this secret, the three Americans must now die. First, however, the Nandous agree to make June young so that she can have a few last moments of happiness before her death. To her husband's horror, she chooses him as the sacrificial victim who will supply her with the pineal hormone, thus extracting a measure of revenge for the years of abuse she suffered at his hands as he grew more and more disgusted by her advancing age. The process works, and June becomes young and beautiful. Meanwhile, Garvay just happens to have a case of dynamite with him, which he uses to destroy much of the Nandou village, allowing him and June to escape and head for civilization. On the way, however, she reverts, becoming older than ever; she is thus forced to kill Garvay in order to extract his pineal hormone and again restore her youth.

When June returns to America, she is forced to commit more murders in order repeatedly to restore her youth, which lasts only for a short time between replenishments. Meanwhile, she sets about putting her youth and beauty to good use by seducing her hunky lawyer, Neil Foster (Grant Williams), who believes her to be June's young niece. When Foster's fiancée, Sally Howard (Gloria Talbott), objects, June kills her as well, realizing only later that Sally's death is pointless because the necessary pineal hormone can be extracted only from men. Eventually, the police track June down, and she leaps from a window to her death. On the ground below, we see her body, now horribly withered by age.

Clearly, *The Leech Woman* can be taken as an expression of the threat posed to men by bloodsucking women. On the other hand, June seems a rather sympathetic figure through most of the film, while all of her male victims are extremely unpleasant individuals—one is even attempting to kill and rob her when she kills him instead. Thus, as Vivian Sobchack has argued, the film can be read in different ways. It is a misogynist statement of the dangers posed by demanding women, but it is also a sort of feminist statement, both because June is driven to desire youth by shallow men who want women only for their youth and beauty and because only men serve as sacrificial victims, thus promoting feminine solidarity. Meanwhile, June's motivation is clearly sexual—regardless of whether men are to blame for her leanings, she clearly wants to be young and beautiful mainly in order to be able to enjoy their sexual adoration. In addition, it is impossible to tell, merely by looking, that June is a monster, so she becomes a figure of the sexual threat posed by all women.

Meanwhile, one might see the Nandous as a sort of feminist tribe, as this restoration of feminine youth seems a central part of their culture — and appears to be designed for the pleasure of the women, not the men, who, after all, must provide the pineal hormone. On the other hand, this equation of feminism with the unspeakable rites practiced by savage tribes in darkest Africa is hard to see as a pro-feminist statement. Of course, the equation of primitive savagery and unleashed feminine sexual power is a literary motif that goes back at least as far as Rider Haggard's *She* (1887), which also features an eternally young woman who ages rapidly into death when her African magic runs out. Other 1950s films that draw upon this motif, or at least upon an equation between the feminine and the alien, include such memorable concoctions as *Cat-Women of the Moon* (1953), described by Warren as "alarmingly awful" (1: 105), *The Astounding She-Monster* (1957, featuring an alluring alien woman who, unfortunately, kills any humans she touches), and *Wild Women of Wongo* (1958, focusing on the savage mating practices on a remote island). Perhaps the best known film in this group is the campy cult classic leer-fest, *Queen of Outer Space* (1958), starring Zsa Zsa Gabor and scripted by Charles Beaumont, later the writer of numerous episodes of *The Twilight Zone*, among other things.

If *The Leech Woman* is entirely stereotypical in its treatment of Africa and Africans, such stereotypes were hardly uncommon in science fiction films of the 1950s. Such films often featured monsters or monstrous forces retrieved from Africa or the other dark places of the earth. Further, they tended to equate Africa and other Third World settings with other planets, the inhabitants of both locales being similarly alien to human civilization. For example, in Nathan Juran's *20 Million Miles to Earth* (1957), the stop-action monster created by Ray Harryhausen is fetched back from Venus in a film that is quite transparently based on *King Kong* (1933), who was similarly fetched back from a Pacific island.

Harryhausen's monster lacks Kong's personality, but it is technically one of the best in 1950s film, and *20 Million Miles to Earth* features excellent special effects, producing a number of spectacular scenes of the monster in action. The plot of the film, however, is pretty pedestrian. Soon after arriving on earth (crashing into the sea near Sicily), the creature, referred to by Harryhausen as an "Ymir" (after a giant in Norse mythology), hatches, emerging from its gel-like "egg" looking a lot like a cross between Kong and a dinosaur. It has a long, reptilian tail, but, as a zoologist observes in the film, "the torso is that of a human being." The Ymir thus functions as a sort of missing link between primates and dinosaurs, its humanlike characteristics helping to make it a relatively sympathetic figure.

At first, the creature is quite small and cute as a button, despite its rather alien appearance. It is also harmless and nonaggressive: it eats only sulfur, and will attack only if provoked. Unfortunately, conditions in earth's atmosphere cause the creature to grow rapidly. It escapes from captivity and wanders about the Sicilian countryside looking for sulfur. Predictably, the creature is assaulted several times, causing it to resort to violence, despite its nonviolent nature. As a result, the Italian authorities decide that the creature must be killed, though the virtuous Americans, led by the commander of the original Venus mission, Colonel Robert Calder (William Hopper), insist on trying to capture it instead. They succeed, then take it to Rome for scientific study. Unfortunately, it again escapes. By now, it is big and strong enough to win a wrestling match with an elephant before going on a rampage through Rome. Finally, it is shot from atop the Colosseum (in lieu of the Empire State Building) by tanks and artillery, sending it plunging to its death.

Harryhausen's ability to make such an alien-looking creature seem vaguely cuddly and sympathetic (despite its lack of any real personality) helps the film, however clumsily, to make its point about the human tendency to reject—or, for that matter, kill—anyone or anything that seems different. As Arkansas Senator William Fulbright once complained about American attitudes, reversing the famous declaration of Terence, "Nothing alien is human to us." Many science fiction films of the 1950s address this same topic through the depiction of misunderstood monsters, who mean no harm, but are assaulted by paranoid humans. *20 Million Miles to Earth* moderates the point a bit, however, by making the truly murderous humans Italian, while the American characters are much more compassionate. Indeed, the only truly compassionate Italian is the female lead (i.e., Calder's love interest), medical student Marisa Leonardo (Joan Taylor), who is, incidentally, the only Italian character who does not speak with a really bad Italian accent. She sounds, in fact, entirely American, signaling both her high level of education and her sympathetic nature.

In other films, Americans were the culprits who tormented and killed the hapless monsters. The key figure here is the eponymous creature from the three-film sequence, *The Creature from the Black Lagoon* (1954), *Revenge of the Creature* (1955), and *The Creature Walks among Us* (1956). Clearly reptilian and thus ostensibly just as foreign to the human species as the insects and spiders of *Them!* and *Tarantula*, the creature is nevertheless a biped, essentially humanoid in its overall shape, as is indicated by the tendency of the humans in the films to refer to it as the "Gill Man." It is, in fact, an evolutionary missing link between reptiles and mammals, discovered in the remote Third World setting of the Amazon, where one might expect such primitive beings to live. This evolutionary motif links the creature, like the rhedosaurus of *The Beast from 20,000 Fathoms*, with the degeneration-linked fear of the primitive.

The basic primitive-critter-from-the-Third-World premise of the creature sequence also places those films in the tradition of *King Kong*. More-

over, the creature itself follows very much in the huge footsteps of Kong
in that it is ultimately more sinned against than sinning, so sensitive to
the cruel treatment meted out to it by its human captors that audiences
could not avoid questioning the basic distinction between Us (as sentient,
feeling humans) and Them (as brutish, beastly reptiles). However, the
first film of the sequence, directed by Jack Arnold, is a relatively conventional, if unusually well made, monster flick, in which the creature re-
tains most of its Otherness. The film features the standard monster vs.
team of scientists opposition that was so common in the 1950s. And audiences are clearly meant to root for the team of scientific investigators,
who venture into the deep Amazon jungle in search of fossil evidence of
extinct species, but instead encounter this strange, and deadly, throwback to a species that lived a hundred million years earlier. On the other
hand, it is also clear that the creature was simply minding its own business in its jungle habitat until the scientists came along, so it is not really
all that culpable. Indeed, it kills only five humans in the course of the
film, an extremely small total for 1950s science fiction, which tends to
feature destruction on a planetary scale. And, of those five, four are
South Americans (and thus don't quite count, like all those islanders
stomped and devoured by Kong).

The creature even has its romantic moments, as in its attraction to Kay
Lawrence (Julie Adams), the film's obligatory beautiful young woman
scientist. Thus, when it first looks up from its underwater lair to spot Kay
swimming on the surface of the lagoon (in a scene referenced in 1975 by
Steven Spielberg in the famous signature opening shot of *Jaws*), it is immediately struck by her beauty. Later, when it plucks her off the boat on
which the scientists are traveling and takes her to its secret grotto, it carries her tenderly, in a mode reminiscent of Kong holding Fay Wray.
Luckily, the creature seems to have no genitals, so Kay is spared being
ravished, though it is also clear that the attraction of the creature to her
suggests racist 1950s fears of the sexual inclinations (and sexual power)
of nonwhite men.[6]

Interestingly, the real villain of the film is not the creature, but the
"bad" scientist, Mark Williams (Richard Denning), who is, predictably,
the only white American to be killed by the creature. And, in many ways,
the real conflict of the film is that between Williams and David Reed
(Richard Carlson), the "good" scientist of the film. Reed is interested only
in learning about the world, which he views, in an obvious response to
the 1950s dread of routinization, as a rich and strange place, filled with
wonders we have yet to imagine. Thus, he continually compares out-of-
the-way places like the black lagoon with other planets, tying into the
decade's fascination with the possibility of marvelous discoveries awaiting space travelers by suggesting that similar discoveries are still available right here on earth. Williams, on the other hand, has no such fasci-

nation with the wonders of nature. He is really more of a bureaucrat than a scientist, concerned more with career advancement and with funding for his institute than with any knowledge the institute might gain. Little wonder, then, that he is the villain, representing, as he does, the forces of corporate routinization incarnate.

In the first sequel, also directed by the ubiquitous Arnold, scientists return to the Amazon, this time managing to capture the Gill Man and return him to captivity in "Ocean Harbor Oceanarium," something like Marineland (where many of the scenes were, in fact, filmed). There, scientists study the creature, while crowds of tourists look on. In this installment of the trilogy, sympathy for the creature increases as he is shown chained to the bottom of a tank, repeatedly shocked by a cattle prod as scientists seek to train him. His status as a lone individual, surrounded by strangers who do not understand him is emphasized, particularly when Helen Dobson (Lori Nelson), this film's beautiful young woman scientist tells her professor boyfriend, scientist Clete Ferguson (John Agar again), "I pity him sometimes. He's so alone. The only one of his kind in the world."

In addition, the studies of the scientists show that the Gill Man is far closer, biologically, to humans than they originally suspected. All tests, Ferguson notes, show that he "just misses being human." The Gill Man thus becomes a metaphor for the alienated individual in the modern world, while the chain holding him in place makes him an image of routinization as well. This being the case, there are clear suggestions that the scientists may be overstepping their bounds in treating the Gill Man merely as a laboratory specimen, thus reinforcing the original film's suggestion that there might be some things science just should not probe into. In one scene, Clete tells Helen, "Some things should remain unknown." He is referring to the mysteries of love, but it is also clear that this film seeks to make a statement, in the tradition of *Frankenstein*, that there are limits to the extent to which scientists should try to extend their mastery of the natural world.

Eventually, the Gill Man, always with an eye for the ladies, develops a yen for Helen. He manages to escape from captivity, then to make off with Helen, pursued by a massive police search. At this point, however, the film's sympathy for the creature tends to wane, even though he is shown treating Helen tenderly as he carries her about for no ostensible reason. That he probably has a sexual motivation for the kidnapping (after all, we now know that there appear to be no females of his own species) is left unstated, but seems obvious. Moreover, his plucking of Helen from the arms of Clete resonates with Helen's earlier complaint that, as a woman, she cannot have both a husband and a career in science. The creature thus becomes a metaphor for the dangers that lurk in the workplace for women who wander out of the domestic sphere, while this motif also addresses the converse anxieties of women over the impact on their careers if they try to have a family life.

In the end, the Gill Man is once again apparently killed, and Helen is restored to the arms of Clete, suggesting that family wins out over science. One is clearly meant to expect that Helen, having learned her lesson, will soon give up her scientific aspirations and become Clete's wife, keeping his house and ironing his underwear. He is, after all, a noted professor, while she (like Steve Clayton before her) is merely a graduate student working on her master's thesis. At the most, they will become a team — in which she will serve as Clete's assistant.

This treatment of domesticity takes an interesting turn in John Sherwood's *The Creature Walks among Us* (1956), which again features a noted scientist, Dr. William Barton (Jeff Morrow), this time with a beautiful young wife, Marcia (Leigh Snowden). But Marcia is no scientist, having been married to Barton since she was seventeen and having lived in his shadow ever since. Meanwhile, he seems to be growing increasingly jealous and abusive, not only tyrannizing, but also terrorizing, his young wife. In fact, his treatment of her provides a subplot for the film that helps to identify Barton as the villain of the piece. There is, of course, some potential social commentary in this dramatization of domestic abuse, though the film does not challenge the sanctity of marriage or the American family. Indeed, Barton's abuse of Marcia is clearly identified in the film as an abnormal deviation, and Barton himself is specifically labeled as "disturbed," via the diagnosis of Dr. Thomas Morgan (Rex Reason), who fills the role of the good scientist in this installment.

This third "creature" film returns to some extent to the formula of the first in setting up the structural opposition between the bad (and also mad) scientist, who wants to tinker with nature for his own ends, and the good scientist, who merely wants to learn about nature. As Morgan himself puts it, in an expression of a central perception of the 1950s, the human race is at a crossroads between moving forward to the stars and reverting back to the jungle. He merely wants to help us understand ourselves better so that we can develop our good side (represented by Morgan) and move forward, rather than developing our bad side (represented by Barton) and falling back. Meanwhile, the object of Barton's diabolical experiments is the hapless Gill Man, who, in this episode, is humanized still further — and in more ways than one. As the film begins, Barton and his team of scientists (including Morgan) travel to the Everglades to capture the creature, which has been spotted there. They succeed, though the creature is badly burned in the process. As a result of the burns, the creature's gills are destroyed and his scales fall off. It turns out, however, that he has human skin underneath the scales and a set of lungs that begin to work once the gills are lost.

Thus, the Gill Man emerges from his bandages transformed into a land creature. The once slim and graceful creature also seems to have put on quite a bit of weight, lumbering bulkily about in the tradition of Frankenstein's monster, even as Barton's lack of restraint places him in the tradition of Victor Frankenstein. From this point, Barton works to further the Gill Man's transformation from reptile to human, hoping to gain knowledge that will further his own ambition of modifying the human race so that it will be better suited for the exploration of outer space. As the film proceeds, the opposition between Barton and Morgan is supplemented by the opposition between Barton and the creature, with suggestions that Barton is actually the more savage (and the Gill Man the more human) of the two. The film thus again challenges the easy dichotomy of Us vs. Them, while at the same time continuing the plea for scientific moderation that informed the earlier creature films.

Eventually, the increasingly human Gill Man is put in a pen on Barton's Sausalito ranch and seems to be growing more and more gentle. Even his libido seems to have been curbed: though he occasionally gazes at Marcia tenderly, he never tries to make off with her. Then Barton murders a man he (wrongly) believes to be involved in a dalliance with Marcia and tries to pin the killing on the creature. Enraged, the creature breaks out of his pen, ransacks the Barton house and kills Barton, though leaving Morgan and Marcia untouched. The creature, now clearly an object of pathos, lumbers back to the beach, looks longingly at the water, his former home, then starts forward again, presumably to go into the water, where he will be drowned due to his lack of gills.

If the monster is the definitive Other of 1950s American culture, then the tendency to efface the boundary between humans and monsters in many 1950s films can be taken as a central expression of anxieties over the viability of the kinds of simple polar oppositions that have served as central props for Western culture since the time of the ancient Greeks. Of course, this interrogation of the human/monster boundary is in many ways a time-honored motif of horror fiction, dating back at least to the classics of the nineteenth century. Thus, Frankenstein's monster is made of human parts, Dracula was once human, and Dracula's human victims can become vampires. But the central expression of this motif in nineteenth-century culture is *Dr. Jekyll and Mr. Hyde*, which warns us that we are all part monster and that our inner monsters are always in danger of erupting to the surface.

As with Professor Deemer of *Tarantula*, unrestrained scientific research always threatens, in the science fiction films of the 1950s, to turn humans into monsters. One of the most subtle expressions of the man-as-monster motif in the films of the long 1950s is Edgar G. Ulmer's *The Amazing Transparent Man* (1960). On the surface, this film is banal and clichéd, quite a disappointment from a director famous for his ability to produce interesting films from the most debased (and low-budget) materials. In the film, the megalomaniacal Major Krenner (James Griffith) helps break ace safecracker Joey Faust (Douglas Kennedy) out of prison, then pressures Faust to burgle a high-security facility and steal some "fissionable material" that Krenner needs for his crazed experiments. These experiments are being conducted by Dr. Peter Ulof (Ivan Triesault), a brilliant scientist, who does Krenner's bidding only because Krenner is holding Ulof's young daughter, Maria (Carmel Daniel), hostage. These experiments involve the development of a nuclear-powered invisibility ray that renders humans and animals invisible. Krenner hopes to use the ray, once it is perfected, to create an invisible army with which to conquer the world. Eventually, however, Ulof convinces Faust (who also has a young daughter) that Krenner must be stopped for the good of posterity. In the end, Ulof and Maria escape, while Faust battles Krenner in the lab, causing the fissionable material to ignite in a nuclear explosion that blows up half the county.

Yet the title of *The Amazing Transparent Man* may suggest that we should try to look through these surface layers to see what lies underneath. Indeed, despite this rather unpromising premise, the film is interesting in a number of ways. For one thing, its opposition between Krenner and Ulof produces another variation on the military-versus-science opposition that is often found in 1950s science fiction film. As with most left-leaning versions of this opposition during the decade, science here represents good, but good that is in danger of being perverted by the evils of militarism. In *The Amazing Transparent Man*, however, the implications of the opposition are enriched by the fact that Ulof, during World War II, had been a prisoner in a German concentration camp, where the Nazis forced him to do the experiments that eventually led to the development of the invisibility ray. Ulmer thus draws upon his own anti-Nazi background to make the evil Krenner the direct successor to the Nazis, thereby suggesting that the militarism of the Cold War arms race (in which both sides drew heavily upon German-developed technology) is rooted in the same ruthless quest for power that had driven Hitler and the Nazis to attempt to dominate the world.[7] Meanwhile, the use of the suggestive name Faust serves (perhaps a bit clumsily) to reinforce the German link, while providing allusive support to the notion that some sorts of knowledge are better left unexplored.

If all this were not enough, Ulmer makes the metaphorical link between the invisibility ray and nuclear weapons quite explicit. For one thing, the ray is nuclear powered and eventually produces a nuclear explosion. For another, Ulof, at the end of the film, assumes the role of Oppenheimer and other scientists who warned against the dangers of the nuclear arms race in the 1950s. He explains to an American security agent that he warned Krenner against the danger of the rays, but that

Krenner, with his "deranged mind" (presumably the same deranged mind that informs contemporary militarism, including that of the American variety), refused to be dissuaded. Further, Ulof resists the efforts of the CIA to convince him to help them develop the ray for their own use. He suggests that the ray is simply too dangerous, especially if "it were stolen from us. It has happened before, you know." He then suggests that it might be better to let the secret of the ray die with Krenner and Faust. "It's a serious problem," Ulof says, turning to look into the camera and thus address the audience. "What would you do?"

One of the definitive (and most memorable) science fiction films of the 1950s was *The Incredible Shrinking Man* (1957), based on Richard Matheson's 1956 novel, *The Shrinking Man*. Though it lacks flying saucers, actual monsters, or alien invaders, this film addresses many of the central concerns of 1950s science fiction, as one might expect from a film directed by Jack Arnold. It is, in fact, really two films in one; it breaks neatly into two halves, each approximately 40 minutes in length. In the first segment, protagonist Robert Scott Carey (Grant Williams) is accidentally exposed to a strange, floating, radioactive cloud that causes him to start to shrink, especially after he is subsequently exposed to pesticides. Thus, the film partakes of the 1950s fear of both radioactive and chemical contamination, while focusing on the psychic impact of the shrinkage on Carey, who grows increasingly bitter and withdrawn (even toward his loyal and faithful wife, Louise, played by Randy Stuart) as his decreasing size makes him more and more of a freak. Indeed, this part of the film is a sort of symbolic study in alienation, somewhat along the lines of Kafka's "The Metamorphosis." Reminded that his experience makes him different even from other small people, such as midgets, Carey responds, "Different. That's another way of saying alone, isn't it?"

Of course, Carey's shrinking represents a specific threat to his virility, as the film not so subtly indicates in its various hints that Carey, as he gets smaller and smaller, is unable to fulfill his conjugal obligations to Louise, becoming more a son to her than a husband. Indeed, numerous critics have suggested ways in which this film allegorizes various 1950s anxieties about gender roles.[8] Meanwhile, if the film suggests Carey's masculine fear of being dominated by his wife, it also suggests a very 1950s fear of being overwhelmed by forces larger than oneself, whether those forces involve something as spectacular as fear of being destroyed by a nuclear explosion or something as mundane as fear of loss of individual power and identity through absorption into large corporate entities.

Eventually, Carey becomes so small that even everyday household objects can become dangerous menaces, suggesting the extent to which fear permeated everyday life in the 1950s. The second segment of the film is set into motion when Carey, chased by the family cat, Butch, falls into a box in the basement and is then assumed by Louise to have been eaten by the cat. There is no word on the fate of the cat, but Carey is left alone in the basement to fend for himself in his own new world. From this point on, the film becomes a sort of replay of *Robinson Crusoe*, with Carey demonstrating the resourcefulness that is necessary to become the master of his basement domain. He himself makes the point clear in his voice-over narration: "I resolved that, as man had dominated the world of the sun, so I would dominate my world."

In the end, Carey succeeds, killing a spider that is his only rival for mastery of the basement and thus verifying, as did Defoe's castaway, the amazing capability of the human individual, especially the *male* human individual. Thus, as Hendershot notes, it is not insignificant that, in the novel on which the film is based, Carey reasserts his virility by killing a spider that is specifically identified as a black widow, though this point is not emphasized in the film (87). The second half of the film thus essentially reverses the first, neatly demonstrating the ambivalence of the 1950s. In part 1, Carey is tormented as he becomes more and more alone, an outcast from human society, unable to live up to 1950s ideas of the masculine ideal; in part 2, he triumphs largely because now he is truly alone and able to explore his (masculine) capabilities. The film then tacks on a rather unsatisfying ending that seeks to heal up the rift between these two conflicting tendencies. Continuing to shrink, Carey approaches the infinitesimal, then looks up at the stars and feels that he is being absorbed into the infinite, his ultimate separation from humanity eventually helping to make him at one with the cosmos.

Perhaps following the Swiftian logic of opposing the giant Gulliver in Lilliput to the tiny Gulliver in Brobdingnag (but more likely following the Hollywood logic of trying to cash in on the success of a similar earlier film), *The Incredible Shrinking Man* was quickly followed by Bert I. Gordon's *The Amazing Colossal Man* (1957), in which radiation from a "plutonium bomb" causes Army Colonel (and Korean War hero) Glenn Manning (Glenn Langan) to experience runaway growth, eventually reaching a height of sixty feet. But, if this huge height protects Manning from some of the size-related dangers faced by Carey, it does not save him from becoming an embittered figure of alienation, understandably feeling that he has become a freak and rejecting the attempts of his fiancée, Carol Forrest (Cathy Downs), to stand by him. Indeed, the title comes from Manning's own suggestion that they put him in a circus and bill him as "The Amazing Colossal Man." Meanwhile, all this growth leads to physical problems when Manning's heart grows less rapidly than the rest of him. Not only is Manning thus in mortal danger from the possible failure of his overworked heart, but the resultant poor circulation cuts off the blood supply to his brain and turns him into a deranged monster. As a result, he begins to wreck Las Vegas, leading a policeman to complain to his superior, ordered by the army not to shoot, "Are you going to stand by and let him destroy property?" This may be one of the all-time ludicrous lines of American cinema, but, of course, they do not just stand by, property being sacred in capitalist America. They open fire, and he is driven out of the city. The army eventually trails Manning (carrying Carol in his giant hand) to the Hoover Dam (identified in the film as Boulder Dam, though it was called that only from 1933 to 1947). They convince him to put Carol down, then shoot him off the dam with bazookas, sending him plunging (apparently) to his death, though he would be resurrected in *War of the Colossal Beast*, the unremarkable 1958 sequel.

Like most of Gordon's science fiction efforts from the 1950s, *The Amazing Colossal Man* is plagued by bad writing, bad acting, bad special effects, and an unbelievable premise—yet somehow it turns out to be more interesting than it has any right to be. For one thing, like *Tarantula*, the film taps into the decade's fears that radiation might cause runaway growth or other biological abnormalities. For another, the alienation theme is treated in ways that also resonate with the concerns of the decade. Langan actually turns in a relatively good performance as the tortured soul who feels impossibly abnormal and thus unable to fit in (in this case, quite literally). Moreover, this normal-abnormal dialectic is treated in some interesting ways. At one point, Manning tries to turn the tables, suggesting to a "normal" sergeant that, from his point of view, he, Manning, is really the normal one, while the sergeant is the freak. "I'm not growing," Manning proclaims, "you're shrinking." And this suggestion of the relativity of normality is reinforced when an army scientist assigned to the case develops a device that should be able to return Manning to normal size, producing a miniature camel and elephant to prove the point. The scientist even develops a hilarious gigantic hypodermic needle for use in injecting his serum into Manning. (Of course, Manning, seizes the syringe and uses it as a spear, skewering the scientist.) Thus, science made Manning big and science can make him little—but if size can be that easily modified by technology, what sense does it make to define one size as normal and all others as abnormal? In any case, by the end, Manning has become abnormal mentally as well as physically, so they still have to kill him off, even though they may soon have the technology to shrink him back down.

A similar technology is central to Gordon's 1958 follow-up, *Attack of the Puppet People*, in which a lonely dollmaker, Mr. Franz (John Hoyt), invents a device that allows him to shrink people to the size of dolls, so that he can hold them captive for companionship. The film is thus a variation on the mad scientist theme, even though Mr. Franz is not a scientist, but a former puppeteer, who dropped out of show business after his beloved wife ran away with an acrobat. It is thus not clear how he was able to develop the high-tech device to do the shrinking, unless, of course, he somehow got the idea from the scientists in *The Amazing Colossal Man*. Speaking of which, one of the most interesting moments in *Attack of the Puppet People* occurs when the two young lovers, Bob Westley and Sally Reynolds (John Agar and June Kenny), go to see *The Amazing Colossal Man* at a drive-in. Bob, asked by Sally why he picked this particular film to see, provides a seminal statement of the way in which science fiction films in general provided an escape from routinization. "Oh," he says, "I get tired of the same things all the time."[9]

Of course, this statement gains irony from the fact that Gordon's films tended to be so formulaic, creating a routine of their own. *Attack of the Puppet People* is especially predictable. Franz shrinks Bob and Sally, adding them to his collection, apparently not realizing that Agar, despite his bad acting, always seemed to come out on top in his numerous battles with 1950s science fiction monsters and villains. Late in the film, Franz puts on a puppet show that features Bob and Sally, along with an actual puppet (cleverly designed, in a weak bit of mad-scientist-story intertextuality, so that it can play the roles of both Dr. Jekyll and Mr. Hyde). In a truly weird scene, Bob is offended by this proto-postmodernist mixture of ontological levels, then goes ballistic and literally tears the puppet apart. Bob and Sally then escape, have the requisite close calls with giant (to them) rats, cats, and dogs, and manage to get back to Franz's workroom. There, they go through the machine backward and once again return to normal size; they then go off to report Franz to the cops, even as he arrives and tearfully begs them not to leave him alone and friendless.

Bad as it all sounds, *Attack of the Puppet People* is again surprisingly effective. At some level, the film taps into the genuine creepiness of dolls and puppets, a phenomenon that has fueled numerous horror movies and that informed the characterization by Heinlein and others of communist leaders as puppet masters manipulating their enthralled minions. This creepiness no doubt arises from the similarity of dolls and puppets to human beings, not only problematizing the Self-Other distinction, but presumably raising the question of whether we ourselves might be the playthings of some colossal child, our universe a cosmic toy chest. In addition, within the context of the 1950s, the plight of the doll people obviously resonates with the sense that we are all at the mercy of huge forces beyond our control. In the end, however, it is not the predicament of the dolls, but rather that of their maker, that is the most interesting and affecting aspect of the film. Franz, after all, is the quintessential alienated individual, so embittered at his betrayal by human beings that he has withdrawn from all human intercourse, preferring to interact only with human dolls, whom he can control at will. What makes this alienation theme work, despite everything, is John Hoyt's genuinely moving performance as the moist-eyed Franz. Hoyt creates a very real pathos and radiates the pain and fear of his loneliness in a way that is entirely believable, unbelievable context notwithstanding.[10]

The final major entry in the shrinking-and-growing genre of the late 1950s was *Attack of the 50 Foot Woman* (1958), directed by Nathan Juran, perhaps best known for his film *The Seventh Voyage of Sinbad* (1958), one of the decade's leading examples of the escape-from-routine-through-fantasy-adventure genre. In this film, one of true cult favorites of 1950s science fiction film, heiress Nancy Fowler Archer (Allison Hayes) meets up with a giant from outer space, who seems to be looking for diamonds to use as fuel for his spacecraft, described in the film as a "satellite." As it happens, Nancy owns the famous "Star of India" diamond (and seems to wear it routinely about), making her a natural target. The bald giant (who looks a bit like Glenn Manning) takes the diamond, in the process inflicting radioactive scratches on Nancy's neck. These scratches then cause her to become a giant as well, after which she lumbers into town, menaces the locals, and has to be shot down by the local sheriff.

This brief plot summary suggests some of the reasons why this film has a reputation for being hilariously awful. However, there are underlying issues in the film that make it more interesting (perhaps inadvertently) than it first appears. For one thing, the Star of India motif may be more meaningful than it seems. The real Star of India is a star sapphire, not a diamond, but in any case it is a large and valuable gem, acquired by the American industrialist and financier J. P. Morgan as part of his turn-of-the-century program of scarfing up as many of the world's treasures as possible to take them back home to the United States. It thus serves as an image of American appropriation of Third World wealth. Such gems are also renowned as images of the riches plundered from the Third World by Western imperial powers, including the famous Koh-i-Noor diamond, taken as booty by British troops in India in the nineteenth century. That diamond was presented to Queen Victoria in 1850 in celebration of the 250th anniversary of the British East India Company, then displayed in London's Crystal Palace in the Great Exhibition of 1851, one of the most important of the various nineteenth-century spectacles that were designed to demonstrate the power and splendor of the British Empire.[11] The Koh-i-Noor is now the central jewel in the crown of Queen Elizabeth II. If, as I have suggested, aliens in 1950s science fiction films are often images of the threat posed to America by the Third World, then the meaning of the Star of India motif in *Attack of the 50 Foot Woman* becomes clear. When a huge, powerful alien suddenly appears in America and takes the Star of India from Nancy, we are reminded that Third Worlders may someday appear on our doorsteps, demanding a return of the vast wealth that has been extracted from them by American corporations and their British imperial predecessors.[12]

Meanwhile, though the rich and beautiful Nancy, as the inheritor of a $50 million fortune, is hardly the typical girl next door, she nonetheless suffers from a range of typical 1950s feminine problems. She is a former mental patient with a drinking problem and a philandering husband, Harry Archer (William Hudson), who spends most of his time running around with Honey Parker (Yvette Vickers), his blond bimbo girlfriend. Indeed, the film suggests that Harry's cruelty and infidelity are the primary causes of Nancy's mental problems, though the venerable Dr. von Loeb (Otto Waldis), a German doctor brought in to help diagnose her emotional ailments, suggests that her case is a fairly typical result of life in the fast-paced modern world, "not infrequent in this supersonic age we live in."

The local authorities habitually humor Nancy, given her great wealth, though it is clear that, when she first reports sighting the giant, they think she's nuts, or at least drunk. The media are not so kind. They pick up the story, and Nancy is mocked in the press, which reminds everyone of her history of emotional instability. Surrounded by doubters, Nancy herself begins to question her own sanity, but then encounters the giant again, this time with Harry as a witness, thus verifying the original sighting. It is at this point that she gets the scratches, becomes a giant, and lumbers into town looking for Harry, who is, by now, back carousing with Honey as usual, despite all that has happened. Nancy wrecks the club where the two are dancing, killing Honey in the process. She then grabs Harry in her gigantic hand and begins to lumber away, at which point the sheriff shoots a high-voltage transformer just as she walks by it, zapping and killing both Nancy and Harry with electricity.

The Attack of the 50 Foot Woman offers itself to all sorts of Freudian interpretations; for example, Hendershot has suggested that the gigantic Nancy is an image of the "powerful, frightening pre-oedipal maternal imago" (61). On a more down-to-earth level, she is an image of the suffering wife, who, in the context of the 1950s, can strike back against her unfaithful husband only by making a spectacle of herself, thereby becoming a threat to the safety and security of the entire community. Granted, one can see the film as a sympathetic (and even pre-feminist) comment on the plight of the embattled 1950s wife. Thus Leonard Wolf calls the film a "moving, and startling, image of modern marital distress" (16). On the other hand, it is significant that, while 50 feet tall, the voluptuous Hayes moves about in an extremely skimpy costume (by the standards of the 1950s, anyway), clearly suggesting a sexual element to the threat that this giant, unleashed, radioactive woman poses to the community.[13] Thus, Welch Everman notes that the film suggests that, "if a woman happens to come by a bit of power, she will use it to destroy the local community and crush her lover to bits" (21).

It is certainly the case that, in the beginning, most of the locals (and presumably, the audience) sympathize with Nancy and think Harry is a heel. On the other hand, much of the support for Nancy arises from respect for her economic power, and no one in town seems to question that she needs to be killed once she grows huge, transgresses the boundaries of acceptably normal (i.e., demure) feminine behavior, and takes action against Harry and Honey. The film thus suggests a masculine fear of feminine energies unleashed, as well as a feminine fear of oppression and betrayal by a masculine world, all within a context in which these fears are somehow exacerbated by radiation. Actually, the film contains elements that support readings of the film as either anti-feminist or pro-feminist, which could be taken as an attempt to achieve the ambiguity so beloved by literary critics in the 1950s. Unfortunately, the film feels more confused than intentionally complex, leading Mark Jancovich to conclude that "the most interesting feature of the film is its ramshackle incoherence" (206).

Other films of the period seemed more intentional in their ambiguity, or at least in their complication of the easy polar opposition between good and evil. Thus, in Kurt Neumann's *The Fly* (1958), well-meaning scientist André Delambre (David Hedison) is also the monster. After developing a teleportation apparatus, Delambre teleports himself as an experiment. Unfortunately, a common housefly accidentally gets into the machine with him, and, when they come out on the other end, their atoms have become intermixed. Delambre now has the head and arm of a fly, while the fly has a human head and arm. These two hybrid creatures thoroughly deconstruct the simple polar opposition between self and Other that had made insects such convenient villains in the monster films of the 1950s. But, except for this deconstruction, *The Fly* is a fairly silly effort that tends to produce comedy just as it tries for pathos—as when Delambre starts to battle against his fly arm in anticipation of the later travails of Kubrick's *Dr. Strangelove*, or when violins start to play as Delambre explains to his loyal wife, Helene (Patricia Owens), that he still loves her, even though his brain is rapidly becoming a fly brain.

Indeed, critics have typically been unkind to *The Fly*, largely on the basis of its unlikely premise and overdone melodramatics. Moreover, as Richard Hodgens notes, the film is built upon a questionable morality as well, ultimately endorsing the killing of both of the hybrid creatures as necessary and logical, because both are merely "Things" (86). Thus, the film misses the opportunity for a thoughtful exploration of the hybridity of human and insect by simply declaring that both hybrids are irreducibly alien and therefore unfit for life. In the meantime, the film also muddles its own warnings about the dangers of undisciplined scientific inquiry by having André's brother, François (Vincent Price), deliver a final speech in praise of the glories of science, which he describes as "the search for truth" and as "the most important work in the whole world and the most dangerous."

Partly because of its very silliness, *The Fly* has become a become a cult classic to later generations of film viewers, who have valued it for its potential as camp. Indeed, the film supplied one of the iconic moments of 1950s science fiction film in a scene near the end in which the fly with a human head, trapped in a spider web, cries out "Help me!" in a tiny voice — only to be smashed with a rock by Police Inspector Charas (Herbert Marshall). Meanwhile, the film, which had relatively high production values for a 1950s science fiction film, rewarded its producers with huge profits at the box office. As a result of this success, the film was followed by a less interesting sequel, *Return of the Fly* (1959) and, eventually, a more interesting remake, David Cronenberg's *The Fly* (1986).

The success of *The Fly* also inspired imitations, such as Roger Corman's *The Wasp Woman* (1959). However, if the unrestrained quest for scientific knowledge brings on the undoing of André Delambre, it is a quest for pure profit that undoes the title character of *The Wasp Woman*. This low-budget effort again deconstructs the strict Otherness of insects by having its female protagonist, Janice Starlin (Susan Cabot), transform into a humanoid queen wasp, though the wasp costume is incredibly bad and the film, in general, is not much better. The most interesting moment in the film is probably the one in which Starlin, feeling herself turning into the wasp woman, cries out, "Help me!" in a tiny voice reminiscent of the one at the end of *The Fly*. Otherwise, the film actually has more in common with *The Leech Woman* than with *The Fly*. Starlin is an aging cosmetics magnate, whose fortune has been built on her own great beauty. Desperate, she seeks the help of eccentric scientist Dr. Eric Zinthrop (Michael Mark), who is developing an anti-aging formula based on "royal jelly" extracted from queen wasps. The formula works, making the fortyish Starlin look much younger. But, when she takes excessive doses to try to speed the process, she begins periodically to transform into the wasp woman, killing human victims and eating their flesh. The film thus addresses many of the same issues as *The Leech Woman*, potentially criticizing our society's emphasis on feminine youth and beauty, while at the same time acknowledging the threat presented to male domination by sexually attractive women. However, Starlin is more CEO than siren, and the film puts a strongly economic spin on the motif: she seems to want youth and beauty, not to attract male lovers (she has none in the film), but to attract customers (and thus profits) to her line of cosmetics. Feminine youth and beauty, the film tells us, are highly salable commodities, a lesson advertisers in the 1950s had already learned well.

Starlin is also a typical figure of the 1950s in the way that she ultimately sacrifices her identity in her quest for economic success. In this sense, she resembles Tom Rath, the protagonist of *The Man in the Gray*

Flannel Suit, except that Rath (perhaps because he is male) finally manages to keep both his identity and his financial prospects. Still, the crisis in subjectivity that so centrally informed American experience in the 1950s was triggered, as much as anything, by the suspicion that success required a selfless devotion to one's corporation and a ruthless determination to squelch the competition, both of which were felt to be incompatible with genuine selfhood. This suspicion that capitalism is by its nature inimical to ethical selfhood goes back at least as far as the work of Balzac, who made this very suspicion his central theme. Nevertheless, it took on a particular intensity in America in the 1950s, when the potential rewards of success were greater than ever, and the prospect of failure amid all this prosperity was perceived as more and more shameful.

Numerous other factors also contributed to the growing instability of identity in the 1950s, which might also be described as a gradually increasing alienation. Much of this increase can be attributed to problems of cognitive mapping for Americans, who were suddenly urged, for a variety of reasons, to establish an unprecedented sense of participation in a global community. This difficulty might be described as a breakdown in the conventional American sense that Americans were Us and everyone else was Them. It thus participates in a general dissolution of conventional polar oppositions of the kind on which Western Aristotelian thought had long been based. The popularity of monster films in the long 1950s can, in turn, be taken as a defensive reaction against this dissolution, just as the intensity of American anticommunist paranoia can be at least partly related to a strong need on the part of Americans to find polar oppositions in which they could still believe. Yet, the anxiety over the opposition between Self and Other in the decade was so radical that even the opposition between humans and monsters was difficult to maintain, resulting in humans who became monsters (such as the Teenage Werewolf) or in sympathetic monsters (such as the creature from the Black Lagoon) who seemed more human than the humans to whom they were opposed.

In short, the crisis in subjectivity of the long 1950s was closely related to the general breakdown in the stability of conventional dualistic thought. Both of these phenomena are among the clearest signs of the growing power of capitalism, the inherent contradictions of which, when taken to their full extreme, begin to cause simple dualistic logic to dissolve. It is primarily in this sense that the monster movies of the decade reflect the logic of late capitalism and thus participate in the rise of postmodernism, though the campiness of films, such as those of Roger Corman, in the second half of the decade suggested a parodic self-consciousness that was also clearly postmodern. That these films are also related to the anxieties of the Cold War is obvious, but that may not be a case of overdetermination so much as a suggestion of the extent to which the Cold War was itself a part of the historical phenomenon of late capitalism. Cold War anxieties helped to determine many of the characteristics of postmodernism, but the postmodern logic of late capitalism also helped to determine the course and characteristics of the Cold War.

It is beyond the scope of this book to attempt a full exploration of the interrelationships between the Cold War and the rise of late capitalism. However, this study should at least make it clear that such an exploration is needed. While the science fiction novels and films of the long 1950s are transparently related to their context in the Cold War, it is clear that most of the characteristics of American science fiction during this period can be understood as consequences of the globalization of capital, without any direct reference to the Cold War. Indeed, if one views late capitalism as, not only the global phase of capitalism, but also the global phase of Enlightenment modernity, it is not at all clear whether the opposition of the socialist bloc provided resistance to capitalist globalization or whether it actually furthered that phenomenon by helping to spread modern ideas around the world. Additional, broader studies of American culture in the long 1950s should help to determine whether that culture was driven primarily by the Cold War or by the growing (postmodernist) hegemony of late capitalism. In turn, such studies should contribute to our understanding of the true historical dynamics of the period and of whether the dialectical opposition driving history during the period of the Cold War was really that between capitalism and communism or merely the opposition between a modernization propelled by the principles of the Western Enlightenment and a tradition surviving primarily in the non-Western parts of the world.

Notes

INTRODUCTION

1. See Kenneth C. Davis for a study of the history of the paperback industry in America, in which he notes that 32 of the 50 most important books in this history appeared between 1946 and 1964 (391–92). For a particularly interesting study of pulp crime fiction (which was marginal even to the paperback industry as a whole), see Geoffrey O'Brien.

2. See MacDonald's essay, "A Theory of Mass Culture,'" for a particularly negative view of mass culture. MacDonald moderates this view somewhat in a modified version of this essay, published as "Masscult & Midcult" in his *Against the American Grain*.

3. On this topic, see the work of Scott Bukatman and the collection edited by Larry McCaffery. See also Brian McHale's *Constructing Postmodernism*, which pays substantial attention to cyberpunk science fiction.

4. Boyer provides a good discussion of the precipitous decline in the level of nuclear fear around 1964, noting that "in 1959, 64 percent of Americans listed nuclear war as the nation's most urgent problem. By 1964, the figure had dropped to 16 percent" (355).

5. This particular anxiety has been addressed by historians such as Richard Hofstadter and S. M. Lipset under the rubric of "status politics," built largely, as Daniel Bell summarizes it, on the idea that "groups that are advancing in wealth and social position are often as anxious and politically feverish as groups that have become *déclassé*" (*End* 111).

6. There is a large and diverse literature on American labor history. For a number of insightful commentaries on this particular phenomenon, see the essays in the collection edited by Ginger and Christiano.

7. For a more grass-roots example of Gandhi's influence, see Halberstam's fascinating treatment, in *The Children*, of Nashville civil rights leader James Lawson, who studied for three years with Gandhi's followers in India before returning to begin his work in America.

8. By the 1960s, the obvious similarities between Vietnam and the American West were noticed by American popular culture, leading to the production of numerous Western films that were at least partly allegories about Vietnam. Such films include *The Professionals* (1966), *The Wild Bunch* (1969), *Soldier Blue* (1970), *Two Mules for Sister Sara* (1970), *Little Big Man* (1970), and *Ulzana's Raid* (1972).

9. On the siege of Dien Bien Phu, see Fall.

10. From this perspective, *I Love Lucy* would seem to be an exception—and certainly the most daring sitcom of the decade. Both of those it might have been, but Desi's Latino background and Lucy's ambition to get into show business were fairly safely contained by being depicted as forms of buffoonery.

11. On the phenomenon of suburbanization, see Kenneth T. Jackson's informative *Crabgrass Frontier*.

12. On the work of Packard, see Horowitz.

13. Of course, Mills's critique of American society from the Left also had its counterparts on the Right, as in Friedrich von Hayek's *The Road to Serfdom*. Hayek's book, first published in 1944, went largely unnoticed until after World War II, when, with its warnings that the true enemy of American prosperity and freedom was not corporate power, but the welfare state, the book became, as Diggins puts it, "the gospel of American conservatives" (228).

14. For a succinct summary of Mumford's battle with Levitt, see Halberstam (*The Fifties* 139–41). For a further critique of Levittown, see Keats.

CHAPTER 1

1. Compare Frederik Pohl's argument that "there is no *good* science fiction at all, that is not to some degree political" ("Politics" 7).

2. Jameson here draws heavily upon the important work of Kevin Lynch, who explores the difficulty of cognitive mapping in complex urban settings in *The Image of the City*.

3. See, for example, the essay by Andrew Butler.

4. Compare Scott Bukatman's discussion of "reality-slippage" as a key postmodernist strategy in Dick's 1969 novel *Ubik* (93)

5. Asimov returned to the series in the 1980s with great commercial success, though novels such as *Foundation's Edge* (1982) were typically disappointing to Asimov purists.

6. Asimov was never strong on the creation of compelling aliens. On the other hand, the absence of nonhumans from the trilogy is partly due to its genesis in the magazine *Astounding Science Fiction*, whose editor, John W. Campbell, Jr., refused to publish stories depicting aliens who were superior to humans.

7. It is probably fortunate that the Second Foundation cannot be demonstrably linked to the Soviets, at least for Asimov. Had anyone in the 1950s made this connection, Asimov's positive depiction of the ability of the Second Foundation to manipulate the minds of the leaders of the First Foundation would have made the Soviet-born author a perfect target for the McCarthyite purges.

8. Gunn notes, in passing, Asimov's participation in the Futurians, but describes them as a "fan group" and makes no mention of their politics (9). See Damon Knight for a detailed study of the Futurians.

9. As Elkins notes, Asimov himself argues in his essays on science fiction that the whole point of the genre is to describe the historical changes that might be wrought by scientific progress—yet Elkins also notes that Asimov consistently tends to deny the possibility of historical change in his fiction (Elkins 98–99).

10. For a succinct discussion of the technological optimism of 1930s science fiction, see Andrew Ross (101-35). For a representative nonfiction statement of technological optimism in the 1930s, see Lewis Mumford's *Technics and Civilization* (1934). Also representative was the dark turn taken by Mumford's view of technology by the time he published *In the Name of Sanity* in 1954. This new view of technology as a dehumanizing tool of the antidemocratic forces of the military-industrial establishment would culminate in Mumford's 1964 publication of *The Myth of the Machine*.

11. On Pohl and his collaborator Cyril Kornbluth as Swiftian satirists, see Hassler.

12. Compare Dick's *The World Jones Made*, in which a colony is established on Venus to give humanity a fresh start after it proves impossible to overcome fanaticism, religiosity, and demagoguery on earth.

13. Such fears would continue to be current throughout the long 1950s. For a simplified and condensed treatment of this theme more than a decade after *Player Piano*, see the late *Twilight Zone* episode, "The Brain Center at Whipple's" (May 15, 1964), in which a factory owner replaces all of his employees by machines, then is himself replaced by a robot.

14. Note that book 1 of *They Shall have Stars* begins with an epigraph from Oppenheimer, quoting from Thomas Jefferson to extol the importance of the free flow of information.

15. Religion plays an even more central role in Blish's *A Case of Conscience* (1958), perhaps the most extended critical examination of religion to appear in the science fiction of the 1950s. But see also Dick's *The World Jones Made*, in which the demagogue Jones ascends to power by making himself the locus of a new religious enthusiasm, thus playing on the gullibility of those who are hungry for belief.

16. Pohl, incidentally, confirms this insight firsthand, noting in "The Politics of Prophecy" that science fiction often functions as a "political cryptogram" that allows writers to "say things in hint and metaphor that the writer dares not say in clear" (10).

17. Note that this book, much admired by hippie peaceniks, was also cited by Charles Manson as one of the inspirations for his program of mass murder.

18. Pohl goes so far as to characterize this book, which he admires greatly, as "anarchist" ("Politics" 14).

19. The book would also seem to have been ideal fodder for film adaptation, except that a good rendition of Heinlein's story would have required special effects technology (and budgets) not available in the 1950s. Actually, a weak (uncredited) adaptation was attempted in 1958 as *The Brain Eaters*, leading Heinlein to sue the film's producers for copyright infringement. It was not until 1994 that

a full-scale film adaptation (with Heinlein's original title) could be made, complete with very effective alien parasites, but without the overtly anticommunist subtext.

20. See H. Bruce Franklin's discussion of the "paranoid ... anti-Communist frenzy" that informs this and other Heinlein works of the early 1950s, including the stories "The Year of the Jackpot" and "Project Nightmare" (98–105).

21. See Endicott and Hagerman for a detailed study of the charges by Chinese and North Korean officials that the U.S. employed germ warfare during the Korean conflict. American officials have long denied the charges, but Endicott and Hagerman conclude that the bulk of available evidence supports the Chinese/North Korean position.

22. Much of Dick's *The World Jones Made* is structured around precisely this reversal. Here, the sinister (and cynically opportunistic) Jones rises to power largely by stirring up a genocidal campaign against the harnless "drifters," organisms from outer space that begin to land on earth.

23. See Dolman for a review of some of this criticism of Heinlein's novel. However, Dolman himself concludes that the book is neither fascist nor racist, but merely overly idealistic (211–12).

24. Oddly enough, especially for Heinlein, the final cataclysmic war that swept away the old order is pictured as a confrontation, beginning in 1987, between the "Russo-Anglo-American Alliance" on one side and the "Chinese Hegemony" on the other. Of course, swarming hordes of Chinese are, for Heinlein, the ultimate communist nightmare, a virtual human equivalent to the Bugs of *Starship Troopers*.

CHAPTER 2

1. In the first volume of *Capital*, Marx notes how Crusoe carefully apportions his time, creating a sort of one-man division of labor, after which he "commences, like a true-born Briton, to keep a set of books" (Marx and Engels 325). Meanwhile, Georg Lukács identifies Crusoe as a paradigm of the "individual, egoistic bourgeois isolated artificially by capitalism" (*History* 135).

2. For an amusing science fiction lampoon of this kind of primitivist utopia, see Robert Sheckley's *Journey Beyond Tomorrow* (1962), which presents the utopian community of Chorowait as a ridiculous project designed by comically inept academics. (Stewart, by the way, was a professor of English at the University of California.)

3. For another post-holocaust work with a feminine perspective, see Helen Clarkson's *The Last Day* (1959). Clarkson's heroine-narrator, however, takes refuge on an island retreat off the Massachusetts coast, rather than in suburbia. Even this isolation, incidentally, does not finally protect her from the consequences of the nuclear war. The novel ends as the narrator herself nears death from radioactive fallout. Indeed, the novel explicitly critiques the literary romanticization of nuclear holocaust, which Clarkson sees as part of the "American ... cult of the happy ending" (37).

4. This entry in the encyclopedia was written by David Pringle, who also includes *Limbo* in his *Science Fiction: The 100 Best Novels*.

5. Compare Sheckley's later *Journey Beyond Tomorrow* (1962), which employs a similar comic-satiric strategy, though in a mode more reminiscent of Voltaire than of Swift.

6. Wolfe, of course, was not alone in this insight. A conventional criticism of McCarthyism, for example, was that it was making America indistinguishable from the Stalinist Soviet Union. For a similar fictional statement, published a year before *Limbo*, see Norman Mailer's *Barbary Shore* (1951), which envisions a coming American-Soviet war as a "conflict between two virtually identical forms of exploitation," both sides having succumbed to the same bureaucratic routinization (278).

7. The dystopian tradition has, of course, continued in the postmodern era. See my chapter on postmodernist dystopias in *The Dystopian Impulse in Modern Literature* (141–71).

8. Bradbury's rather puerile sentimentalism can also be seen in the *Twilight Zone* episode, "I Sing the Body Electric" (May 18, 1962), scripted by Bradbury from his short story of the same title. That episode, about a kindly robot grandmother, is notorious as one of the most sentimental ever to appear on the series.

9. *I Am Legend* was a bit too frightening for film audiences in the 1950s, so it was not adapted to the screen at the time, despite Matheson's film connections. In 1964, however, it was adapted as the Vincent Price vehicle, *The Last Man on Earth*; in 1971, it was more loosely adapted as *The Omega Man*, with Charlton Heston as Neville and the vampires replaced by technology-hating albino zombies.

10. For a good idea of Asimov's attitude toward religion, see *Asimov's Guide to the Bible*, which presents both the Old and New Testaments essentially as collections of myths, contradictions, and just plain silliness.

11. For a good study of American society in the 1950s that pays special attention to the role of organized religion in the decade, see Oakley.

12. For another example of a turn to postmodernist absurdism in the treatment of the holocaust theme, see Vonnegut's *Cat's Cradle* (1963). Here, Vonnegut plays on the old theme of the heat death of the universe by having an unrestrained scientist develop "ice nine," which runs amok and freezes the entire earth.

13. Compare the later *The World, the Flesh, and the Devil* (1959), which similarly deals with race in a post-holocaust context. At one point in this film, the seemingly last man on earth is black and the last woman white, but the film backs away from dealing with the racial implications of this scenario by introducing a white man as well and refusing to stipulate which of the men will ultimately mate with the woman.

14. In the original novel, of course, this opposition would be in terms of the colonized world versus a colonizing Britain. However, Wells's time traveler tends to associate the Morlock-Eloi opposition with class conflict, relating them to the working class and a spoiled bourgeoisie, respectively. The film, like most American cultural products of the 1950s, shies away from such class issues.

15. Graphic on-screen depictions of the actual effects of nuclear war were rare until the mid-1980s, when a spate of such films appeared, including *The Day After* (1983), *Testament* (1983), and *Threads* (1985), the latter a British entry.

CHAPTER 3

1. See Joyce Evans for a useful book-length study of Hollywood science fiction films that places those films within the context of the pressures faced by the film industry in the 1950s.

2. Actually, in the original novel, written just after World War II, the bad guys were Nazis. That the bad guys are Soviets by the time of the film is transparently clear.

3. The notion that the destruction of the earth has a therapeutic, cleansing effect is supported by the film's continual comparisons of the spaceship to Noah's ark.

4. For a succinct discussion of the film's debt to Shakespeare, see Knighten.

5. For more on the film's ambivalence toward technology, see Telotte (111–29).

6. *Red Planet Mars* thus bears out Daniel Bell's suggestion that the level of hysteria that informed American anticommunism in the 1950s can be linked to a traditional American tendency toward religious zeal and that "the attacks on communism were made with all the compulsive moral fervor which was possible because of the equation of communism with sin" (*End* 120).

7. The film thus suggests, not entirely inaccurately, that many of the impressive scientific advances made by the Russians in the postwar years were propelled by former Nazi scientists spirited away from Germany after the war. There is no mention, of course, of the fact that such scientists, including Werner von Braun, were also central to American advances during these years. Indeed, the Soviets had to spirit Calder away from an American prison, where he was being punished for his crimes, in order to put him to work.

8. Producer Howard Hawks apparently provided considerable assistance to Nyby in directing the film, which would make Hawks the most prestigious director to have worked on any of the science fiction films of the 1950s. Indeed, Warren concludes that "there's no doubt the guiding mind behind the entire enterprise was that of Howard Hawks" (1, 48). On the other hand, there have long been rumors that Orson Welles may have had a behind-the-scenes hand in the direction.

9. For other examples of monsters from the plant kingdom, see *From Hell It Came* (1957), whose monster is basically an ill-tempered tree stump, and *The Day of the Triffids* (1963), in which giant man-eating plants (brought to earth on meteorites) almost overrun the globe.

10. The Thing was probably this way for technical reasons. In the original John W. Campbell, Jr., story on which the film is based, the Thing was a telepathic shape-changer, which made it much more interesting, but a lot harder to put on the screen. John Carpenter's 1982 remake, with access to much better special-effects technology, is much truer to the original story.

11. Contrast Jack Arnold's *The Space Children* (1958), in which the kids are aligned with an alien brain that comes to earth to stop the arms race—and against their warmongering parents, who are all too anxious to blow the Russkies to kingdom come.

12. The ultimate filmic representation of this motif, of course, would be John Frankenheimer's *The Manchurian Candidate* (1962).

13. Spencer attempted to exempt his contemporary England from this narrative by arguing that Victorian society was a unique hybrid that epitomized the achievements of industrial society, but still maintained the raw energy and drive that he associated with primitive or "militant" societies. Yet this hybrid vision of Victorian England had its drawbacks as well, implying that the Victorians maintained strong vestiges of their primitive past, reinforcing fears that these primitive characteristics might somehow come back to the fore.

14. There are also vague religious resonances at the end of Wells's novel, and this last line is a near-quote from Wells's text. The same line was quoted in the Mercury Theatre radio broadcast. However, the religious elements are not foregrounded in the novel or the radio broadcast to the extent that they are in the film. For example, Wells's unnamed narrator-protagonist, realizing what has killed the Martians, muses on possible religious analogues, noting that "for a moment I believed that the destruction of Sennacherib had been repeated, that God had repented, that the Angel of Death had slain them in the night." This "for a moment," however, is crucial, suggesting the later rejection of this explanation.

15. Such fears were not restricted to America. See, for example, Honda's *The Mysterians* (1959) for a Japanese take on the aliens-need-earth-women genre. The Japanese, of course, had their own reason to feel that larger forces were closing in on them, destroying their racial and cultural purity, in the postwar years. In this case, ironically, the principal source of impurities would be the United States.

16. For a slightly different take on this film as an example of "feminine paranoia," see Hendershot (56–60).

17. This element is almost entirely missing in the considerably less interesting 1998 made-for-TV remake, Nancy Malone's *I Married a Monster*, though even here, the alien (now named Nick) does finally declare his love for his wife (now named Kelly) as he melts.

18. Paul Buhle describes *The Black Cat* as perhaps the leading contribution to the horror-film genre by a leftist filmmaker, demonstrating as it does "the moral bankruptcy of capital" (108). R. Barton Palmer, meanwhile, calls *Detour* "undoubtedly the finest example of purely noir thriller" (108).

19. More accurate as an assessment of the film's politics is James Shaw's description of it, based on interviews with several of the film's principals, including Wise, screenwriter Edmund North, and producer Julian Blaustein, as a "rational response to the McCarthy era," arising from the politics of the New Deal (50). See also Barone, who sees Klaatu as an image of the "New Deal intellectual," thus a problematic figure in the anti-intellectual climate of the McCarthy era (208).

20. Asteroids were a principal source of outer-space monsters in the 1950s. See also *The Monolith Monsters* (1957), in which the asteroids themselves transform into towering rock monsters in the California desert, emerging to destroy everything in their path as they seek silicon for food, meanwhile turning humans into stone. Incidentally, the monolith monsters, described by Sobchack as resembling "German Expressionist skyscrapers," are far more interesting and convincing looking than they sound (100).

21. See also the Japanese entry, *The H-Man* (1959), directed by the formidable Inoshiro Honda, best known for his direction of many of the Godzilla movies, including the first of the series, *Godzilla, King of the Monsters*, in 1954. For a particularly interesting take on this motif, see the British entry *The Quatermass Experiment* (1955), in which an infection from outer space transforms a human into a bloblike mass.

22. If these films tended to drift from science fiction into the gothic, the late 1950s also produced such science fiction efforts as Tom Graeff's *Teenagers from Outer Space* (1959) and Roger Corman's post-holocaust *Teenage Cave Man* (1958).

23. Jancovich notes that horror films of the 1950s were frequently self-conscious and self-parodic, especially when they were designed to appeal to teenagers. He notes that such films "repeatedly reflect on their status as cinema with their monsters striking at victims in dark theatres or drive-ins" (201).

CHAPTER 4

1. The beast thus resembles the better known Godzilla, another prehistoric monster who was awakened by nuclear testing.

2. Byron Haskin's *Naked Jungle* (1954) draws on this same insight, featuring a young Charlton Heston doing battle against an army of normal-sized ants (red ones, of course).

3. Insect imagery is also used to suggest dehumanization in Yevgeny Zamyatin's classic dystopian novel, *We*. In fact, Zamyatin probably derived the imagery from Dostoevsky's *Notes from Underground*, which suggests that the modern emphasis on rationality is making humans more and more like insects.

4. Seed notes that authors such as Poul Anderson and Norman Spinrad, writing during the Cold War, employed anthills as metaphors for Soviet society (2).

5. *Beginning of the End* threatens to introduce an interesting female character, in the person of journalist Audrey Aimes (Peggie Castle), who defies the local authorities in her quest to get the story of the giant locusts. Never fear, though: as soon as she meets the brilliant-but-manly Wainwright, Aimes grows submissive and recedes passively into the background.

6. Hendershot notes the element of male sexual insecurity in the film, but suggests that this insecurity is related to fears about the atomic bomb (94).

7. Ulmer, incidentally, makes Krenner a sort of all-purpose representative of militarism and is careful not to align him with any particular side. Asked early in the film which army he served in, he simply replies that he has served in many.

8. See, for example, Hendershot (86–88), Jancovich, Knee, Tarratt, and Paul Wells.

9. There are other links between the two films as well. *Attack of the Puppet People* was generally distributed as part of a double feature with *War of the Colossal Beast*.

10. Not all of Gordon's films have such redeeming features. For a truly awful film, which combines a ludicrous premise with bad acting, a bad script, and some of the worst special effects of all time, see his early effort, *King Dinosaur* (1955).

11. On such exhibitions, see Greenhalgh.

12. Fears that frightening aliens might appear to reclaim the jewels and other wealth taken from the East to the West have been reflected in Western culture at least since 1868, when Wilkie Collins published *The Moonstone*, a novel about sinister Indians who come to England to reclaim a sacred Indian diamond stolen by the British. Such fears may also partly account for the fact that many such jewels (most notably the Hope diamond, also from India) are reputed to be cursed.

13. Indeed, elaborating on his diagnosis, von Loeb concludes that Nancy's emotional difficulties may be caused by sexual frustration.

Works Cited

BOOKS AND ARTICLES

Asimov, Isaac. *Asimov's Guide to the Bible*. 2 vols. New York: Equinox-Avon, 1968.
———. *The Caves of Steel*. New York: Doubleday, 1954.
———. *The Foundation Trilogy. Three Classics of Science Fiction:* Foundation, Foundation and Empire, *and* Second Foundation. 1951, 1952, 1953. Garden City, NY: Doubleday, 1963.
———. *Foundation's Edge*. New York: Ballantine, 1982.
———. *The Naked Sun*. New York: Doubleday, 1957.
Bakhtin, M. M. *The Dialogic Imagination*. Ed. Michael Holquist. Trans. Caryl Emerson and Michael Holquist. Austin: U of Texas P, 1981.
———. *Problems of Dostoevsky's Poetics*. Trans. and ed. Caryl Emerson. Minneapolis: U of Minnesota P, 1984.
Barone, Dennis. "Klaatu Was No Angel: A Historical-Contextual Analysis of *The Day the Earth Stood Still*." *Studies in the Humanities* 23.2 (1996): 202–12.
Barth, John. *The Sot-Weed Factor*. 1960. Garden City, NY: Anchor-Doubleday, 1987.
Barzman, Ben. *Twinkle, Twinkle Little Star*. New York: G. P. Putnam's Sons, 1960.
Baudrillard, Jean. *Selected Writings*. Ed. Mark Poster. Stanford, CA: Stanford UP, 1988.
Baxter, John. *Science Fiction in the Cinema*. New York: A. S. Barnes, 1970.
Bell, Daniel. *The Cultural Contradictions of Capitalism*. 1976. New York: Basic Books, 1996.
———. *The End of Ideology: On the Exhaustion of Political Ideas in the Fifties*. 1960. Cambridge, MA: Harvard UP, 1988.
Benjamin, Walter. *Illuminations*. Trans. Harry Zohn. Ed. Hannah Arendt. New York: Harcourt, Brace and World, 1955.
Berger, Albert I. "Love, Death, and the Atom Bomb: Sexuality and Community in Science Fiction, 1935–55." *Science-Fiction Studies* 8.3 (1981): 280–95.
Bester, Alfred. *The Demolished Man*. 1953. New York: Vintage-Random House, 1996.
———. *The Stars My Destination*. 1957. New York: Vintage-Random House, 1996.

Biskind, Peter. *Seeing Is Believing: How Hollywood Taught Us to Stop Worrying and Love the Fifties*. New York: Pantheon, 1983.

Blish, James. *A Case of Conscience*. New York: Ballantine, 1958.

———. *They Shall Have Stars*. 1956. *Cities in Flight*. 1970. New York: Overlook P, 2000. 1–124.

Blish, James (as William Atheling, Jr.). *More Issues at Hand*. Chicago: Advent, 1970.

Bloom, James D. *Left Letters: The Culture Wars of Mike Gold and Joseph Freeman*. New York: Columbia UP, 1992.

Booker, M. Keith. *Colonial Power, Colonial Texts: India in the Modern British Novel*. Ann Arbor: U of Michigan P, 1997.

———. *The Dystopian Impulse in Modern Literature: Fiction as Social Criticism*. Westport, CT: Greenwood P, 1994.

Boyer, Paul. *By the Bomb's Early Light: American Thought and Culture at the Dawn of the Atomic Age*. New York: Pantheon, 1985.

Bradbury, Ray. *Fahrenheit 451*. New York: Ballantine Books, 1979.

———. *The Martian Chronicles*. Garden City, NY: Doubleday, 1950.

Brosnan, John. *Future Tense: The Cinema of Science Fiction*. New York: St. Martin's, 1978.

Buhle, Paul. "The Hollywood Left: Aesthetics and Politics." *New Left Review* 212 (1995): 101–19.

Bukatman, Scott. *Terminal Identity: The Virtual Subject in Postmodern Science Fiction*. Durham, NC: Duke UP, 1993.

Burroughs, William S. *Naked Lunch*. 1959. New York: Grove, 1966.

Butler, Andrew. "Science Fiction as Postmodernism: The Case of Philip K. Dick." *Impossibility Fiction: Alternativity, Extrapolation, Speculation*. Ed. Derek Littlewood and Peter Stockwell. Amsterdam: Rodopi, 1996. 45–56.

Cantril, Hadley. *The Invasion from Mars: A Study in the Psychology of Panic*. 1940. New York: Harper and Row, 1966.

Caute, David. *The Great Fear: The Anti-Communist Purge under Truman and Eisenhower*. New York: Simon and Schuster, 1978.

Clarens, Carlos. *An Illustrated History of Horror and Science-Fiction Films: The Classic Era, 1895–1967*. 1967. New York: De Capo P, 1997.

Clarkson, Helen. *The Last Day: A Novel of the Day after Tomorrow*. New York: Dodd Mead, 1959.

Clute, John, and Peter Nicholls, eds. *The Encyclopedia of Science Fiction*. 2nd ed. New York: St. Martin's, 1995.

Collins, Wilkie. *The Moonstone*. 1868. London: Penguin, 1986.

Coover, Robert. *The Public Burning*. New York: Viking, 1977.

Davis, Kenneth C. *Two-Bit Culture: The Paperbacking of America*. Boston: Houghton Mifflin, 1984.

Defoe, Daniel. The Life and Strange and Surprising Adventures of Robinson Crusoe. 1719. New York: Penguin, 1994.

Deleuze, Gilles, and Félix Guattari. *Anti-Oedipus: Capitalism and Schizophrenia*. Trans. Robert Hurely, Mark Seem, and Helen R. Lane. Minneapolis: U of Minnesota P, 1983.

Dick, Philip K. *Dr. Bloodmoney, or How We Got Along after the Bomb*. 1965. New York: Carroll & Graf, 1988.

———. *Dr. Futurity*. 1960. New York: Berkley, 1984.

———. *Do Androids Dream of Electric Sheep?* 1968. New York: Ballantine, 1982.

———. *The Man in the High Castle*. 1962. New York: Vintage-Random House, 1992.

———. *The Man Who Japed*. New York: Ace, 1956.

———. *Martian Time-Slip*. 1964. New York: Vintage-Random House, 1995.

———. *The Penultimate Truth*. New York: Belmont P, 1964.

———. *Time Out of Joint*. 1959. New York: Carroll and Graf, 1987.

———. *Ubik*. 1969. New York: Vintage-Random House, 1991.

———. *Vulcan's Hammer*. New York: Ace, 1960.

———. *We Can Build You*. 1972. New York: Vintage-Random House, 1994.

———. *The World Jones Made*. 1956. New York: Vintage-Random House, 1993.

Diggins, John Patrick. *The Proud Decades: America in War and in Peace, 1941–1960*. New York: W. W. Norton, 1988.

Disch, Thomas M. *The Dreams Our Stuff Is Made Of: How Science Fiction Conquered the World*. New York: Free P, 1998.

Doherty, Thomas. *Teenagers and Teenpics: The Juvenilization of American Movies in the 1950s*. Boston: Unwin Hyman, 1988.

Dolman, Everett Carl. "Military, Democracy, and the State in Robert A. Heinlein's *Starship Troopers*." *Political Science Fiction*. Ed. Donald M. Hassler and Clyde Wilcox. Columbia: U of South Carolina P, 1997. 196–213.

Dostoevsky, Fyodor. *Notes from Underground*. Trans. Mirra Ginsburg. New York: Bantam Books, 1976.

Elkins, Charles. "Asimov's *Foundation* Novels: Historical Materialism Distorted into Cyclical Psychohistory." *Isaac Asimov*. Ed. Joseph D. Olander and Martin Harry Greenberg. New York: Taplinger, 1977. 97–110.

Endicott, Stephen, and Edward Hagerman. *The United States and Biological Warfare: Secrets from the Early Cold War and Korea*. Bloomington: Indiana UP, 1998.

Evans, Joyce A. *Celluloid Mushroom Clouds: Hollywood and the Atomic Bomb*. Boulder, CO: Westview P, 1998.

Everman, Welch. *Cult Horror Films: From* Attack of the 50 Foot Woman *to* Zombies of Mora Tau. New York: Citadel, 1993.

Fall, Bernard. *Hell in a Very Small Place: The Siege of Dien Bien Phu*. Philadelphia: Lippincott, 1967.

Foley, Barbara. *Radical Representations: Politics and Form in U.S. Proletarian Fiction, 1929–1941*. Durham, NC: Duke UP, 1993.

Foucault, Michel. *Discipline and Punish: The Birth of the Prison*. Trans. Alan Sheridan. New York: Vintage-Random House, 1979.

Frank, Pat. *Alas, Babylon*. 1959. New York: HarperPerennial-HarperCollins, 1999.

———. *Forbidden Area*. Philadelphia: Lippincott, 1956.

———. *How to Survive the H-Bomb, and Why*. Philadelphia: Lippincott, 1962.

———. *Mr. Adam*. Philadelphia: Lippincott, 1946.

Franklin, H. Bruce. *Robert A. Heinlein: America as Science Fiction*. New York: Oxford UP, 1980.

Freedman, Carl. *Critical Theory and Science Fiction*. Hanover, NH: Wesleyan UP, 2000.

Friedan, Betty. *The Feminine Mystique*. 1963. New York: W. W. Norton, 1997.

Fromm, Erich. *The Sane Society*. Greenwich, CT: Fawcett, 1955.

Gaddis, William. *The Recognitions*. 1955. New York: Penguin, 1985.

Gibson, William. *Neuromancer*. New York: Ace, 1984.

Ginger, Ann Fagan, and David Christiano, eds. *The Cold War against Labor*. 2 vols. Berkeley, CA: Meiklejohn Civil Liberties Institute, 1987.

Goffman, Erving. *Asylums: Essays on the Social Situation of Mental Patients and Other Inmates*. New York: Anchor-Doubleday, 1961.

Greenhalgh, Paul. *Ephemeral Vistas: The* Expositions Universelles, *Great Exhibitions and World's Fairs, 1851–1939*. Manchester, UK: Manchester UP, 1988.

Gunn, James. *Isaac Asimov: The Foundations of Science Fiction*. Rev. ed. Lanham. MD: Scarecrow P, 1996.

Habermas, Jürgen. "Modernity versus Postmodernity." *New German Critique* 22 (1981): 3–14.

Haggard, Rider. *She*. 1887. New York: Oxford UP, 1991.

Halberstam, David. *The Children*. New York: Random House, 1998.

———. *The Fifties*. New York: Villard, 1993.

Haldeman, Joe. *The Forever War*. 1974. New York: Avon, 1991.

Harrison, Harry. *Bill, the Galactic Hero*. London: Gollancz, 1965.

Harvey, David. *The Condition of Postmodernity: An Enquiry into the Origins of Cultural Change*. Cambridge, MA: Blackwell, 1990.

Hassler, Donald M. "Swift, Pohl, and Kornbluth: Publicists Anatomize Newness." *Political Science Fiction*. Ed. Donald M. Hassler and Clyde Wilcox. Columbia: U of South Carolina P, 1997. 18–25.

Hawkes, John. *The Beetle Leg*. 1951: New York: W. W. Norton, 1967.

———. *The Lime Twig*. New York: New Directions, 1961.

Heinlein, Robert A. *The Moon Is a Harsh Mistress*. 1966. New York: Orb-Tom Doherty Associates, 1997.

———. *The Puppet Masters*. 1951. New York: Del Rey-Ballantine, 1990.

———. *Rocket Ship Galileo*. New York: Scribner's, 1947.

———. *Starship Troopers*. 1959. New York: Ace-Berkley, 1987.

———. *Stranger in a Strange Land*. 1961. New York: Ace, 1987.

Hendershot, Cyndy. *Paranoia, the Bomb, and 1950s Science Fiction Films*. Bowling Green, OH: Bowling Green U Popular P, 1999.

Henriksen, Margot A. *Dr. Strangelove's America: Society and Culture in the Atomic Age*. Berkeley: U of California P, 1997.

Hersey, John. *Hiroshima*. New York: Knopf, 1946.

Hodgens, Richard. "A Brief, Tragical History of the Science Fiction Film." *Focus on the Science Fiction Film*. Ed. William Johnson. Englewood Cliffs, NJ: Prentice-Hall, 1972. 78–90.

Hoover, J. Edgar. *Masters of Deceit: The Story of Communism in America and How to Fight It*. 1958. New York: Pocket Books, 1959.

Horkheimer, Max, and Theodor W. Adorno. *Dialectic of Enlightenment*. Trans. John Cumming. New York: Seabury P, 1972.

Horowitz, Daniel. *Vance Packard and American Social Criticism*. Chapel Hill: U of North Carolina P, 1994.

Huxley, Aldous. *Brave New World*. 1932. Brave New World *and* Brave New World Revisited. New York: Harper and Row, 1965.

Huyssen, Andreas. *After the Great Divide: Modernism, Mass Culture, Postmodernism*. Bloomington: Indiana UP, 1986.

Jackson, Kenneth T. *Crabgrass Frontier: The Suburbanization of the United States.* New York: Oxford UP, 1985.

Jameson, Fredric. "After Armageddon: Character Systems in *Dr. Bloodmoney.*" *Science-Fiction Studies* 5 (1975): 31–42.

———. *The Political Unconscious: Narrative as a Socially Symbolic Act.* Ithaca, NY: Cornell UP, 1981.

———. *Postmodernism, or, the Cultural Logic of Late Capitalism.* Durham, NC: Duke UP, 1991.

———. "Postmodernism and Consumer Society." *The Anti-Aesthetic: Essays on Postmodern Culture.* Ed. Hal Foster. Port Townshend, WA: Bay P, 1983. 111–26.

———. "Progress or Utopia, or, Can We Imagine the Future?" *Science-Fiction Studies* 9.2 (1982): 147–58.

———. *Signatures of the Visible.* New York: Routledge, 1992.

Jancovich, Mark. *Rational Fears: American Horror in the 1950s.* Manchester, UK: Manchester UP, 1996.

Keats, John. *The Crack in the Picture Window.* Boston: Houghton Mifflin, 1957.

Kershner, R. B. "Degeneration: The Explanatory Nightmare." *Georgia Review* 40 (1986): 416–44.

Kinsey, Alfred C. *Sexual Behavior in the Human Male.* 1948. Bloomington: U of Indiana P, 1998.

Kinsey, Alfred C., et al. *Sexual Behavior in the Human Female.* 1953. Bloomington: U of Indiana P, 1998.

Knee, Adam. "The Metamorphosis of the Fly." *Wide Angle* 14.1 (January 1992): 20–34.

Knight, Damon. *The Futurians.* New York: John Day, 1977.

Knighten, Merrell. "The Triple Paternity of *Forbidden Planet.*" *Shakespeare Bulletin* 12.3 (1994): 36–37.

Kornbluth, C. M., and Judith Merril (as Cyril Judd). *Gunner Cade.* 1952. New York: Dell, 1969.

Kornbluth, C. M., and Judith Merril. *Outpost Mars.* New York: Dell, 1952.

Lears, Jackson. "A Matter of Taste: Corporate Cultural Hegemony in a Mass-Consumption Society." *Recasting America: Culture and Politics in the Age of Cold War.* Ed. Lary May. Chicago: U of Chicago P, 1989. 38–57.

Lukács, Georg. *The Historical Novel.* Trans. Hannah Mitchell and Stanley Mitchell. Lincoln: U of Nebraska P, 1983.

———. *History and Class Consciousness.* Trans. Rodney Livingstone. Cambridge, MA: MIT P, 1971.

Lynch, Kevin. *The Image of the City.* Cambridge, MA: MIT P, 1960.

Lyotard, Jean-François. *The Postmodern Condition: A Report on Knowledge.* Trans. Geoff Bennington and Brian Massumi. Minneapolis: U of Minnesota P, 1984.

MacDonald, Dwight. *Against the American Grain: Essays on the Effects of Mass Culture.* New York: Vintage, 1962.

———. "A Theory of Mass Culture" *Mass Culture: The Popular Arts in America.* Eds. Bernard Rosenberg and David Manning White. New York: Free P, 1957. 59–73.

Mackey, Douglas A. *Philip K. Dick.* Boston: Twayne, 1988.

Mailer, Norman. *Barbary Shore.* 1951. New York: Vintage-Random House, 1997.

Maland, Charles. "*Dr. Strangelove* (1964): Nightmare Comedy and the Ideology of Liberal Consensus." *Hollywood as Historian: American Film in a Cultural Context.* Rev. ed. Ed. Peter C. Rollins. Lexington: UP of Kentucky, 1998. 190–210.

Mandel, Ernest. *Late Capitalism.* Trans. Joris De Bres. London: NLB, 1975.

Marcuse, Herbert. *One-Dimensional Man: Studies in the Ideology of Advanced Industrial Society.* Boston: Beacon P, 1964.

Martin, Ernest F. "*Five.*" *Nuclear War Films.* Ed. Jack G. Shaheen. Carbondale: Southern Illinois UP, 1978. 11–16.

Marx, Karl, and Friedrich Engels. *The Marx-Engels Reader.* Ed. Robert C. Tucker. New York: Norton, 1978.

Masters, Dexter, and Katherine Way, eds. *One World or None.* New York: McGraw-Hill, 1946.

Matheson, Richard. *I Am Legend.* 1954. New York: Orb-Tom Doherty Associates, 1997.

———. *The Shrinking Man.* 1956. Republished as *The Incredible Shrinking Man.* New York: Tor, 1995.

McCaffery, Larry, ed. *Storming the Reality Studio: A Casebook of Cyberpunk and Postmodern Fiction.* Durham, NC: Duke UP, 1991.

McHale, Brian. *Constructing Postmodernism.* London: Routledge, 1992.

———. *Postmodernist Fiction.* New York: Methuen, 1987.

Merril, Judith. *Shadow on the Hearth.* Garden City, NY: Doubleday, 1950.

Miller, Walter M., Jr. *A Canticle for Leibowitz.* Philadelphia: J. B. Lippincott, 1959.

Mills, C. Wright. *The Power Elite.* London: Oxford UP, 1956.

———. *White Collar: The American Middle Classes.* New York: Oxford UP, 1951.

Mumford, Lewis. *In the Name of Sanity.* New York: Harcourt, Brace and Co. 1954.

———. *The Myth of the Machine.* 2 vols. New York: Harcourt, Brace, and World, 1964.

———. *Technics and Civilization.* New York: Harcourt, Brace, and Co., 1934.

Murphy, James F. *The Proletarian Moment: The Controversy over Leftism in Literature.* Urbana: U of Illinois P, 1991.

Nelson, Cary. *Repression and Recovery: Modern American Poetry and the Politics of Cultural Memory, 1914–1945.* Madison: U of Wisconsin P, 1989.

Nietzsche, Friedrich. *The Birth of Tragedy.* 1872. Trans. Douglas Smith. New York: Oxford UP, 2000.

Nordau, Max. *Degeneration.* 1895. Trans. anon. New York: Appleton, 1905.

Oakley, J. Ronald. *God's Country: America in the Fifties.* New York: Dembner Books, 1986.

O'Brien, Geoffrey. *Hardboiled America: Lurid Paperbacks and the Masters of Noir.* Expanded ed. New York: Da Capo, 1997.

Orwell, George. *Nineteen Eighty-four.* 1949. New York: New American Library, 1961.

Palmer, R. Barton. *Hollywood's Dark Cinema: The American Noir Film.* New York: Twayne, 1994.

Pells, Richard H. *The Liberal Mind in a Conservative Age: American Intellectuals in the 1940s and 1950s.* New York: Harper and Row, 1985.

Pierce, Hazel. "Philip K. Dick's Political Dreams." *Philip K. Dick.* Ed. Martin Harry Greenberg and Joseph D. Olander. New York: Taplinger, 1983. 105–35.

Pierce, John J. *Foundations of Science Fiction: A Study in Imagination and Evolution.* Westport, CT: Greenwood P, 1987.

Pietz, William. "The 'Post-Colonialism' of Cold War Discourse." *Social Text* 19–20 (Fall 1988): 55–75.

Pohl, Frederik. "The Politics of Prophecy." *Political Science Fiction.* Ed. Donald M. Hassler and Clyde Wilcox. Columbia: U of South Carolina P, 1997. 7–17.

Pohl, Frederik, and Lester Del Rey. *Preferred Risk.* 1955. New York: Ballantine, 1980.

Pohl, Frederik, and C. M. Kornbluth. *Gladiator-at-Law.* New York: Ballantine, 1955.

———. *The Space Merchants.* 1952. New York: St. Martin's, 1987.

Porter, Jeffrey. "Narrating the End: Fables of Survival in the Nuclear Age." *Journal of American Culture* 16.4 (1993): 41–47.

Potter, David M. *People of Plenty: Economic Abundance and the American Character.* Chicago: U of Chicago P, 1954.

Pringle, David. *Science Fiction: The 100 Best Novels.* New York: Carroll & Graf, 1985.

Riesman, David, with Reuel Denney and Nathan Glazer. *The Lonely Crowd: A Study of the Changing American Character.* New Haven, CT: Yale UP, 1950.

Robinson, Kim Stanley. *The Novels of Philip K. Dick.* Ann Arbor, MI: UMI Research P, 1984.

Roshwald, Mordecai. *Level 7.* New York: McGraw Hill, 1959.

Ross, Andrew. *Strange Weather: Culture, Science, and Technology in the Age of Limits.* London: Verso, 1991.

Said, Edward. *Orientalism.* New York: Vintage-Random House, 1979.

Schickel, Richard. *Brando: A Life in Our Times.* New York: Atheneum, 1991.

Seed, David. *American Science Fiction and the Cold War: Literature and Film.* Chicago: Fitzroy Dearborn, 1999.

Shaw, James. "*The Day the Earth Stood Still:* Dramatizing a Political Tract." *Creative Screenwriting* 5.4 (1998): 50–53.

Sheckley, Robert. *Journey beyond Tomorrow.* New York: Dell, 1962.

Simak, Clifford D. *Ring around the Sun.* 1953. New York: Avon, 1967.

Sobchack, Vivian. *Screening Space: The American Science Fiction Film.* 2nd ed. New Brunswick, NJ: Rutgers UP, 1997.

Sontag, Susan. "The Imagination of Disaster." *Against Interpretation and Other Essays.* New York: Farrar, Straus and Giroux, 1966. 209–25.

Spanos, William V. *Repetitions: The Postmodern Occasion in Literature and Culture.* Baton Rouge: Louisiana State UP, 1987.

Steinbeck, John. *The Grapes of Wrath.* 1939. *John Steinbeck: The Grapes of Wrath and Other Writings, 1936–1941.* New York: Library of America, 1996. 207–692.

Stephenson, Neal. *Snow Crash.* New York: Bantam, 1992.

Stevenson, Robert Louis. *The Strange Case of Dr. Jekyll and Mr. Hyde.* 1886. New York: Bantam, 1981.

Stewart, George. *Earth Abides.* 1949. New York: Fawcett-Ballantine, 1983.

Suvin, Darko. "Artifice as Refuge and World View: Philip K. Dick's Foci." *Philip K. Dick.* Ed. Martin Harry Greenberg and Joseph D. Olander. New York: Taplinger, 1983. 73–95.

———. *Metamorphoses of Science Fiction: On the Poetics and History of a Literary Genre*. New Haven, CT: Yale UP, 1979.

Tarratt, Margaret. "Monsters from the Id." *Film Genre Reader*. Ed. Barry Keith Grant. Austin: U of Texas P, 1986. 104–14.

Telotte, J. P. *Replications: A Robotic History of the Science Fiction Film*. Urbana: U of Illinois P, 1995.

von Hayek, Friedrich. *The Road to Serfdom*. Chicago: U of Chicago P, 1944.

Vonnegut, Kurt, Jr. *Cat's Cradle*. New York: Delacorte, 1963.

———. *Player Piano*. New York: Delacorte, 1952.

Wald, Alan. *Writing from the Left: New Essays on Radical Culture and Politics*. London: Verso, 1994.

Warren, Bill. *Keep Watching the Skies! American Science Fiction Movies of the Fifties: Vol. 1, 1950–1957*. Jefferson, NC: McFarland, 1982.

———. *Keep Watching the Skies! American Science Fiction Movies of the Fifties: Vol. 2, 1958–1962*. Jefferson, NC: McFarland, 1986.

Weart, Spencer R. *Nuclear Fear: A History of Images*. Cambridge, MA: Harvard UP, 1988.

Weber, Max. *The Protestant Ethic and the Spirit of Capitalism*. 1904–1905. Trans. Talcott Parsons. 1930. London: Routledge, 1995.

Wells, H. G. *The Time Machine*. 1895. New York: Ventura, 1980.

———. *The War of the Worlds*. 1895. New York: Oxford UP, 1993.

Wells, Paul. "The Invisible Man: Shrinking Masculinity in the 1950s Science Fiction B-Movie." *You Tarzan: Masculinity, Movies, and Men*. Ed. Pat Kirkham and Janet Thurman. New York: St. Martin's, 1993. 181–99.

Whyte, William. *The Organization Man*. New York: Simon and Schuster, 1956.

Wilson, Sloan. *The Man in the Gray Flannel Suit*. New York: Simon and Schuster, 1955.

Wolf, Leonard. *Horror: A Connoisseur's Guide to Literature and Film*. New York: Facts on File, 1989.

Wolfe, Bernard. *Limbo*. New York: Random House, 1952.

Wollheim, Donald A. *The Universe Makers: Science Fiction Today*. New York: Harper and Row, 1971.

Wymer, Thomas L. "Machines and the Meaning of Human in the Novels of Kurt Vonnegut, Jr." *The Mechanical God: Machines in Science Fiction*. Ed. Thomas P. Dunn and Richard D. Erlich. Westport, CT: Greenwood P, 1982, 41–52.

Zamyatin, Yevgeny. *We*. Trans. Mirra Ginsberg. New York: Avon, 1983.

Zicree, Marc Scott. *The Twilight Zone Companion*. 2nd ed. Los Angeles: Silman-James P, 1992.

Zipes, Jack. "Mass Degradation of Humanity and Massive Contradictions in Bradbury's Vision of America in *Fahrenheit 451*." *No Place Else: Explorations in Utopian and Dystopian Fiction*. Ed. Eric S. Rabkin, Martin H. Greenberg, and Joseph D. Olander. Carbondale: Southern Illinois UP, 1983. 182–98.

FILMS

The Amazing Colossal Man. Dir. Bert I. Gordon. Perf. Glenn Langan, Cathy Downs, and William Hudson. American International, 1957.

The Amazing Transparent Man. Dir. Edgar G. Ulmer. Perf. Marguerite Chapman, Douglas Kennedy, James Griffith, and Ivan Triesault. American International, 1960.

The Astounding She-Monster. Dir. Ronald V. Ashcroft. Perf. Robert Clarke, Kenne Duncan, and Marilyn Harvey. American International, 1957.

Atomic Café. Dir. Jayne Loader, Kevin Rafferty, and Pierce Rafferty. The Archives Project, 1982.

The Atomic Kid. Dir. Leslie H. Martinson. Perf. Mickey Rooney, Robert Strauss, and Elaine Davis. Republic, 1954.

Attack of the Crab Monsters. Dir. Roger Corman. Perf. Richard Garland, Pamela Duncan, and Russell Johnson. Allied Artists, 1957.

The Attack of the 50 Foot Woman. Dir. Nathan Juran. Perf. Allison Hayes, William Hudson, and Yvette Vickers. Allied Artists, 1958.

Attack of the Giant Leeches. Dir. Bernard L. Kowalski. Perf. Ken Clark, Yvette Vickers, Jan Shepard, and Michael Emmett. American International, 1960.

Attack of the Killer Tomatoes. Dir. John De Bello. Perf. David Miller, Sharon Taylor, and George Wilson. Four Square, 1977.

Attack of the Puppet People. Dir. Bert I. Gordon. Perf. John Hoyt, John Agar, and June Kenny. American International, 1958.

The Beast from 20,000 Fathoms. Dir. Eugène Lourié. Perf. Paul Christian, Paula Raymond, Cecil Kellaway, and Kenneth Tobey. Warner, 1953.

Beginning of the End. Dir. Bert I. Gordon. Perf. Peter Graves, Peggie Castle, and Morris Ankrum. Republic, 1957.

Big Jim McLain. Dir. Edward Ludwig. Perf. John Wayne, Nancy Olson, and James Arness. Wayne, 1952.

The Black Cat. Dir. Edgar G. Ulmer. Perf. Boris Karloff and Bela Lugosi. Universal, 1934.

The Black Scorpion. Dir. Edward Ludwig. Perf. Richard Denning and Mara Corday. Warner, 1957.

Blade Runner. Dir. Ridley Scott. Perf. Harrison Ford, Rutger Hauer, and Sean Young. Warner, 1982.

The Blob. Dir. Irwin S. Yeawroth, Jr. Perf. Steve McQueen and Aneta Corseaut. Paramount, 1958.

The Brain Eaters. Dir. Bruno Ve Sota. Perf. Ed Nelson, Cornelius Keefe, Alan Frost, Joanna Lee, and Jody Fair. American International, 1958.

The Brain from Planet Arous. Dir. Nathan Juran. Perf. John Agar, Joyce Meadows, and Robert Fuller. Howco International, 1957.

The Brain That Wouldn't Die. Dir. Joseph Green. Perf. Jason Evers, Virginia Leith, and Adele Lamont. American International, 1963.

Cat-Women of the Moon. Dir. Arthur Hilton. Perf. Sonny Tufts, Victor Jory, and Marie Windsor. Astor Pictures, 1953.

Conquest of Space. Dir. Byron Haskin. Perf. Eric Fleming, Walter Brooke, Mickey Shaughnessy, William Hopper, and Ross Martin. Paramount, 1955.

The Creature from the Black Lagoon. Dir. Jack Arnold. Perf. Richard Carlson, Julie Adams, and Richard Denning. Universal International, 1954.

The Creature Walks among Us. Dir. John F. Sherwood. Perf. Jeff Morrow, Rex Reason, and Leigh Snowden. Universal International, 1956.

Daughter of Horror. Dir. John Parker. Perf. Adrienne Barrett, Richard Barron, and Ed McMahon. Exploitation Pictures, 1955.

The Day After. Dir. Nicholas Meyer. Perf. Jason Robards, John Cullum, JoBeth Williams, and John Lithgow. ABC Motion Pictures, 1983.

The Day of the Triffids. Dir. Steve Sekely. Perf. Howard Keel, Nicole Maurey, and Kieron Moore. Philip Yordan, 1963

The Day the Earth Caught Fire. Dir. Val Guest. Perf. Edward Judd, Janet Munro, and Leo McKern. British Lion, 1962.

The Day the Earth Stood Still. Dir. Robert Wise. Perf. Michael Rennie and Patricia Neal. TCF, 1951.

The Day the World Ended. Dir. Roger Corman. Perf. Paul Birch, Richard Denning, Mike Connors, and Lori Nelson. American Releasing Corporation, 1955.

The Deadly Mantis. Dir. Nathan Juran. Perf. Craig Stevens, William Hopper, and Alix Talton. Universal International, 1957.

Destination Moon. Dir. Irving Pichel. Perf. Warner Anderson, John Archer, Tom Powers, and Dick Wesson. Universal, 1950.

Detour. Dir. Edgar G. Ulmer. Perf. Tom Neal, Ann Savage, Claudia Drake, and Edmund McDonald. PRC, 1945.

Donovan's Brain. Dir. Felix Feist. Perf. Lew Ayres, Gene Evans, and Nancy Davis. United Artists, 1953.

Dr. Strangelove, or, How I Learned to Stop Worrying and Love the Bomb. Dir. Stanley Kubrick. Perf. Peter Sellers, George C. Scott, Sterling Hayden, and Keenan Wynn. Columbia, 1963.

Dracula. Dir. Tod Browning. Perf. Bela Lugosi, Helen Chandler, and David Manners. Universal, 1931.

Earth vs. the Flying Saucers. Dir. Fred F. Sears. Perf. Hugh Marlowe, Joan Taylor, Donald Curtis, and Morris Ankrum. Columbia, 1956.

Ed Wood. Dir. Tim Burton. Perf. Johnny Depp, Martin Landau, Sarah Jessica Parker, and Patricia Arquette. Buena Vista, 1994.

Fail-Safe. Dir. Sidney Lumet. Perf. Henry Fonda, Walter Matthau, and Dan O'Herlihy. Columbia, 1964.

Five. Dir. Arch Oboler. Perf. William Phipps, Susan Douglas, James Anderson, Charles Lampkin, and Earl Lee. Columbia, 1951.

The Fly. Dir. Kurt Neumann. Perf. Vincent Price, David Hedison, and Patricia Owens. TCF, 1958.

The Fly. Dir. David Cronenberg. Perf. Jeff Goldblum and Geena Davis. TCF/Brooksfilm, 1986.

Forbidden Planet. Dir. Fred M. Wilcox. Perf. Walter Pidgeon, Anne Francis, and Leslie Nielsen. MGM, 1956.

Frankenstein. Dir. James Whale. Perf. Boris Karloff, Colin Clive, and Mae Clarke. Universal, 1931.

From Hell It Came. Dir. Dan Milner. Perf. Tod Andrews, Tina Carver, and Linda Watkins. Allied Artists, 1957.

Godzilla, King of the Monsters. Dir. Inoshiro Honda. Perf. Raymond Burr, Takashi Shimura, and Momoko Kochi. Toho, 1954.

The H-Man. Dir. Inoshiro Honda. Perf. Yumi Shirakawa and Kenji Sahara. Toho, 1959.

How to Make a Monster. Dir. Herbert J. Strock. Perf. Robert H. Harris, Paul Brinegar, and Gary Conway. American International, 1958.

I Married a Monster. Dir. Nancy Malone. Perf. Richard Burgi, Susan Walters, and Tim Ryan. Paramount, 1998.

I Married a Monster from Outer Space. Dir. Gene Fowler. Perf. Gloria Talbott, Tom Tryon, and Ken Lynch. American International, 1958.

I Was a Communist for the FBI. Dir. Gordon Douglas. Perf. Frank Lovejoy, Dorothy Hart, and Phil Carey. Warner, 1951.

I Was a Teenage Frankenstein. Dir. Herbert J. Strock. Perf. White Bissell, Phyllis Coates, and Gary Conway. American International, 1958.

I Was a Teenage Werewolf. Dir. Gene Fowler. Perf. Michael Landon, White Bissell, and Yvonne Lime. American International, 1957.

The Incredible Shrinking Man. Dir. Jack Arnold. Perf. Grant Williams and Randy Stuart. Universal International, 1957.

Invaders from Mars. Dir. William Cameron Menzies. Perf. Helena Carter, Arthur Franz, Leif Erickson, and Hilary Brooke. Edward L. Alperson, 1953.

Invasion of the Body Snatchers. Dir. Don Siegel. Perf. Kevin McCarthy, Dana Wynter, Larry Gates. Allied Artists, 1956.

Invasion U.S.A. Dir. Alfred E. Green. Perf. Dan O'Herlihy, Gerald Mohr, and Peggie Castle. Columbia, 1952.

The Invisible Boy. Dir. Herman Hoffman. Perf. Richard Eyer, Philip Abbott, Harold J. Stone, and Diane Brewster. MGM, 1957.

It Came from Beneath the Sea. Dir. Robert Gordon. Perf. Kenneth Tobey, Faith Domergue, and Donald Curtis. Columbia, 1955.

It Came from Outer Space. Dir. Jack Arnold. Perf. Richard Carlson, Barbara Rush, and Charles Drake. Columbia, 1953.

Jaws. Dir. Steven Spielberg. Perf. Robert Shaw, Roy Scheider, and Richard Dreyfuss. Universal, 1975.

Killer Klowns from Outer Space. Dir. Stephen Chiodo. Perf. Grant Cramer, Suzanne Snyder, and John Allen Nelson. Trans World Entertainment, 1988.

King Dinosaur. Dir. Bert I. Gordon. Perf. William Bryant, Wanda Curtis, and Douglas Henderson. Lippert, 1955.

King Kong. Dir. Merian C. Cooper. Perf. Robert Armstrong and Fay Wray. RKO, 1933.

Kronos. Dir. Kurt Neumann. Perf. Jeff Morrow, Barbara Lawrence, John Emery, and George O'Hanlon. 1957.

The Last Man on Earth. Dir. Ubaldo Ragona and Sidney Salkow. Perf. Vincent Price, Franca Bettoya, and Giacomo Rossi-Stuart. American International, 1964.

The Leech Woman. Dir. Edward Dein. Perf. Colleen Gray, Phillip Terry, and Grant Williams. Universal, 1960.

Little Big Man. Dir. Arthur Penn. Perf. Dustin Hoffman, Martin Balsam, and Faye Dunaway. Stockbridge/Hiller/Cinema Center, 1970.

Living It Up. Dir. Norman Taurog. Perf. Dean Martin, Jerry Lewis, and Janet Leigh. Paramount, 1954.

Lost Continent. Dir. Sam Newfield. Perf. Cesar Romero, John Hoyt, Hugh Beaumont, Whit Bissell, and Sid Melton. Lippert, 1951.

The Man from Planet X. Dir. Edgar G. Ulmer. Perf. Margaret Field, Raymond Bond, and William Schallert. United Artists, 1951.

The Manchurian Candidate. Dir. John Frankenheimer. Perf. Frank Sinatra, Laurence Harvey, and Janet Leigh. United Artists, 1962.

Mighty Joe Young. Dir. Ernest Schoedsack. Perf. Terry Moore, Ben Johnson, and Robert Armstrong. RKO, 1949.

The Monolith Monsters. Dir. John F. Sherwood. Perf. Grant Williams, Lola Albright, Les Tremayne, and Trevor Burdette. Universal International, 1957.

The Mummy. Dir. Karl Freund. Perf. Boris Karloff, Zita Johann, and David Manners. Universal, 1932.

The Mysterians. Dir. Inoshiro Honda. Perf. Kenji Sahara and Yumo Shirakawa. Toho, 1959.

Mystery Science Theater 3000: The Movie. Dir. Jim Mallon. Perf. Michael J. Nelson, Trace Beaulieu, Jim Mallon, and Kevin Murphy. Gramercy Pictures, 1996.

The Naked Gun: From the Files of Police Squad. Dir. David Zucker. Perf. Leslie Nielsen, Priscilla Presley, Ricardo Montalban, and O. J. Simpson. Paramount, 1988.

The Naked Jungle. Dir. Byron Haskin. Perf. Charlton Heston and Eleanor Parker. Paramount, 1954.

The Omega Man. Dir. Boris Sagal. Perf. Charlton Heston, Rosalind Cash, and Anthony Zerbe. Warner, 1971.

On the Beach. Dir. Stanley Kramer. Perf. Gregory Peck, Ava Gardner, Fred Astaire, and Anthony Perkins. United Artists, 1959.

Panic in Year Zero. Dir. Ray Milland. Perf. Ray Milland, Jean Hagen, Frankie Avalon, and Joan Freeman. American International, 1962.

Plan 9 from Outer Space. Dir. Edward D. Wood, Jr. Perf. Gregory Walcott, Mona McKinnon, Tor Johnson, and Bela Lugosi. Distributors Corporation of America, 1956.

The Professionals. Dir. Richard Brooks. Perf. Burt Lancaster, Lee Marvin, Robert Ryan, and Jack Palance. Columbia, 1966.

The Quatermass Experiment. Dir. Val Guest. Perf. Brian Donlevy, Jack Warner, and Margia Dean. Hammer, 1955.

Queen of Outer Space. Dir. Edward Bernds. Perf. Zsa Zsa Gabor, Eric Fleming, and Laurie Mitchell. Allied Artists, 1958.

Rebel without a Cause. Dir. Nicholas Ray. Perf. James Dean, Natalie Wood, Jim Backus, and Sal Mineo. Warner, 1955.

Red Planet Mars. Dir. Harry Horner. Perf. Herbert Berghof, Peter Graves, Andrea King, and Marvin Miller. United Artists, 1952.

Return of the Fly. Dir. Edward Bernds. Perf. Vincent Price, Brett Halsey, and John Sutton. Bernard Glasser/TCF, 1959.

Revenge of the Creature. Dir. Jack Arnold. Perf. John Agar and Lori Nelson. Universal International, 1955.

Robinson Crusoe on Mars. Dir. Byron Haskin. Perf. Paul Mantee, Adam West, and Vic Lundin. Paramount, 1964.

Rocketship X-M. Dir. Kurt Neumann. Perf. Lloyd Bridges, Osa Massen, John Emery, and Hugh O'Brian. Lippert, 1950.

Seven Days in May. Dir. John Frankenheimer. Perf. Kirk Douglas, Burt Lancaster, Fredric March, and Ava Gardner. Seven Arts, 1964.

The Seventh Voyage of Sinbad. Dir. Nathan Juran. Perf. Kerwin Mathews, Kathryn Grant, and Torin Thatcher. Columbia, 1958.

Soldier Blue. Dir. Ralph Nelson. Perf. Candice Bergen, Peter Strauss, and Donald Pleasance. Avco, 1970.

The Space Children. Dir. Jack Arnold. Perf. Adam Williams, Michel Ray, and Peggy Webber. Paramount, 1958.

Star Wars. Dir. George Lucas. Perf. Mark Hamill, Harrison Ford, Carrie Fisher, and Alec Guinness. TCF, 1977.

Tarantula. Dir. Jack Arnold. Perf. Leo G. Carroll, John Agar, and Mara Corday. Universal International, 1955.

Teenage Cave Man. Dir. Roger Corman. Perf. Robert Vaughn, Sarah Marshall, and Leslie Bradley. American International, 1958.

Teenagers from Outer Space. Dir. Tom Graeff. Perf. Tom Graeff, Dawn Anderson, and Bryant Grant. Warner Brothers, 1959.

The Terminator. Dir. James Cameron. Perf. Arnold Schwarzenegger and Linda Hamilton. Orion, 1984.

Testament. Dir. Lynne Littman. Perf. Jane Alexander, William DeVane, Ross Harris, Roxana Zal, and Lukas Haas. American Playhouse, 1983.

Them! Dir. Gordon Douglas. Perf. Edmund Gwenn, James Whitmore, Joan Weldon, and James Arness, 1954.

The Thing. Dir. John Carpenter. Perf. Kurt Russell, Wilford Brimley, David Clennon, and Richard Dysart. Universal, 1982.

The Thing from Another World. Dir. Christian Nyby. Perf. Kenneth Tobey, Robert Cornthwaite, and Margaret Sheridan. RKO, 1951.

This Island Earth. Dir. Joseph Newman. Perf. Rex Reason, Jeff Morrow, and Faith Domergue. Universal International, 1955.

Threads. Dir. Mick Jackson. Perf. Karen Meagher, Reece Dinsdale, David Brierly, and Rita May. BBC, 1985.

The Time Machine. Dir. George Pal. Perf. Rod Taylor, Yvette Mimieux, and Alan Young. MGM, 1960.

Tobor the Great. Dir. Lee Sholem. Perf. Charles Drake, Karin Booth, Taylor Holmes, and Billy Chapin. Republic, 1954.

Touch of Evil. Dir. Orson Welles. Perf. Orson Welles, Charlton Heston, Janet Leigh, and Marlene Dietrich. Universal International, 1958.

20 Million Miles to Earth. Dir. Nathan Juran. Perf. William Hopper and Joan Taylor. Columbia, 1957.

The 27th Day. Dir. William Asher. Perf. Gene Barry, Valerie French, and George Voskevec. Columbia, 1957.

Two Mules for Sister Sara. Dir. Don Siegel. Perf. Clint Eastwood and Shirley Maclaine. Universal, 1970.

2001: A Space Odyssey. Dir. Stanley Kubrick. Perf. Gary Lockwood and Keir Dullea. MGM, 1968.

Ulzana's Raid. Dir. Robert Aldrich. Perf. Burt Lancaster, Bruce Davison, Jorge Luke, and Richard Jaeckel. Universal, 1972.

War of the Colossal Beast. Dir. Bert I. Gordon. Perf. Sally Fraser, Roger Pace, and Duncan Parkin. American International, 1958.

War of the Worlds. Dir. Byron Haskin. Perf. Gene Barry, Ann Robinson, and Les Tremayne. Paramount, 1953.

The Wasp Woman. Dir. Roger Corman. Perf. Susan Cabot, Anthony Eisely, Barboura Morris, William Roerick, and Michael Mark. Allied Artists, 1959.

When Worlds Collide. Dir. Rudolph Maté. Perf. Richard Derr, Barbara Rush, Larry Keating, Peter Hanson, and John Hoyt. Paramount, 1951.

The Wild Bunch. Dir. Sam Peckinpah. Perf. William Holden, Ernest Borgnine, Robert Ryan, and Edmond O'Brien. Warner, 1969.

Wild Women of Wongo. Dir. James L. Wolcott. Perf. Jean Hawkshaw, Johnny Walsh, and Mary Ann Webb. Wolcott Productions, 1958.

The World, the Flesh, and the Devil. Dir. Ranald MacDougall. Perf. Harry Belafonte, Inger Stevens, and Mel Ferrer. MGM, 1959.

World without End. Dir. Edward Bernds. Perf. Hugh Marlowe, Rod Taylor, and Nancy Gates. Allied Artists, 1956.

Index

About the Author

M. KEITH BOOKER is Professor of English at the University of Arkansas. His many books include *The Dystopian Impulse in Modern Literature: Fiction as Social Criticism* (1994); *Dystopian Fiction: A Theory and Research Guide* (1994); *Bakhtin, Stalin, and Modern Russian Fiction: Carnival, Dialogism, and History* (1995); *The Modern British Novel of the Left: A Research Guide* (1998); *The Modern American Novel of the Left: A Research Guide* (1999); *Film and the American Left: A Research Guide* (1999); and *Ulysses, Capitalism, and Colonialism: Reading Joyce after the Cold War* (2000), all available from Greenwood Press.